The Power of Wagging Tails

A Doctor's Guide to Dog Therapy and Healing

The Power of Wagging Tails

A Doctor's Guide to
Dog Therapy and Healing

Dawn A. Marcus, MD

demos HEALTH

New York

ISBN: 978-1-936303-12-0
E-ISBN: 978-1-6-17050-65-7

Visit our web site at www.demoshealthpub.com

Acquisitions Editor: Noreen Henson
Cover Design: Carlos Maldonado
Compositor: Newgen Imaging
Printer: Bang Printing

Medical information provided by Demos Health, in the absence of a visit with a healthcare professional, must be considered as an educational service only. This book is not designed to replace a physician's independent judgment about the appropriateness or risks of a procedure or therapy for a given patient. Our purpose is to provide you with information that will help you make your own healthcare decisions. The information and opinions provided here are believed to be accurate and sound, based on the best judgment available to the authors, editors, and publisher, but readers who fail to consult appropriate health authorities assume the risk of any injuries. The publisher is not responsible for errors or omissions. The editors and publisher welcome any reader to report to the publisher any discrepancies or inaccuracies noticed.

Library of Congress Cataloging-in-Publication Data

Marcus, Dawn A.
   The power of wagging tails: A doctor's guide to dog therapy and healing /
Dawn Marcus.
      p. cm.
   Includes bibliographical references and index.
   ISBN 978-1-936303-12-0
   1. Dogs—Therapeutic use. 2. Human-animal relationships.   I. Title.
   RM931.D63M37 2011
   615.8'5158—dc22   2011004857

Special discounts on bulk quantities of Demos Health books are available to corporations, professional associations, pharmaceutical companies, health care organizations, and other qualifying groups. For details, please contact:

Special Sales Department
Demos Medical Publishing
11 W. 42nd Street
New York, NY 10036
Phone: 800–532–8663 or 212–683–0072
Fax: 212–941–7842
E-mail: rsantana@demosmedpub.com

Made in the United States of America
11 12 13 14 15   5 4 3 2 1

CONTENTS

PREFACE

As a medical doctor, it took a little getting used to playing second fiddle to the newest member of my team. After all, he was really just a young upstart—very young. And he'd only completed a year's worth of training before passing the certification that put him with me at patients' bedsides, unlike my four years of college, four years of medical school, three years residency, and then many years as a university professor. But there was no doubt about it: When we'd walk through the halls in the hospital or enter a patient's room, people no longer seemed to see me. Instead, they'd focus all eyes and attention on my colleague. With his soulful eyes, listening ear, and gentle touch, I was just no match for his charms. Did I mention, my new colleague is a Soft-Coated Wheaten Terrier therapy dog?

There's just something about a dog in the room. That's what my patients and people we visit tell me over and over. And they're right. When I walk alone through the hospital, people usually scurry by, intent on reaching their destination. But when Wheatie is at my side—he *is* the destination! It's like a wave of joy, peace, and calm follows in our wake as we pass people who—if only for the briefest of moments—take a break from the day's stress, burdens, and worries and pull strength and peace from a few minutes petting a silly little pup.

Believe it or not, doctors have been fascinated for years by—and probably a little jealous of—the amazing healing power of therapy dogs. Doctors and others have been watching, recording, and analyzing what happens when a patient meets a therapy dog. And the verdict is in—there really *is* something about a dog in the room!

The Power of Wagging Tails: A Doctor's Guide to Dog Therapy and Healing highlights the medical research proving what we therapy dog handlers already know: Therapy dog visits are good for your healing and recovery. As you read through this research and the personal accounts of people who make visits with therapy dogs and those folks who've been on the receiving end of those visits, you, too, will be amazed at the healing power of seemingly ordinary dogs. This book shares stories from people using therapy dogs across the United States and in Canada. Although, in most cases, the patients' names have been changed to protect their privacy, the powerful responses to the therapy dog visits haven't been altered. As you read people's similar experiences with therapy dogs of all different breeds, who see all types of patients across the continent, you'll be convinced about the incredible healing power of a simple dog. And, with any luck, you may decide that you'll get involved in therapy dog work, too, so you can also share an incredible life journey on the lucky end of a therapy dog's leash.

Dawn A. Marcus, MD

ACKNOWLEDGMENTS

Through researching this project, I have met an incredible group of people and their dogs from California to Toronto to the United Kingdom. Their stories have become inspirations to me, and I hope they will inspire you also.

I am indebted to the expertise and wisdom shared with me by dog experts Carol Lea Benjamin, Patricia Bednarik, and Judy Fridono. I would also like to thank my friends at Animal Friends, Gabriel's Angels, and Angel Paws, especially Ann Cadman, Pamela Gaber, and Patti Shanaberg. Thanks also go to the staff at Therapy Dogs International and the Delta Society for their assistance and guidance. Another thanks needs to go to my aerobics experts, Dawn Celapino and Janet Atutes, whose knowledge and enthusiasm will, I hope, encourage everyone to make exercising more fun and rewarding.

Thank you to those professional photographers who graciously shared their images with me: Jasmine Goldband from the *Tribune-Review* in Pittsburgh, Pennsylvania, Joshua J. Grenell, Patricia A. M. Ingram from Ingram Portrait Design, Natalie Larocco, Stephen Lennard, Tamandra Michaels from Heart Dog Studios, Jolene Miklas, Cindy Noland, Rob Ochoa from Pawmzing Pets, Ron Paglia, and Tomek Sewilski from L'Arche Daybreak in Richmond Hill, Ontario, Canada.

This book couldn't have been written without the wonderful experiences of so many magnificent people and their dogs. Therapy dog handlers across the United States and in Canada opened their hearts to share stories of their own amazing dogs. Hearing these stories has been both touching and eye-opening. As a therapy dog handler, I often leave a visit thinking, "Did I *really* see what I thought I saw? I know my dog's special, but did he *really* do that?" Hearing dog handlers from California to Toronto describe experiences that mirror my own and each other's has reinforced the amazing healing power of therapy dogs. We've all seen our dogs work their magic—often when we were least expecting it!

Nearly every conversation started the same: "I'm not sure this is anything special or much of a story, but..." And then I would hear stories that made me smile, laugh, shake my head in wonder, and cry. The bonds formed between owner and dog and the service performed by therapy dog–handler teams are priceless, and it has truly been a blessing that so many people opened their lives, hearts, and homes to me to share their stories and beautiful images of their precious dogs: Gloria Aiello and Rosebud; Susan Ambridge and Binx; Alyssa Applequist and Troy; CJ Anderson and the Chihuahuas; Marleen Ashton and Lannie; Shelley Bates and Bentley; Barbara Bishop and Rufus; Jennifer Blanchard and Ike; Olivia and Janet Brendel with Chloe and Lacey; Debbie Brown with Natalie and Hayley; Miki Carlin and Spinner; Deborah Cooper with Tucker; Anita DeBiase and Louie; Danielle Di Bona and Naomi; Carol Estades and Phoebe; Cindy Etling with Charlie, Winston, and Lady; Kad Favorite and Lucy; Margaret Foxmoore with Lord Argyle and Miss Maisy; Marion Francis and Reina; Judy Fridono with Rina and Ricochet; Pauline Glagola with dogs Chip, Rocky, and Sigmund, and their one cat who snuck into this dog book named Clyde; DJ Goodell with Kelly, Gracie, Poly, Baylor, and Roy; Sandy Grentz and Callie; Diana Hare and Sonia; Mary Ann Hirt and Thom Harding with dogs Baron, Hobie, Holly, Cooper, Sam, Walker, and Siena; Donna Kaczynski and Noah; Becky Kikukawa and Mattie; the Klipas and little Liesel; Sue London with Rocky, Molly, Willy, and Gus; Janet Malinsky with Lindsey, Brittney, and Courtney; Sherry Meininghaus and her Beardies and Louie; Jane and Beth Miller with Sadie; Marlene Miller, Mitsu, and Zeus; David Mitchell with Lucy and Ricky; Rose Mary Mulkerrin and Lucky D; Mariann and Jim Murrin with Rocky and Sammie; Cheryl Noethiger and Honey Bear; Gabe O'Neill and Charlie; Ron Paglia; Allen Parton with Endal; Barbara and Emil Pohodich with Lexi and Sadie; Claire Rumpler and Makena; Ruth Salvador and Birdie; Lisa Saroyan and Minnie; Clyde Schauer and Crystal; Mary Ann Seman and Latte; Patti Shanaberg and Sami;

Sue Showalter and Buddy; Jacque Speed and Reilly; Kerri Stamas with Dillon; Richard Statman and Pandora; Nancy Torres; Jodi Tuckett and Suzy; Dana Wilson and Noel; and Andrew Yori and Hector. I extend a special thanks to all those special people who helped introduce me to the wonderful folks above. I would also like to thank the Hermans for allowing me to use their mother Cilly's name to share her incredible story of perseverance with grace and charm through a very difficult life to become a beloved wife, mother, and friend to Pittsburgh.

I am deeply indebted to each of you and offer you my sincerest thanks—with ear and belly scratches for your amazing pups!

The Power of Wagging Tails

A Doctor's Guide to
Dog Therapy and Healing

BRINGING HEALING DOGS INTO OUR LIVES

1

Living With Healing Dogs

What do you call a healing volunteer with four legs, a wagging tail, and a slobbery grin? A therapy dog. You don't have to be around a therapy dog long to recognize the amazing power of these precious dogs for healing the bodies and souls of those they visit.

Tail Waggin' Tip

Florence Nightingale recognized the healing power of pets: "A small pet is often an excellent companion for the sick or long chronic cases."

Nurse Elaine Smith made therapy dogs a formal part of the healing process after noticing benefits for patients visited by a chaplain and his Golden Retriever. In 1976, Smith founded Therapy Dogs International, a volunteer organization that focuses on testing and registering therapy dogs and their owners and promoting therapy dog work. Today, Therapy Dogs International–certified volunteers can be found in all 50 United States and in Canada, with over 20,000 therapy dogs on the roster.

Tail Waggin' Tip

According to the American Kennel Club, about 45,000 dogs receive their Canine Good Citizen therapy dog certification each year.

As a typical medical doctor, I was used to prescriptions and medical therapies for my patients. For the last couple of decades, I'd been caring for patients with chronic pain problems—arthritis, migraines, fibromyalgia, low back pain, and more. Although I'd been trained to embrace traditional medical treatments, I soon learned that my bag of pills and remedies barely made a dent in these patients' lives—and I was re-educated about the need for a more holistic approach that addressed lifestyle, social, and emotional issues in addition to simply physical ailments. At our clinic, we encouraged our patients to get involved with nondrug and nontraditional therapies. Despite what I thought was a pretty comprehensive knowledge about alternative treatments, I'd never heard of therapy dogs until my veterinarian commented during a puppy visit that my Soft-Coated Wheaten Terrier—appropriately named Wheatie—would make be a terrific dog for visiting patients.

Like my terrier, I'm a bit stubborn. OK—for those of you reading this book who know me—quite a bit stubborn! And when I get an idea in my head, I'm like a dog with a bone. And I'll confess I had three reasons to pursue therapy dog work. First, Wheatie's very social and loves people. Second, I was already enrolled in obedience classes with Wheatie, and he really seemed to enjoy practicing his skills, so I knew we'd both enjoy the therapy dog training. And, finally, I had a purely selfish reason: I knew I'd enjoy taking Wheatie to work with me at the hospital. After Wheatie had been making visits for a couple of years, a second Wheaten Terrier, Toby, joined our family. Toby followed in Wheatie's pawprints, earning his therapy dog certification, too, and giving me a therapy dog team.

I have spent my medical career working at a university, focused on research and continuing to learn new ways to help improve the lives of my patients, so it was only natural that I didn't jump into therapy dog work without investigating whether there was really anything to people's claims about the healing power of therapy dogs. Sure, dogs are cute, and I was always happier when I was around my dog. But could something as seemingly simple as a therapy dog visit made a real, measurable, medical difference for real patients? Study after study convinced me the answer was a resounding "Yes."

Once I started making my own visits, I'd have moments where I'd look at Wheatie and say, "That was so amazing! Did you see what just

Figure 1.1. My Soft-Coated Wheaten Terrier, Toby, brightens a patient's day while making his hospital rounds. Photo by Jasmine Goldband, courtesy of the (Pittsburgh, PA) *Tribune-Review*.

happened?" Or I'd leave a room, choked up with emotion that had washed over to me from the person Wheatie had just visited. And I'd think, "Is there really something to this, like all the research says, or am I just a dog nut who's reading more into these visits than there is?" The answer is that I may be a dog nut—but therapy dogs are amazing. As I've talked with handlers from California to Ontario, I keep hearing the same line over and over: "I don't know if this is really anything or not. But...." And then I hear stories of peace, joy, and comfort driven by a seemingly ordinary pup at the end of a leash. These seemingly ordinary dogs with seemingly ordinary handlers have seen the extraordinary—witnessing smiles and seeing people reached in ways that have mystified close relatives and professionals.

WHAT IS A THERAPY DOG?

A *therapy dog* is a dog that has been trained, tested, and certified to be able to consistently and safely provide comfort and affection to people in nursing homes, assisted living facilities, hospitals, and schools. A therapy dog needs to be social, engaging, and responsive to contact with strangers. People can engage in unpredictable behavior around dogs, especially when they're sick or confused, or they are young children unfamiliar with dogs. So the therapy dog first and foremost needs a temperament that will make visits safe and positive experiences for both the dog and the humans the dog visits.

Test Your Knowledge

Pick the true statement from those below:

1. Any dog can visit patients in nursing homes and hospitals, as long as he's friendly and on a leash.
2. Therapy dogs can go anywhere their owners go—into schools, hospitals, buses, and restaurants.
3. The most important part of the therapy dog visit is the conversation the dog's owner has with the patient.
4. Getting a visit from a therapy dog will likely put a smile on your face, but there won't be any real health benefits.
5. You can describe a working dog as a therapy dog or service dog. These two terms mean about the same thing.

If you spotted all of these statements as false—you're right. And you probably have or know a therapy dog.

A therapy dog is trained to work with a particular human, called the *handler*. The dog and handler become a team that visits patients together. The handler is there to assist the dog during visits—but the visits are all about the dog. When I was visiting a hospital with Wheatie, my volunteer supervisor had a twinkle in her eye when she told me, "I let the charge nurse on 4 West know that you and Wheatie would be visiting today. The nurse's face brightened at the mention of Wheatie's name, 'Oh, we just *love* Wheatie! But I don't think we've ever met Dawn.'" We both understood—it's *all* about the dog.

WHAT DOES A THERAPY DOG ACTUALLY DO?

When I'm riding on elevators in the hospital with Wheatie or Toby wearing his volunteer badge, people often ask me about therapy dogs. Here's a typical conversation:

> *"Why is there a dog in the hospital?"*
>   *"This is Toby—he's one of the hospital's therapy dogs. He visits patients."*
> *"Oh—so what does he do?"*
>   *"He visits patients and cheers them up."*
> *"Yeah—but what does he DO?"*

I know they're asking if he performs tasks for patients or entertains them with tricks. I just gaze fondly at my little terrier that has by now captured the attention of everyone in the elevator. Scowling faces have been replaced by smiles as stressed-out staff and worried visitors take a break from their concerns to look at Toby, give him some ear scratches, and start talking with each other about their own wonderful dogs. So I simply reply: "This is it—he's doing it right now."

For those of us who are lucky enough to be part of a therapy dog–handler team, seeing the joy that blossoms when our dogs meet with patients and the long-lasting comfort patients can get from these brief visits is especially rewarding. Wheatie and I had visited a young woman, Lia, in an intensive care unit weekly over several months. Lia had a Yorkie at home and had told the staff she missed seeing her dog. On most of our visits, Lia was very ill and able to open her eyes for only a few seconds. Despite this, Wheatie stood calmly by her bedside, nuzzling Lia's hand and letting us rub Lia's hand over his head and back. One week when we arrived at Lia's room, she was no longer in her bed, and we feared the worst. A couple months later, Wheatie and I were walking into the hospital elevator when I heard a petite woman calling, "Wheatie!" She said, "You probably don't remember me, but Wheatie visited me in intensive care and those visits really helped me pull through. You have no idea how much they meant to me." Lia looked so vibrant and healthy—so different from the young woman in the hospital bed hooked up to a breathing machine and countless intravenous tubes. Seeing her walking out of the hospital truly made our day. Do I think Wheatie's visit affected Lia's recovery? Absolutely. And while

I know Lia's own inner strength, her medical team, and the treatments she received should be primarily credited for her return to good health, I am blessed to know that those little visits from a shaggy dog made a positive impact and, in some small way, helped Lia return home to her Yorkie with tales to tell of the healing touch of a little pooch.

ANIMAL-ASSISTED THERAPY VERSUS ANIMAL-ASSISTED ACTIVITIES

Trained animals can be used therapeutically for animal-assisted therapy or animal-assisted activities. *Animal-assisted therapy* refers to a specific treatment intervention to a select patient that's designed to produce a specific goal. For example, a psychologist might include therapy dogs during sessions for children with a fear of dogs to help them overcome their fear, or a medical team might measure the effects of visits with a therapy dog on reducing heart stress in patients who recently had a heart attack. The more typical daily encounters that therapy dogs have with patients are termed *animal-assisted activities*. Animal-assisted activities, often dubbed *pet therapy*, are more casual encounters between therapy dogs and people with a wide range of needs. Animal-assisted activities are designed to provide comfort and companionship. The benefits from animal-assisted activities are more difficult to measure, but the impact is no less profound for many of those lives touched by the therapy dog. Animal-assisted therapy and activities can be performed with a wide range of animals, most commonly dogs and sometimes cats. Other domesticated animals have also been trained for pet therapy, although they are not discussed here.

 Founder of therapy dog organization Angel Paws, Patti Shanaberg, understands the power of therapy dogs: "Animals, with their complete lack of agenda, have a unique capacity to reach people on a whole new level many people under-estimate. The therapeutic benefits of animal-assisted therapy and activities go far beyond the entertaining diversion people often first think of."

In this book, you'll hear about carefully designed research studies of animal-assisted therapy as well as casual, everyday animal-assisted activity visits that prove the research is right on track. In this book, I use the term *therapy dog visit* to include both animal-assisted therapy and activities.

THERAPY DOGS PROVIDE UNCONDITIONAL ACCEPTANCE AND LOVE

The therapy dog's mission is to help others. Ann Cadman is the Health and Wellness Coordinator at Animal Friends, a no-kill shelter in Pittsburgh, Pennsylvania. Ann's face glows as she talks about the work of the program's therapy dogs:

> *Working with a therapy dog is a chance to give back to others— especially those largely forgotten people in nursing homes, assisted living facilities, and hospitals who so desperately need a healing touch. Therapy dogs are very special for these people—they give them unconditional acceptance and love. The therapy dog doesn't care what you look like, what problems you may have, or what you can do. The dog looks through the outer shell and focuses on the real person inside. There are no strings attached—the dog asks for nothing from the person and is ready to give that person everything.*

Wheatie showed me the power of this unconditional acceptance and love when we visited our first hospital patient, Sarah, together. Sarah was a 52-year-old lady and the unfortunate victim cer. In a final effort to prolong 1ove much of the tumor, result- her cheek and jaw. The surgical n open, seeping wound. Before hey were having trouble getting Sarah, because her surgery had :ing my own patients as a doctor d have no problem visiting this eatie and I came to Sarah's open

In Transit Slip

Transit library: APPOQUIN
Title: The power of wagging tails : a doctor's guide to
Transit date: 4/1/2016,10: 02
Transit to: GREENWOOD

door and I knocked to ask permission to enter. She was lying with her right side facing the door and appeared quite normal from this angle. When she heard the knock and turned to face us, it was difficult not to start when first seeing the extent of the surgical wound. Wheatie, however, happily jaunted into the room and raced up to Sarah. Although it was hard to understand many of her words, Sarah chatted with and caressed Wheatie for a long time, clearly thrilled to have a visitor who came in without an expression of regret, foreboding, or fear at her appearance. We visited her several more times during her stay, and each time her eyes brightened when Wheatie came to her doorway. He asked for nothing—and gave everything. And for those brief moments when Sarah and Wheatie gazed deeply into each other's eyes, nose to snout, the world of cancer, surgery, and pain melted away for Sarah, replaced by an island of acceptance, peace, and unconditional love.

LOOK—IT'S A WORKING DOG

People often confuse the terms *service dog* (called *assistance dogs* in Europe) and *therapy dog*. When we're visiting in the hospital, I often hear mothers reprimand their children as they approach Wheatie or Toby, "Don't bother him—he's a working dog." And others enviously tell me how lucky I am to have a dog I can take into restaurants with me (service dogs are allowed in restaurants but therapy dogs are not). A friend once told me the sad story of a disabled woman with a service dog who wasn't allowed to bring her dog on the bus because she mistakenly told the bus driver she had a therapy dog.

A *service dog* is highly trained to meet the unique, varied, and individual needs of the person he or she serves. A service dog is "on duty" most of the time—vigilant and attentive to the needs of his or her person. A therapy dog, however, usually performs his or her work for an hour or so, a couple of times a week. When a therapy dog leaves the facility where he or she works, that dog is free to become a pet and behave "just like a regular dog" again. For my dogs, thirty minutes to one hour is their limit for seeing patients.

Service Dog Versus Therapy Dog

A service dog is a dog that has been trained to do work or perform tasks for the benefit of a specific individual with a disability. Federal laws protect the rights of individuals with disabilities to be accompanied by their service dogs in public places, as they are not considered "pets."

Therapy dogs are not legally defined by federal law and are typically a person's pet. After completion of training and evaluation, therapy dogs and their handlers visit people where dogs are typically not allowed— hospitals, assisted living, hospice, schools, domestic-violence shelters, physical rehabilitation, and many other places.

The benefits of therapy dog visits are vast including both physical (lower blood pressure, reduce anxiety, inspire exercise, etc.) and psychological (minimize depression, provide a sense of joy, companionship, etc.).

In a sense, a person can think of a service dog as being in a one-to-one relationship—one dog helping one person. Therapy dogs help in a one-to-many relationship—one dog provides joy, comfort, and inspiration to many people.

—JoAnn Turnbull, Delta Society

WHAT DO SERVICE DOGS DO?

One of my favorite books to read to my sons was *Follow My Leader*, by James B. Garfield. This touching and inspirational story follows the courageous journey of Jimmy, a boy blinded in a firecracker accident who regained his confidence and independence with the help of a guide dog he renamed "Leader." According to the International Guide Dog Federation, historical ruins show images of dogs leading the blind as early as the first century AD. During World War I, German doctor Gerhard Stalling began training dogs to guide soldiers blinded from mustard gas and other injuries. In 1929, the first guide dog school, called The Seeing Eye, opened in North America. The Seeing Eye continues to flourish, with a 60-acre campus in Washington Valley, New Jersey. Today, service dogs provide a wide range of tasks for those they serve.

To better understand service dogs, I spoke with my favorite dog trainer and author, Carol Lea Benjamin. Carol has written the addictive Rachel Alexander and Dash mystery series and a number of practical training books. Carol's book *Mother Knows Best: The Natural Way to Train Your Dog* (1985) is by far the most down-to-earth and practical resource for taking you through all stages of puppy and young dog training. I've reread, highlighted, and taken notes from my very dog-eared copy before each new puppy comes to my house. Carol clearly explained to me the unique role of the service dog:

> *Service dogs help their partners with a disability. Sometimes you can see what they are doing—pulling a wheelchair, opening a door, fetching a dropped item, alerting someone to a sound such as the doorbell or the ringing telephone and, the first job of service dogs, leading the blind. Other times, the dog's partner has what is called an "invisible disability"—meaning you cannot see what the disability is by merely observing the person. In that case, what the dog is doing is watching and waiting to see if he is needed. In these cases, dogs can help with pain, alert people about oncoming seizures, monitor blood sugar for diabetics, etc. You usually cannot see what the dog is doing because most of what he is doing is paying careful attention. In fact, even when these dogs are doing the more active parts of their jobs, alerting a seizure or helping with pain, most people would not know that the dog was working. He would appear to be pawing his partner for attention or perhaps leaning against his partner. At those times, the dog is unobtrusively providing help when it is most needed.*

HOW IS A SERVICE DOG DIFFERENT FROM A THERAPY DOG?

Because service dogs are usually on duty working for their human partner, Carol Lea Benjamin notes that other people need to avoid interacting with the working dog:

> *No service dog should be talked to, called away from his owner, or handled when he is working—even if the work is as invisible as the*

Figure 1.2. Carol Lea Benjamin with service dogs Sky (on the bench) and Monk. Photo courtesy of Stephen Lennard.

disability. Interacting with the dog distracts him from his important job.

With therapy dogs, things are reversed. In this case, the dog's partner has encouraged the dog to relate to others. The work of these dogs is to be handled, petted, and kissed by strangers—people in the hospital, a nursing home, or some other institution where the visit of a trained, well-behaved, sociable dog can work miracles. Therapy dogs can change the energy and the mood in a room and bring smiles where there were tears. Therapy dogs bring warmth and cheer to people in need, sometimes allowing people to relate who could not do so before the dog's visit. In these cases, the dog may become a bridge from the patient to the dog handler. Therapy dogs can often be petted when they are out and about, but one should always ask first.

Understanding the Differences Between Working Dogs

How are therapy and service dogs similar?
Both therapy dogs and service dogs undergo special training, testing, and certification.

How are therapy and service dogs different?

Therapy dogs	Service dogs
Serve many people	Serve one person
Usually work once a week or once a month	Are "on duty" most of the time
Are trained to show generally calm, obedient behavior	Are trained to complete specific, complex tasks needed based on their human's disability
Are permitted in some hospitals, nursing homes, hospices, schools, and libraries, but only during the times when they are providing therapy services	Are permitted wherever their human might go—buses, restaurants, stores, and so on
People are encouraged to interact with a therapy dog.	People should avoid distracting a service dog from his work.

WHAT'S INVOLVED IN TRAINING A SERVICE DOG?

To get the scoop on how service dogs are trained, I spoke with Judy Fridono, founder and executive director of Puppy Prodigies, a program in San Diego, California that begins the initial training of service dog puppies during their first 8 weeks of life:

> *Although every program trains their dogs a little differently, service dog puppies typically go to a puppy raiser around eight weeks of age*

and stay with the puppy raiser for about fifteen months. This is really a time for the dogs to mature. At that point, the dogs undergo six months of advanced training, teaching them how to perform specific tasks. Success in a service program is less about the dog learning tasks and more about identifying whether the dog has an appropriate temperament, personality, and behaviors to fulfill the rigorous needs of the service dog.

Tail Waggin' Tip

Only about three of every five dogs who start service dog training will successfully become certified to work as service dogs.

A SERVICE DOG CAN BE A TRUE LIFELINE

Like so many who serve their country, Allen G. Parton returned home from the Gulf War a changed man. He had been seriously injured in 1991 while serving with the Royal Navy and came home unable to speak, write, or walk. After years of intensive rehabilitative therapy, Allen was still disabled and profoundly discouraged:

I found myself in the darkest pit of despair where any human can find himself. My time in rehab and hospital was my worst nightmare. I had spent twenty years in the Royal Navy having worked my way up through the ranks to officer. I was a weapons electronics engineering officer, designing new weapons. I traveled the world to repair systems that had gone down on ships that were deployed. And I had always been the provider, the carer for my family. And then suddenly I found myself totally dependent on others—it was horrible and beyond my control.

After a despondent Allen returned home in a wheelchair, his devoted wife, Sandra, decided to help train puppies for a service dog charity. Allen attended these classes with Sandra, although he sat in his wheelchair in the corner of the room, remaining unengaged. One day, a trainee Labrador Retriever named Endal changed all that:

> *Endal saw something on the floor by my wheelchair, trotted over, picked it up like he'd been trained, and proudly put it in my lap. I didn't acknowledge, thank, or reward what he'd done—and that hacked him off to no end. Apparently determined to show he was a great worker, Endal found something else and put it in my lap—but I thought I could be more stubborn than him and he still got no reaction from me. Endal kept loading my lap up with anything he could find and, just before I completely disappeared behind a mountain of stuff, I smiled for the very first time in six years.*

Thus began a 13-year rewarding relationship between service dog and his initially reluctant charge. Endal helped Allen regain his independence—Endal could bring Allen his keys, a pen, and the telephone. Endal could reach up to take packages off store shelves, insert a card into an ATM machine, and pay clerks. Endal could even open doors—doors to the laundry machine, doors to the front of the house, and doors in the outside world that allowed Allen to again participate in and enjoy those same daily activities most of us take for granted.

Many dog owners can't imagine life without their canine buddy—but for Jennifer Blanchard, her Labradoodle service dog, Ike, is an

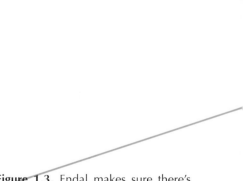

Figure 1.3. Endal makes sure there's no door un-opened to individuals with disabilities.

essential lifeline. Jennifer has a rare, incurable immune disorder similar to angioedema. *Angioedema* literally means "swelling from leaky blood vessels"—and this swelling can be very severe and painful. Even the seemingly smallest injury can set off a severe bout of swelling for Jennifer: "I can bump my leg on the coffee table and end up in surgery twelve to twenty-four hours later." And Jennifer has had lots of surgeries. When I talked with Jennifer in the summer of 2010, she had already had 95 surgeries—no, that's not a typo: ninety-five. With so many surgeries, complications from infections and daily painful dressing changes only added to Jennifer's disability. These surgeries left her with limited mobility and feeling disheartened after her doctor told her she'd never walk without a walker and may be confined to a wheelchair:

> When I lost muscles in my legs from my injuries and surgeries, my doctors told me I would never walk unassisted again. They said I'd have to either be in a wheelchair or use a walker or leg braces. I tried the leg braces and they actually caused so much irritation I ended up back in surgery. I was 39 at the time and was unable to come to grips with those realities. I also thought about all the times I had both arms and legs operated on at the same time, making me totally incapacitated and unable to do anything for myself. My doctor also told me I could never use crutches again because the pressure from carrying my weight caused my arms to swell too much. It was all so humbling. Life seemed very sad for me.

Into Jennifer's life walked service dog Ike:

> Before Ike, there were so many things I thought I'd never be able to do again. Ike has changed my life completely. First and foremost, Ike brings a smile to my face every morning when he sneaks up onto my bed, wet beard dripping on my face. He leans over me ever so gently and plants a big wet beard kiss on me. He does this every morning without fail. When I am in the hospital and Ike comes in to visit, he climbs onto my hospital bed and gently places his head on my chest and sighs. He knows where he belongs.

Ike also helps Jennifer accomplish daily physical tasks:

> Ike picks up things I drop. He turns lights on and off. He can give a cashier my credit card when I am in a wheelchair and can't reach.

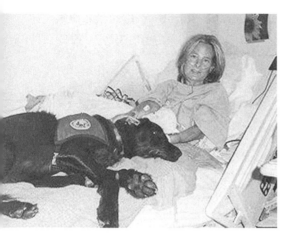

Figure 1.4. Service dog Ike tends to Jennifer's physical and emotional needs—he's a constant source of support and strength through good times and bad. After recent hand surgery, Ike found Jennifer's hospital room, planted himself firmly on her bed, and refused to leave without her.

He can press elevator buttons and open electronic handicapped doors. Ike opens drawers and even takes my socks off when I have had hand or arm surgeries and need an extra paw. When I am able to walk, Ike provides constant stability for me. He wears a rigid harness that I hold onto and he guides me through my day, providing necessary extra steadiness that allows me to walk safely. He also shields me from large crowds of people to avoid me getting bumped or bruised.

Ike has changed my life one hundred and twenty percent. I was afraid to leave the house before I got him, afraid of crowds and people. I was sad and depressed about losing my job, my ability to walk, my life as I knew it. Now I have the confidence to get back out there—to live my life as best as I can, knowing that I have a steward, leading me, loving me, without waver.

HOW DO THERAPY DOGS HELP PEOPLE?

When we read stories of service dogs like Endal and Ike, it's easy to see very clearly how they help their partners. But what about the therapy dog? Does a visit from a furry pooch really make a difference in medical care? Doctors have been asking this for many years and conducting research to answer that very question. What do these research studies show? Study after study shows the same thing: Therapy dogs have healing powers that improve both the physical and emotional health of those whom they visit.

Pet therapy provides a special time in the lives of my mom and the other residents at the assisted living facility where she lives. Mom and her friends look forward to each visit and the special programs the dog handlers, Pauline and Mike Glagola, put together, like Bow Wow Bingo. I am so grateful to Pauline and Mike for the time, energy, and compassion they bring, brightening the days (and evenings) of my mother and the other residents.

As soon as the dogs arrive, everyone's face just lights up. Seeing these dogs gives the seniors joy today and helps bring back memories of pets they had in their younger days. One of the first therapy dogs my mom met was Chip—a handsome, friendly, and loving Cocker Spaniel. It was almost as though Chip knew he had a special his role as a certified therapy dog. He'd proudly strut into the room, eyes alert and tail wagging, and snuggled up to everyone he visited. He really conveyed a message to each resident, "I came here special today—just so I could see you." It's difficult to put into words the joy he brought into their lives—but you could sure see that happiness when you'd see each smiling face greeting Chip.

—Ron Paglia

The power of the therapy dog becomes apparent as he walks down any crowded hall—overworked, stressed expressions on scurrying staff and frightened, anxious looks on patients and visitors are replaced by curious glances, tender smiles, and the always-heard cheer of the therapy dog, "Awwww. Look how sweet. It's a dog!" It's as though the therapy dog turns on light switches of joy as he struts down the hall. Seeing a neighbor smile and coo, the next person looks over and follows suit, until a stress-relieving wave of cheerfulness accompanies the therapy dog as he proudly marches forward, intent on his healing work.

Researchers at Massachusetts General Hospital carefully studied the effects of therapy dog visits to adults in their hospital (Coakley & Mahoney, 2009). Fifty-nine patients were evaluated before and after a therapy dog visit. Each visit lasted ten minutes. Immediately following the dog visit, patients were calmer. They had slower breathing, lower pain scores, and dramatically improved moods. People became less tense, anxious, angry, tired, depressed, and dejected after petting the dog.

Health Benefits After a Ten-Minute Therapy Dog Visit (Coakley & Mahoney, 2009)

- Three percent slower breathing rate
- Twenty-two percent drop in pain severity
- Nineteen percent boost in energy
- Fifty-three percent drop in anxiety
- Forty-eight percent decrease in depression
- Sixty-four percent drop in feelings of anger
- Thirty-nine percent decrease in fatigue

Being a hospital patient is tough, frustrating, and sometimes boring work. A visit from a dog can inject a much-needed break into a patient's routine. In the Massachusetts General Hospital study, patients commented that the therapy dog visit was calming and comforting, that visits brightened their day, and that the visit gave them a break from worrying about their problems. This study highlights what I find when making hospital rounds with Wheatie or Toby. Once patients' eyes light on a terrier, there's a change in their whole demeanor—they look brighter and more alert and even sit up straighter in their beds. Do you enjoy seeing a child's eyes light up when seeing Santa or a stack of birthday gifts? You can see that same look every day in the face of a needy patient who gets a therapy dog visit. There's nothing like a smiling pooch to make someone temporarily forget about the fears, loneliness, and discomfort of being a patient. When making a therapy dog visit one day to a man and his family, the man turned to his wife and announced, "I can't believe it. Seeing this dog took me out of myself. This is the first time since I've been in the hospital that I stopped worrying about myself. I can't believe how much better I feel." And all from a few minutes with a therapy dog.

Research Proves It

Therapy dog visits improve patients' moods and their sense of well-being. These visits also reduce pain, stress levels, and patients' sense of isolation.

Check out what expert researchers (Kawamura, Niiyama, & Niiyama, 2009; Sobo, Eng, & Kassity-Krich, 2006) hear from patients after a therapy dog visit:

- Therapy dog visits give patients a welcome distraction from illness, symptoms, and worry.
- Therapy dogs have a calming effect.
- Snuggling with or petting a dog is comforting.
- Therapy dogs bring patients a positive "piece of home."
- Therapy dogs bring happiness to patients.
- Therapy dogs give people something to talk about with their visitors, fellow patients or nursing home residents, and staff members.

The effects from therapy dog visits last longer than just the few minutes spent between dog and human. A research study of older nursing home residents, aged sixty-seven to ninety-four years, found that including therapy dog visits resulted in residents becoming more interested in themselves, fellow residents, and their surroundings (Kawamura et al., 2009). These results come as no surprise to Marlene Miller. For Marlene's mother-in-law, eighty-nine-year-old Dorothy Miller, visits from Marlene's Keeshond therapy dog, Mitsu, helped brighten her day and gave her an easy way to get involved with her fellow retirement home residents. Dorothy and her husband had always been a team, but when he died five years ago, Dorothy found herself alone. Marlene recalled to me how Mitsu helped fill an important hole in Dorothy's life:

Mom was very social when she was with her husband. But being the only one left can be very sad. All that changed when I started bringing Mitsu to visit. Suddenly, Tuesday evenings became the time when everyone wanted to come visit Dorothy and my beautiful Mitsu. Mitsu became a bit of a status symbol for Mom, and there was never a problem for Mom making conversation—everyone wanted to know all about Mitsu! In the days between visits, other ladies would invite Mom to join them for chats and tea, with talk often turning to tales about Mitsu. Suddenly, Mom felt like an important member of a community again, rather than the only one in her family who was left.

Many scientific studies have proven that therapy dogs help many people—from pediatric to geriatric patients. Therapy dogs have been shown to reduce pain in children and adults, reduce heart stress in patients with heart failure, increase positive communication in seniors with Alzheimer's disease, and reduce depression in cancer sufferers getting chemotherapy.

Tail Waggin' Tip

Here's what the experts are saying: "With the current intense focus on health care reform, increased use of animals as therapy may serve as a cost-effective strategy for improving and maintaining health in older adults" (Cangelosi & Sorrell, 2010, p. 19).

THERAPY DOGS CAN OPEN DOORS

Therapy dogs touch people and their families deeply. Working as a doctor, I've walked with patients and their families through times of great joy, when I delivered their baby or was able to share good news, and through times of great sorrow, when talking about a newly diagnosed terminal illness or sitting at a bedside while someone's mom took her final breaths. During these times, the doctor shares some of the family's emotions. Before I'd done therapy dog work, I'd had many of these moments and really thought I'd seen it all. So I wasn't quite prepared for the depth of emotion commonly experienced by the therapy dog handler.

The presence of the therapy dog seems to erase the careful masks people place on their emotions to avoid making others uncomfortable and you can, at times, almost feel like you can see right into someone's soul. Jacque Speed and her seven-year-old Golden Retriever therapy dog, Reilly, have come to expect these times of great emotional sharing and healing:

> *During one hospital visit, Reilly and I walked into a room that was full of family huddled together in a circle on one side of the room. On the other side, an elderly, frail woman lay quietly in the hospital bed. Reilly immediately captured the family's attention and each member, in turn, told her how beautiful she was and enjoyed petting her soft fur. My attention turned to the woman still lying alone in the bed. She raised a crooked finger and moved it back and forth, as though silently summoning Reilly to her. Before I could turn back to Reilly, my perceptive therapy dog responded to this small gesture by marching proudly to the woman's bed and lowering her head to the woman's hand. The woman immediately began stroking Reilly's silky ear, the woman's mouth forming a huge, blissful smile. Soon, a tear of joy rolled down her cheek. It all happened so fast, and it was only a moment in time. But the love and joy that that woman got from that moment was priceless. Throughout this encounter, I'd been totally focused on Reilly and her patient. I had stopped watching the family. But the family hadn't stopped watching Reilly—they too were touched by this simple yet profound bond between their loved one and the dog and they were also all crying. "We can't remember the last time Gran smiled."*

Those few minutes with a dog opened doors that had been shut for a long time.

THERAPY DOGS HELP CAREGIVERS TOO

Although a lot of medical studies have proved the benefit to patients from therapy dog visits, the effects on others who meet therapy dogs have not been studied. Any therapy dog handler, however, will tell you that the therapy dog reduces the stress level of everyone who greets it—facility visitors, housekeepers, therapists, nurses, and doctors. Much of the time dogs actually spend during visits will be ministering to the needs of family and staff. My therapy dogs and I can't walk through the hospital without being repeatedly stopped by visitors and staff alike all saying the same thing, "Oooo! A therapy dog! Come over here. I could *really* use some therapy today." And improvements in stress levels and mood for patient caregivers will likely result in better, more cheerful care given to their patients.

One of the most memorable visits for Jacque Speed and Golden Retriever therapy dog Reilly was with John, a man who used to own Golden Retrievers who was dying at a hospice center:

> *When we arrived, John was in his bed, surrounded by his wife, daughter, and granddaughter. When he spotted Reilly, John became so excited that he sat up in bed, fed Reilly the snacks we had brought, hugged her, stroked her ears and face, smiled, laughed, and shared stories with me and his family. Watching the joy on John's face while petting Reilly, his daughter and granddaughter snapped pictures, smiling from ear to ear, with tears running down their faces.*
>
> *This visit lasted only about twelve minutes, and John's family tried to apologize for making me come all that way for only a few minutes of time with John. But those few minutes erased a lot of pain. John's family said that they couldn't remember the last time they had seen John smile and laugh and enjoy something so thoroughly. Four days later, I received a phone call from John's wife. John had passed. But those twelve minutes with Reilly were the memory of John's final days that will stay with us all forever.*

WHAT'S THE SCIENCE BEHIND THE HEALING POWER OF THERAPY DOGS?

Sure, we can see that having a dog visit gives us a nice cheery distraction when we're sick, lonely, or bored. But can a dog *really* affect our health? Isn't therapy dog work just about feeling emotionally better?

We medical researchers apparently have lots of time on our hands to ponder these types of questions—and then design research studies to find out the answers. And these studies show that the benefits from therapy dogs are biological, not just emotional.

Figure 1.5. Jacque sits back while Golden Retriever therapy dog Reilly works his magic, spreading joy and easing pain.

When you interact with a friendly dog, there is a physiological change that takes place. Petting a dog makes you feel calmer *and* reduces the harmful physical response to your body that occurs from stress. In one unique experiment, one hundred twenty healthy adults were put into stressful situations with both mental stress from doing math calculations and physical stress (Allen, Blascovich, & Mendes, 2002). Researchers measured heart responses to stress by monitoring increased heart rate and blood pressure. Increases in heart rate and blood pressure show that the mental or physical stress is also causing stress on the heart. Having a friendly dog in the room during times of physical stress or when making math calculations significantly decreased the stress response: You feel better *and* your physiology is healthier.

So how does a dog visit make you healthier? Dr. J. S. Odendaal helped to answer this question in a research article published in the *Journal of Psychosomatic Research* titled "Animal-Assisted Therapy—Magic or Medicine?" In this study, Odendaal measured biological changes—both blood pressure and levels of stress chemicals—in people and dogs during a positive interaction. Stress chemicals are messengers in the brain and nervous system that signal different organs in the body to react to stress; they include cortisol, oxytocin, prolactin, and endorphins. When cortisol levels increase, this revs up the stress response and the negative effects this stress has on the body. Endorphins, on the other hand, are important to help improve our mood and feelings of well-being and reduce pain. In this experiment, after spending a few minutes with the dog, the humans' stress response decreased:

- The humans' blood pressure was significantly reduced—helping to show their stress response was positively affected and the heart was less stressed.
- Stress chemicals were lowered in the humans.
- Endorphin levels increased in both the humans and the dogs, showing that both enjoyed their time together and felt better being together.
- Cortisol levels dropped in the humans, showing that the encounter helped curb stress effects.
- Cortisol levels in the dogs, however, didn't decrease, showing us that visits are stressful work for the dog.

This study highlights two important features of a therapy dog visits. First, a brief visit reduces biological stress chemicals and the negative effect of stress on the body in the human who receives the visit. Second, these visits are work for the dog, whose stress system remains active during visits. It's important to understand and respect that the therapy dog is not enjoying an afternoon of play but is working hard when greeting strangers and sharing a healing gift.

 What Does Science Say About the Effects of Therapy Dog Visits?

- A therapy dog visit results in real, measurable, physical changes in brain chemicals and the heart. These changes make us healthier.

- These positive changes occur after just a few minutes with the dog. Researchers recommended that therapy dog visits last about 10 to 15 minutes to give people optimal health benefits.
- Both dogs and the people they visit enjoy these encounters and find their sessions spiritually lifting and emotionally comforting.
- Although stress is reduced in the people dogs visit, making visits is stressful work for dogs. Therefore, it's important to limit both the duration of each visit and the number of visits a dog makes on any given day. Because people improve after brief visits with the dog, there's generally no reason to make long visits that might increase the stress on the therapy dog.

So, is it magic or medicine? Without question, the benefits from therapy dog visits are real medicine. Science proves it.

2

Making Fido a Member of Your Personal Treatment Team and Support Network

Most dog owners will insist their dog is an important part of the family. When there's a health problem in the family, companion pets can do important healing work for their human pack members. But what does the research show? Does having a dog actually improve your health?

Tail Waggin' Tip

According to a 2004 survey by the American Animal Hospital Association, half of pet owners surveyed would choose their pet if they could only have one companion on a deserted island.

Decades of medical research into the effects of sharing your home with a furry friend have concluded that having a dog at your side is good for your health (Barker & Wolen, 2008):

- Dog owners are generally healthier than people who don't own dogs.

- Petting a dog lowers your blood pressure and the stress on your heart.
- Having a dog helps people with heart disease stick with their rehabilitation therapy.
- Having a dog to walk helps people keep their weight in check.
- Seniors with pets stay active, healthier, and happier longer than seniors without a pet.
- Having a dog helps people stay socially engaged with others and reduces loneliness and isolation.

New research published in the British medical journal *Clinical and Experimental Allergy* showed that having a dog in the household helps develop the immune system (Lappalainen et al., 2010). A healthy immune system is critical for staying healthy and being able to fight off diseases. Levels of immune factors changed significantly when young children had had contact with dogs very early in their development, for example, when a dog was living in the house while the mom was pregnant or during the baby's first year of life. This change was thought to possibly prevent these babies from developing abnormal immune reactions as they grew up. Having a cat in the house didn't affect the immune system. The importance of this research is highlighted by an earlier report in this same journal that showed that toddlers who had had a dog living in the home when they were babies had significantly lower risks for developing allergy and immune problems (Bufford et al., 2008). Having a dog in the house during the first year of life reduced the risk of developing an itchy, allergic skin condition linked to asthma (called *atopic dermatitis*) by fifty-six percent. Risk for developing wheezing dropped by forty-seven percent.

Having a dog in one's life can also ease the emotional suffering that goes along with medical illnesses. Mark Doty learned first hand how having companion dogs can ease the suffering of illness, detailing the vital role played by his Golden Retriever and Black Labrador Retriever when facing the death of his partner from AIDS. In his best-selling book, *Dog Years: A Memoir*, Doty (2007) described the important role for his canine companions in easing his suffering:

> *How useful Arden and Beau were to me after Wally died—not only because their daily needs kept me tethered to the ordinary world...,*

but because I could talk and cry...and they didn't mind in the least, never found me morbid...[or] indicated that I should get over it. (pp. 32–33)

Research has repeatedly shown that dogs can help when people are coping with illnesses. But having a companion dog is also a lot of responsibility that may be too much for a household already over-burdened from caring for someone who's sick. Understanding what to expect from a companion dog—both the benefits and the work involved—and understanding what's needed when adding a new dog to a home that includes illness are important for making this addition successful.

COMPANION DOGS HAVE HEALING POWERS

Medical research supports what dog owners have long suspected: The pet dog fills a vital, healing role for his humans. Codirector of the Chicago Center for Family Health and a professor at the University of Chicago, Froma Walsh, MSW, PhD, has researched the important role that pets play in families. Walsh has received awards for her contributions to family therapy from the American Psychological Association, the American Association for Marriage and Family Therapy, and the American Family Therapy Association. In a recent review of this important topic, Walsh (2009) noted that companion dogs provide their owners with stability and resilience when life turmoil occurs or illness strikes. Dogs provide a sense of comfort and security when families need to move, experience the death of a loved one, or go through a divorce, and during times of illness a pet dog can become a real lifeline.

Tail Waggin' Tip

Walsh (2009) noted that "Pets are often the 'glue' in the family—they promote greater interaction and communication" (p. 483).

COMPANION DOGS UNDERSTAND HOW TO BEST HELP US THROUGH ILLNESS

For Maggie Foxmoore, a Wheaten Terrier became her lifeline when faced with a debilitating illness. Having a terrier for comfort and support made all the difference when she was sick. Maggie's an artist, with two wonderful models for her paintings: ten-year-old Lord Argyle and six-year-old Miss Maisy.

Despite their proper-sounding names, Lord Argyle and Miss Maisy are typical, exuberant Wheaten Terriers. Maggie has come to expect the usual "Wheaten greetin'" that's characteristic of this breed. "Normally with Wheaten Terriers, you can't just walk into the house and get a subdued welcome. Wheatens give you a greeting like Tigger from *Winnie-the-Pooh* stories—all bounce and joy!"

When Maggie had a bout of severe vertigo, she wasn't up for bounces. Vertigo is a severe sensation of moving or spinning that makes it hard to stand or walk. It is like the world's worst case of motion sickness, and most people need to stay in bed while they recover from it. Maggie's vertigo was caused by severe damage to her inner ear that required a trip to specialists in another state and major reconstructive surgery.

While Maggie was getting her hospital treatments, Lord Argyle felt lost:

> *My husband told me Argyle was a mess while I was gone and spent the few nights I stayed in the hospital carrying on a vigil on the sofa— just looking out the window all night long. When it was time to come home, I still felt miserable. My head was killing me and the slightest movement gave me intense vertigo. All I could do was lie quietly. When I arrived home, we were both a bit worried—expecting an enthusiastic greeting from my usually energetic Lord Argyle who'd been missing me so. Instead, the minute I got to the house, Lord Argyle sensed something was different and immediately became a restrained Wheaten I never would have imagined was possible. He calmly walked up to me, gently licked my hand, and then stuck to me through my recovery like glue!*

Wherever Maggie was, Lord Argyle positioned himself in a protective position behind her legs, leaving her side only when her husband dragged him out for potty breaks and meals.

Figure 2.1. Maggie's art captures the supportive power of nature's perfect nurses as her terriers surround her to give comfort in times of greatest need.

Since then, Maggie has had other times when she has struggled with health problems, and her Wheatens have remained her steadfast nurse crew. "When I am laid up in bed or if I am in horrific discomfort—my terriers sense it and come close to me." The support she gets from her Wheatens is reflected in Maggie's art:

> *Some of my paintings show my Wheatens sustaining me. They seem to instinctively read what's going on with my body and, at times, seem more in tune with my health than me! My Wheatens are always there to listen and, without a word, act as anchors of support 100% of the time.*

HOW DO PEOPLE WITH MEDICAL PROBLEMS BENEFIT FROM A COMPANION DOG?

As we saw with Maggie Foxmore and Lord Argyle, dogs can provide comfort, companionship, and a shoulder to cry on when you have a health problem. When health problems are chronic, a companion dog can help people achieve a more normal routine and provide important distractions from health symptoms:

- Companion dogs can keep people more active by giving them a built-in walking buddy and playmate. People may skip their own exercise routine, but the responsibility of caring for Fido will often make them get out and moving even on days that they might have otherwise stayed on the couch or in bed.
- Companion dogs may make people with visible illnesses or disabilities more approachable. People may walk by someone sitting quietly in a wheelchair or resting her cane next to a park bench, but few can resist coming over to check out the cute dog at the person's side.
- Companion dogs are cute and hilarious, and spending time with them can distract people from their own concerns, lift their spirits, and brighten their moods.
- Spending time with a dog can effectively relieve the negative effects of high stress.

If you or a loved one has a medical condition, you may wonder about adding a dog to your pack. There are a lot of issues to consider before bringing a dog into a family, especially when that family may already have extra burdens from an illness. The following are some questions to consider:

- Will the dog be too much for us?
- Dogs are cute, but do I really have the time and energy for a new puppy?
- Should we add a dog to our family at this time?

To get straight answers to these questions and more, I turned to Patricia A. Bednarik. If you ask Pat about her qualifications, she'll tell you, "I'm a long-time dog mom who enjoys dogs and helping others become dog parents." Pat serves on the board of directors for Animal Friends, a no-kill shelter in Pittsburgh, Pennsylvania, and is a foster parent and foster mentor for Cairn Terrier breed rescue. Her ten years working in rescue have given her important insights into deciding when to add a dog into a household—and when adding a dog

Figure 2.2. Pat Bednarik and nine-year-old Cairn Terrier Petunia, who spent her first four years confined to a cage in a puppy mill as a breeding dog before being rescued by Pat.

probably won't be successful. Pat's also a multiple sclerosis (MS) certified specialist who blended her understanding of dogs and medical disabilities to spearhead the MS PAWS (Pets Are Wonderful Support) Program, which provides temporary care on an emergency basis for the pets of people with MS. So, Pat's an expert placing dogs and understanding the physical and emotional needs of people with chronic medical problems.

Pat knows first hand when adding a dog is likely to work, how to bring a dog into a home when someone has health issues, and what needs to be done to make sure the dog continues to be a happy and well-cared-for member of that household:

A dog should never be added to a household on a whim or without a lot of thought and consideration. When someone in the home has special needs, it's essential to also consider that person's needs, the needs

*of other members of the household, and the needs of a dog when decid-
ing whether it's appropriate to bring a dog into the home. Adding
a dog to the household should only be considered when everyone's
needs can be met—both human and dog. And those needs can be met
day in and day out—on good days and bad.*

Adding a dog to the family is a big job and a lot of work. Every
dog needs training to be a good family member and neighbor. Pat cautions that it's important to make sure this is the right time to add a dog
before bringing one home:

*In some situations, the main caregiver for someone with a serious
health problem will also be the person primarily responsible for the
dog. In these cases, it's important to make sure that adding a dog
will not overburden the person's caregiver. This is especially important to think about when the person's medical condition is unstable
or progressive and the duties of that person's caregiver are likely to
increase.*

Taking the time to carefully evaluate the needs of *everyone* in the household is important to make sure adding a dog is successful for both the
dog and humans in the pack.

Questions to Ask Before Deciding to Get a Dog

- Is everyone in the household interested in and committed to
  getting a dog?
- Is there someone at home who can reliably take on the responsibility of caring for a dog every day?
- Will the dog be able to get enough daily exercise? Can someone give the dog daily walks? Is there a fenced yard, secure tie
  out, or runner for the dog?
- Can you commit to making sure the dog is adequately trained?
  Do you have the time, motivation, and stamina to stick with a
  training program?

- Will someone be able to make sure the dog is housetrained and able to clean up any unexpected accidents in the house and droppings outside?
- Does the person who will care for the dog have a temporary or stable health problem? If the condition is a degenerative and progressive illness, is there a second person who will also be responsible for caring for the dog?
- Do you have the extra money to pay for the dog—vet bills, food, boarding, grooming, and so on?

Make sure you can answer "yes" to each question before bringing a dog home.

Once you have decided that it's the right time to add a dog to your home, you need to make sure you choose the right dog and reassess the situation to make sure you're ready to have a dog join your family. Before bringing a dog home, you must carefully consider typical dog behaviors and needs as well as any special circumstances of members in your household.

After considering the factors discussed so far, you may decide a dog in the home is not for you. You and your loved one with a medical condition can still benefit from the healing power of dogs, even if this isn't the right time to bring a dog into your home. When the full-time responsibility of dog ownership is too much, think about arranging for visits from a certified therapy dog and the dog's handler. These can often be arranged by contacting local dog shelters and dog clubs that train dogs for therapy dog work.

Tail Waggin' Tip

People with medical illnesses who can't have their own dogs can still benefit from the healing power of a dog by arranging for visits from a certified therapy dog and the dog's handler, who can ensure the safety and care of the dog.

CHOOSING THE RIGHT DOG

When trying to decide what type of dog you should get, Pat suggests considering dog size, age, and the typical characteristics of different breeds:

Size of the dog is important. People often think about a small dog for the older, frail person, but a small dog can easily trip an older person, especially if they have impaired vision. And for people adjusting to new blindness, a service dog is often a better choice compared with a pet dog.

The dog's age is an important consideration. Puppies are cute, but puppies are babies and they're totally focused on themselves. For someone with a health problem, an older dog who is already housebroken, trained, and less energetic is often a better choice. Puppies also require detailed training throughout their puppyhood. Each week is critical in the developmental process to help the puppy become a good dog. If the puppy's caregiver has a health problem that may interfere with their training during these critical weeks, important lessons may be lost that the puppy may have needed. It's also easier to judge personalities and temperaments of the older dog to make sure they'll meet your lifestyle and needs.

There are certain breeds Pat wouldn't pick as first choices for people with medical needs, including dogs that are highly protective, territorial, likely to have high energy levels, or are generally difficult to train:

Breed can be important, but you also need to consider an individual dog's personality and temperament. While high-energy, territorial, or stubborn dogs are usually not the best choice, a lot depends on the motivation of the owner—how much time and effort that person is willing to invest in training their dog. Although terriers can be stubborn and difficult to train, there's a wheelchair-bound lady who has a Jack Russell Terrier mix that she brings to small dog socials at the shelter. The lady's in a power chair and she has her dog trained so that when she gives a signal, the dog immediately runs over to her, jumps up on her lap, and then sits on her shoulder where it quietly rides once the chair is moving. It's amazing to watch and, knowing terriers, I know the tremendous effort this lady put into training her dog. You need to commit to training every dog—some dogs will just need more effort.

If you have a particular breed in mind, it's best to talk it over with people who raise and show that breed of dog in American Kennel Club competitions. These people are a wealth of knowledge when it comes to knowing the type of home that best suits the needs of their breed of dog.

Breeds to consider when someone has special needs:	**These highly protective, territorial, high-energy, and difficult-to-train breeds are not generally first choices when someone in the house has a medical problem:**
Bichon Frise	Akita
Cavalier King Charles Spaniel	Border Collie
Cocker Spaniel	Chihuahua
Adult English Setter	Chow Chow
Golden Retriever	German Shepherd
Greyhound (if a fenced yard is available)	Husky
Irish Wolfhound	Terrier
Adult Labrador Retriever	
Pomeranian	
Pug	

After considering size, age, and breed, you need to make sure the individual dog is a good match for the family. Pat especially recommends that you choose a dog that seems to initially bond with the person for whom you're getting the dog:

Make sure the family member who most needs therapeutic benefit from the dog meets the dog before the dog has been selected to come to your home. The dog should go up to this individual and prefer him to others in the family. If the dog shies away from the person with a health condition during this time, he'll probably continue to do so after the dog is home, too. Make sure you bring any devices the person uses—canes, walkers, wheelchairs, motorized scooters, speech-generating devices, etc. Make sure you test the dog's reaction to each of these. If a particular dog is fearful of these at the initial meeting, you may wish to look for a different dog who will be more accepting.

Pat cautions that you can't expect a dog to provide therapeutic benefit when it first joins your household. This is particularly true for younger dogs, which will require more training and care:

When a dog first comes to the home, the focus will need to be on making sure the dog's needs are being met—the dog will need to adjust to the new family and receive appropriate training and companionship. And the dog shouldn't be expected to provide companionship to people in the household all the time—he'll need time to play, work out his own energies, and relax. It might be better to arrange for visits from a certified therapy dog if you need a dog who will instantly be in tune with the needs of people in the household and who can provide therapeutic benefits right away.

Pat also encourages another realistic look at the extra workload that a dog brings to any home. This additional work may be too much in some homes, especially if someone with a health problem has a lot of needs:

Before a dog comes into a household, it's important to make sure that adding a dog will not give excess work to someone who is already overburdened caring for someone with an illness. This can be another great time to set up visits from a therapy dog rather than adding the responsibility of dog ownership to the home.

DOGS CAN BE WONDERFUL...BUT

There's no question that Pat loves dogs, and nothing brightens her face like talking about a successful rescue for one of her foster Cairns into a happy, forever home. But Pat is also a realist, with no-nonsense, down-to-earth tips on deciding when to add a pet to a household—and a thorough understanding of when a dog may not be the right choice for a certain individual or family:

> *Dogs are wonderful, but sometimes a dog is not the right pet. Sometimes, people who had dogs can no longer fulfill the responsibilities needed to care for a dog. In some cases, a cat may be a better choice. Other times, the best pet is no pet.*

 ## If You Live Alone, Think Twice Before Getting a Dog If

- you can't physically take care of yourself
- you can't financially manage the extra expenses of having a dog (veterinary care, licensing, food, grooming, boarding, etc.)
- you frequently need to go into the hospital
- there's no way for you to exercise a dog
- you can't provide adequate companionship for a dog
- you have no *reliable* backup plan to care for your dog should you need it

In some cases, having certain health problems makes it difficult, if not impossible, to care for a dog. A dog needs care each and every day—not just on good days. A dog should never be added to a home when there are concerns that the dog might not be safe or well cared for. A dog should never be added to a home where it might be hurt or neglected. Pat describes a few specific health problems that suggest a dog is not the right choice:

> *Dogs are very sensitive to people's emotions and a pet dog should probably not be added to the household when someone in the house is not emotionally stable or has significant anger control issues. Dogs can be very helpful for people with depression, but should not be given to people prone to violence. This doesn't mean that people with*

psychiatric illnesses can't benefit from dogs. This might be an ideal time to look for someone with a therapy dog to come and make visits, rather than adding a pet to the home.

Patients with dementia are also not good candidates to be care-givers for a dog. The dog is not only there to help the person—the person needs to be able to reliably care for the dog. Just because Grandpa enjoys cuddling with your Yorkies when you come to visit and they seem to cheer and calm him, that doesn't mean he can assume the responsibility of caring for his own dog. This is another great opportunity to bring your dogs over for regular visits or arrange for visits from therapy dogs whose handlers can make sure the dogs' needs are also met.

Pets can also cause people to fall. A recent report in the *Journal of Safety Research* described injuries related to falling caused by pets (Stevens, Teh, & Haileyesus, 2010). Falls occurred from chasing pets, falling or tripping over pets, or being pulled or pushed by pets. It's especially important to consider possible risks from pets—especially smaller and more active pets—for older seniors and individuals with balance or mobility problems. As Stevens et al. (2010) noted, under-standing what may precipitate falls and attending to obedience train-ing can minimize fall risks.

Living with a health problem helps you expect the unexpected given that your symptoms may flare up or progress. You may have times when it's harder to manage daily needs. You may need to make unexpected trips to the hospital. While your health problems are wors-ening, Fido will still need to get the same care—he'll still need his daily walks and exercise, meals, potty breaks, companionship, and so on.

Tail Waggin' Tip

Before adding a dog to the home, make sure you have planned for the dog's needs, understand the training and effort that will be needed to care for the dog, and have plans for dog care when health problems may prevent you from caring for the dog.

Pat's patient Dan is a young man with MS, a progressive neurological illness that unpredictably hits different parts of the nervous system. Loss of nerve functions can come and go or progressively get worse. Adding a dog to the household was successful for Dan because both he and his wife are dedicated to providing daily dog care:

> *Dan is confined to a wheelchair, and when he adopted Ginger—it was a match made in heaven. When Dan was first introduced to Ginger, she came right up to him and wasn't intimidated by his chair. They really seemed to bond and Dan became totally invested in caring for Ginger and making sure she had everything she needed. He made sure she got fed, played with, and brushed—and was given time to rest. Taking care of Ginger gave Dan a new purpose and it really brought him out of himself and focusing on his own limitations. But Dan couldn't do everything for Ginger himself. His wife was also committed to caring for Ginger—making sure Ginger was put out in the fenced yard, making sure the yard was kept poo-free, and caring for Ginger on Dan's bad days.*

Everyone can have the occasional emergency that happens unexpectedly. You can't predict most accidents or emergencies. But if you have a health problem that's unstable or progressive, the occasional episode when you can't take care of a dog may become more frequent. Sometimes you can predict that you'll frequently need extra help. When this is the case, you also have the added responsibility of making solid arrangements with reliable adults or dog professionals for Fido's care when the unexpected happens.

3

Getting Involved With Pet Therapy

Therapy dog work involves a close relationship between the trained dog and his dedicated handler. Philosophers have actually debated the ethics of using pets for human therapy: Is it fair to the dog to ask him to help people? Their analysis supports that the therapy dog–handler relationship benefits the dog, his handler, and those lucky enough to have a therapy dog visit (Zamir, 2006). Because dogs are very social by nature, philosophers believe that they will enjoy the social aspects of therapy work as well as the positive bonding that occurs through dog–handler training.

I started life with the therapeutic benefit of a companion dog. When my parents decided it was time to adopt their second child, they made two adoptions: a noisy, blue-eyed girl with curls and a slobbery English Springer Spaniel puppy to provide comfort and companionship to my older brother. After having my own children, I'm still amazed at how my mom cheerfully cared for a 2-year-old, a new baby, and a puppy! Although the puppy, Skipper, was intended for my brother, his annoying little sister staked a claim on the dog, and Skipper and I were inseparable for our twelve years together. Skipper helped raised me, teaching me valuable lessons about dogs and life.

Growing up, our home was always filled with dogs. My artist mom painted portraits of show dogs, and my dad trained hunting dogs. So I naively thought I knew everything I needed to know about dogs and dog training. When I decided to add a therapy dog to my medical team, I was a bit surprised to discover that there's a lot involved before making that first therapy visit. In addition to learning obedience commands, I needed to thoughtfully evaluate my dog's temperament to see whether he was a good match for therapy work—and then find what type of work might be best for him. We started with a reading program for children, then added nursing home visits, and he finally found his niche seeing hospital patients. When you're thinking about therapy dog work, you need to answer several questions:

- Is therapy dog work right for you and your dog?
- Can you make the training commitment needed to become certified as a therapy dog–handler team?
- Do you know where to find other therapy dog handlers to give you advice and help you get started?

Becoming a therapy dog–handler team takes time, training, and commitment. Therapy dog work isn't right for every dog or for every dog owner. But when it is right, you'll find yourself open to an amazing world.

Tail Waggin' Tip

Handler Rose Mary Mulkerrin noted that the training required for her dog, Lucky D, to become a therapy dog has made him a better pet, too—staying on command, leaving dropped items on the floor, and adopting a calm demeanor on request.

IS THERAPY WORK RIGHT FOR YOU AND YOUR DOG?

Ann Cadman, Health and Wellness Coordinator at Animal Friends, a companion animal resource center, has been working with therapy dog handlers for several years. During a three-year period, her therapy dog–handler teams visited over 69,000 lucky people:

It takes a special dog and handler to become a therapy dog team. Therapy dog work's not right for every dog or every handler. I've had lots of dogs through the years, and many of them just didn't have the temperament or stamina to be good therapy dogs. It's important to learn what's needed for a therapy dog so you plan this work with the right dog.

Janet Malinsky and Barbara Pohodich have teamed up not only with their dogs for therapy dog work but also with each other. Janet and Barb are therapy dog handlers who work as a team, making weekly visits together with their pups to lucky residents of nursing homes and hospice centers. Janet has two therapy dogs, both Toy Manchesters, and Barb makes visits with a Toy Poodle and a Maltese.

Janet and Barb take their therapy dog commitment seriously, continuing to attend training classes with their dogs and making visits a priority. They go out of their way to make their visits

Figure 3.1. Janet and Barbara are friends who have become a bubbly team of therapy dog handlers, making weekly visits together. They're joined here by two of the four therapy dogs in their pack: Toy Manchester Courtney and Maltese Sadie.

extra-special—dressing the dogs up for holidays, taking photos of the persons they visit with the dogs, and reminding residents that they thought about them during the days between visits. Janet describes a special bond she and Barb feel with the residents they visit:

> For many of the people we visit, we are their family. They look forward to seeing us and especially our dogs and worry terribly about the dogs if we miss a week. One lady, Grace, expected to see "her dogs" each week. She always enjoyed when we took pictures of her with Courtney, Brittney, Sadie, and Lexi. She framed the pictures and put them up in her room. The "brag book" of pictures she showed everyone she met was filled with pictures of our therapy dogs.

Barb further explains that the bond she and Janet share with the people they visit is a two-way street:

> The people we visit become like family for us, too. Grace became like a grandmother to us. When my daughter graduated from high school, we asked Grace to come to the graduation party. Grace talked about coming to the party for over a month and even went to the beauty parlor for what she called "the works"! It was a big effort for Janet and me to get Grace to the party—helping her get ready, getting her and her wheelchair into the car, and taking care of her while she was with us—but it was worth it for her and for my family. My daughter gained a new grandmother that day.

And just think—it probably wouldn't have happened without the work of a couple of cuddly therapy dogs.

Janet continues, "When you see the same people every week, they become a part of your family." And Janet and Barb are important for the families, too. Barb recalls, "Betty's daughter always appreciated us visiting her mom, since she couldn't visit every day. She always told us, 'Your visit is the highlight of Mom's week.'" When Betty became ill and was moved to hospice, the dogs went to make visits at the hospice, too:

> The first week Betty was at hospice, we came for a visit. The minute Betty's daughter saw the dogs, she started to cry—having "her dogs" with her at the hospice helped bring joy to Betty in her final months.

We didn't know how much it meant until we were presented with beautiful thank you notes one week—addressed to each of our dogs!

Ann Cadman understands what it takes to be a good therapy dog. Therapy dogs need to be well behaved, well adjusted, outgoing, and not afraid of strangers:

It really doesn't matter what the dog's breed, size, or gender is when you're looking for a therapy dog—it's all about temperament and stamina. I have three dogs at home that are wonderful pets, but I'd never consider them for therapy work because they don't have the temperament and stamina that are required of the therapy dog. The therapy dog needs to be people oriented, able to accept touching, not pull on a leash, and not bark or yip when working. Older dogs are often calmer and can make terrific therapy dogs.

Ruth Salvador took Ann's advice to heart when she adopted Birdie, a Border Collie who had been trained for a goose-chasing business. Though an expert herder, Birdie lacked the stamina to chase geese for prolonged periods of time and left her owner at age four to live with retired fifth-grade teacher Ruth. For the last three years, Birdie has found a new career with Ruth as a therapy dog:

I never thought I would spend my retirement years visiting with a therapy dog. After Birdie joined my family, I was amazed how well she interacted with everyone. On our walks, Birdie made sure she gave attention to everyone we passed: adults, children, busy repairmen, someone stepping out of a car, and deliverymen. If Birdie saw them, she couldn't pass up an opportunity to get involved. And most people couldn't resist Birdie, either. She always left them smiling. I just knew Birdie was meant to be a therapy dog.

Today, Birdie visits dementia patients at a nursing home; children at a cancer center; and elementary school children for a reading program. She may not have had the stamina for goose chasing, but what amazing staying power she has for bringing love to so many needy people!

Golden Doodle Lucy has a gentle touch, social nature, and consistent obedience that make her a terrific therapy dog. Like all good

Figure 3.2. Border Collie Birdie was not cut out for herding work, but even a "flawed dog" can become a healing therapy dog. Photo courtesy of Natalie Larocco.

therapy dogs, Lucy seems to be instinctively drawn to people in the most need of her therapeutic touch. Since she was a small puppy, Lucy understood when people needed to be comforted. "She has always been so in tune with people," recalls Lucy's handler, Kad Favorite. "If someone's crying, Lucy will gently walk up to their side and rest her head on the person's hand or lap." Consistent obedience, a social personality, and an open, gentle spirit made Lucy a great candidate for becoming a therapy dog.

Patti Shanaberg, founder of central Ohio's therapy dog organization Angel Paws, suggests practicing your dog's obedience skills in public places as a good way to hone skills during distraction and to make sure your dog is comfortable meeting strangers in public places:

> *Some dogs enjoy greeting people in your home and when walking on the street. But it can be a very different experience going into strange buildings to meet people. It's good to take your dog repeatedly into public places that allow dogs, like pet stores and warehouse stores that permit dogs inside. These experiences help to make sure your dog will be comfortable entering buildings and meeting with the*

strangers in those buildings. These encounters are more like many therapy dog visits than simply greeting people in the open on the street. If you find that your dog is uncomfortable in these situations, continue to work with your dog in a positive way and include these kinds of experiences with indoor practice with strangers to help your dog become more comfortable in these types of environments.

Before visits can start, it is important to test each dog to make sure he's ready for therapy work. Ann Cadman ensures that all dogs complete testing and certification by an outside organization:

People sometimes think that because their dog is happy greeting people at their home, he'll also be a good therapy dog. Many times he will—but it's important to make sure each dog is suited for therapy work by completing specific testing in an unfamiliar environment with unfamiliar humans interacting with the dog before visits are started. This is important for the safety and well-being of the dog and those who the dog will visit. Therapy dogs also act as ambassadors for your volunteer organization and for your dog's breed—so it's important to make sure they're up to the requirements of therapy work.

A list of organizations that test and certify therapy dogs and Web sites that list specific requirements for each group are provided in the Resources section at the back of this book. Contacts at these sites will be able to point you to local therapy dog groups in your area where you will be able to get tips on therapy dog training and suggestions for places in your neighborhood that might be interested in receiving therapy dog visits.

Does My Dog Have What it Takes to be a Therapy Dog?

Check each statement that correctly describes your dog. My dog:

- consistently follows commands for sit, down, stay, and come—even when there are distractions

- walks nicely at my side on a leash, especially through groups of people
- enjoys being greeted by strangers
- is able to be greeted, petted (including clumsy petting), and hugged without jumping, straining, barking, or biting
- is able to avoid sniffing or picking up interesting items (when told "Leave it")
- tolerates crowds, activity, and noise
- tolerates getting bathed, brushed, and having his nails clipped in preparation for visits
- greets new situations, unusual equipment, and strangers of different ages without distress

A therapy dog needs to be able to do *all* of these things. If you can honestly say that each statement describes your dog, you may have a future therapy dog. If your dog struggles with some of these skills, you may want to attend therapy dog training classes, which are offered by many dog clubs and shelters that administer therapy dog testing to help improve your dog's obedience skills.

My own therapy dogs are Soft-Coated Wheaten Terriers. Wheatens are known for being lovable, playful, energetic, *and* jumpy. Talk to a Wheaten owner and you'll soon hear about the "Wheaten greetin'"—a Wheaten's favorite way to say "hello" is to bound straight up in the air and give someone a big smooch on the face. Needless to say, a therapy dog is not permitted to jump on others.

Before starting therapy dog work with her lovable, friendly Wheaten, Hayley, Debbie Brown was worried that Hayley might jump on people when she got excited:

I soon discovered that Hayley understood the difference between play time and therapy visits. She really seemed to understand that the people she was visiting in the nursing home were old, and instead of jumping to greet them, she'd move next to them and lean in for a greeting. She got it!

When I was practicing skills in a pet store with my second Wheaten, Toby, the store owner gave me a curious look, and I explained how I was helping Toby learn to follow commands with distractions in preparation for his therapy dog test. Knowing the typical exuberance of Wheatens, the owner promptly announced, "You'll never get a Wheaten certified for therapy work." To make a long story short, like Hayley, Toby successfully passed his test and I confess that the *first* place we visited after placing Toby's bright yellow "I AM A THERAPY DOG" tag on his collar was the same pet store. Debbie is right—therapy dogs just "get it" and understand when it's time to work their healing magic.

People sometimes wonder if there are certain breeds best suited to become therapy dogs. Ann Cadman will tell you that becoming a therapy dog is more about an individual dog's temperament and training than breed. Pam Gaber, the CEO of Gabriel's Angels, echoes that sentiment. Gabriel's Angels is an organization committed to providing pet therapy for abused, neglected, and at-risk children. Gabriel's Angels was named after its first therapy dog, which was not a typical therapy dog breed—a beautiful grey Weimaraner, Gabriel. Pam's work with Gabriel and other therapy dogs has taught her that great therapy dogs can come from many breeds:

> *When people think about therapy dogs, they often picture Golden Retrievers or Labrador Retrievers. If you're interested in therapy dog work, don't be discouraged just because you don't have a breed that's a popular one for therapy dog work. Other breeds can also become terrific therapy dogs. On the other hand, your individual dog might not be suited for therapy work—even if he is a popular breed for therapy dogs. At Gabriel's Angels, we have lovely therapy dogs from a wide range of breeds—unexpected breeds like Dobermans, Rottweilers, and pit bull mixes, as well as Goldens and Labs. We don't automatically say "no" to these "bully breeds," but we don't always say "yes" either. Over the past ten years, we've found that, while genes play a role, it's the love and healthy environment provided by the owner that play a bigger part in how a dog turns out and whether he'll be suited for therapy dog work.*

The director at one of the programs where I volunteer with my Wheatens recently asked me, "We just got an application from someone

Figure 3.3. Gabriel and Pam Gaber from Gabriel's Angels.

who wants to do pet therapy with a Rottweiler. They have letters that say he's a great dog that has worked so well in nursing homes. But a Rottweiler therapy dog? What do you think?"

I didn't have to think long—Rottweilers can make terrific therapy dogs. A great example is Dillon, a five-year-old who has been making visits with his handler, Kerri Stamas, for the last two years. As a puppy, Dillon spent time in an apartment complex office where renters would come to pay their monthly bills. Kerri remembers how Dillon enjoyed playing with the children:

> People would often have their kids with them and the kids would have fun playing with Dillon. Pretty soon, kids would come to the office by themselves and ask, "Can Dillon come out to play?" I think this early puppy experience taught Dillon to think he was just one of the kids.

Dillon started obedience training at seven weeks of age. In puppy kindergarten, the class practiced "pass the puppy," and Dillon nipped at three people. Kerri took this seriously and worked on training to reduce aggressive behaviors. After a few weeks, Dillon understood how to greet strangers appropriately. Kerri continued to train Dillon over the next four years in obedience and Rally classes that promote teamwork between the dog and handler and help train the dog to crisply perform obedience and other skills on a testing course during competitions. Dillon grew up to be a lovable, social dog, and Kerri trained him for therapy dog work. Dillon has a special affinity for working with children. At one crisis center, Dillon acts as a go-between to help parents reconnect with children who have been living at the center without their parents:

> *Interacting with Dillon is something both the parents and children can do comfortably. Once they're playing with Dillon and talking about him together, it's easier for the parents and kids to start talking with each other about other things, too.*

Despite Dillon's size and muscled body, children don't fear him:

> *When children see Dillon's smiling face, they just light up. Dillon seems to give off a message inviting the children to come and play with him. For most kids, this is irresistible. Dillon just draws children to himself. At one event we attended, booths were set up to showcase different services available for children in need. Dillon and I were at the pet therapy booth and next to us was a lady with marshmallow shooters for the kids—these are little toys that send small marshmallows flying into the air that kids generally can't resist. As kids would walk toward the booths, they'd see Dillon and would pass up the marshmallow shooters so they could pet my dog. The lady at the marshmallow shooter table complained that Dillon was keeping kids from stopping to see her and put up a divider so kids wouldn't be able to see Dillon before they'd stopped at her booth.*

Dillon also has incredible patience. Because children are so attracted to him, he'll often find himself surrounded by large groups of kids—with everyone reaching in to pet, hug, and brush this beautiful dog.

Many people are surprised when they first meet this gentle giant:

> *At one facility, teenage boys had been looking through some books showing different dogs and were commenting that Rottweilers were*

Figure 3.4. Kerri and Rottweiler therapy dog Dillon. Kerri's commitment to training resulted in both a wonderful therapy dog and great helper around the house who picks up dropped items, finds a lost remote or shoes, and even helps carry in the groceries.

mean and ferocious. So the counselor asked us to bring Dillon for a visit. When we got there, a Rhodesian Ridgeback who is a therapy dog at the center came up to Dillon—apparently less than pleased to find another dog in his territory. The Ridgeback gave Dillon a sniff and a quick snap to show him who was boss. Dillon calmly backed away and turned his attention to the teens. The boys looked on in amazement and one exclaimed, "Now that's something I never thought I'd see! A Rottweiler backed down!"

That day, those boys got a great lesson about dogs—and a valuable lesson about handling conflict without fighting. And in case you think Dillon must just be a timid Rottweiler—he's not. When he backed down from the Ridgeback, it wasn't from fear. Dillon made a choice, one that was fostered by good education and excellent manners developed by Kerri's diligent commitment to training.

Dillon's incredible work with children shows that so-called "bully breeds" can be wonderful therapy dogs—these tough-looking dogs can provide a calm strength for those needing support. So should my director consider adding a well-trained, qualified, reliable Rottweiler to our team? Absolutely.

Who could forget when the headlines broke implicating star football player Michael Vick in dog fighting? In August 2007, Vick pleaded guilty to federal charges and the news media covered his sentencing and imprisonment. But while Vick was serving time, what happened to his silent victims, those many unfortunate dogs brutalized through dog fighting? Many of these dogs were given second chances at a better life—and one of those dogs is a pit bull named Hector.

When Vick's dogs were taken in for rescue, Andrew (Roo) Yori, an experienced trainer with a passion for showcasing the positive attributes of pit bulls, contacted the group caring for some of the dogs, the Bay Area Doglovers Responsible About Pit Bulls—also known as BAD RAP. When Roo first met Hector, he could see the external scars from Hector's years in dog fighting. But he also saw that, despite the scars on the outside, Hector was still a wonderful dog on the inside:

> *Hector was around two or three years old when I first saw him. You could tell he'd been thorough a lot by looking at him, with scars on his chest and legs, missing canine teeth, and a notch out of his tongue.*

Figure 3.5. Behind the scars of abuse, Hector's bright eyes and pleasant disposition showed the making of a terrific pet and a future therapy dog. Photo courtesy of Joshua J. Grenell.

But I could also see the dog within and knew Hector would make a wonderful addition to my family.

So on lucky Friday the 13th of June 2008, Hector joined Roo and the rest of the Yori pack:

Although fighting dogs are usually poorly socialized, Hector turned out to be a happy, easygoing dog. We call him "Hector the Inspector" because he likes to sniff and investigate everything. He really takes everything in—it's as though he's making up for lost time when he missed out on exploring the world and meeting others. Because of Hector's demeanor, I knew he'd make a wonderful companion dog and, more than that, I thought he'd be a good therapy dog.

Roo and Hector completed therapy dog training and testing in February 2009, with the test evaluator making a special note of Hector's excellent behavior:

Hector's story is really one that highlights the resilience of dogs. Hector is now enjoying a second chance at life—this time as a therapy dog. Hector makes visits to nursing homes and hospitals, where he really touches people he meets. For our first hospital visit, Hector and I went to a common room where patients who could walk or be wheeled in wheelchairs came to sit in a circle to meet the therapy dog. Hector just bounced from patient to patient, going around the group. Some people really wanted to play with Hector, and he'd lean into them to let them know he understood and was eager for their attention. Others were more tentative about being around a dog. For these people, Hector adjusted his responses to meet their needs and comfort level. It was incredible to witness this dog that had been poorly socialized in early life really understand and connect with such a wide range of people.

As we sat together in the group, the patients really became engaged. They all wanted to hear more about Hector's story and, in some cases, told me their own views of pit bulls changed because of Hector. Perhaps more amazing was watching these patients open up and become connected with each other. After talking about Hector, people around the circle began sharing stories with each other about their dogs at home or dogs they use to have. Hector really helped those people interact and bond with each other rather than feeling like they were alone and isolated in the hospital.

Hector's incredible story shows us how there's more to each individual dog than the breed stereotypes. Hector's story also shows that a wonderful therapy dog may be hidden inside many dogs, even dogs that need a second chance at a good life.

Both large and small dogs can make great therapy dogs. Although it's easier to lift a small dog onto someone's lap, some patients may feel more comfortable with larger dogs. In one study, seniors with dementia were offered visits from a small 11-lb (5-kg) miniature Schnauzer, a medium 35-lb (16-kg) Schnauzer, and a large 44-lb (20-kg) Standard Poodle (Marx et al., 2010). The study yielded the following results:

- Nearly half of the seniors refused a visit from the small dog.
- Two of five seniors refused to see the medium dog.
- Only one in five refused the large dog.

Seniors also chose to spend more time with the larger dogs. The longest a dog was permitted to stay with any one senior was three minutes:

- On average, seniors spent over two and a half minutes with the large dog.
- Seniors spent two minutes with the medium dog.
- Seniors stayed one minute with the small dog.

Seniors also expressed a more positive attitude about visiting with the larger dogs. The results of this study shouldn't discourage you from visiting seniors with a smaller dog. It is important, however, to recognize that some people may feel less comfortable receiving visits from smaller dogs and may require more time observing the dog at a distance before they are comfortable approaching the smaller dog directly for petting. Other people might be intimidated by large dogs.

Recognize that some people might be initially uncomfortable with dogs in general or certain breeds or sizes:

- Always ask permission to provide a visit.
- Approach new people who haven't visited with your dog before slowly and gently.

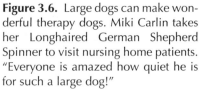

Figure 3.6. Large dogs can make wonderful therapy dogs. Miki Carlin takes her Longhaired German Shepherd Spinner to visit nursing home patients. "Everyone is amazed how quiet he is for such a large dog!"

- Allow the person you're visiting to determine how close he or she wants to come to your dog—perhaps a pat on the head while your dog sits on the floor or maybe an embracing hug with your dog on the bed.
- Don't overstay your welcome—brief visits do provide healing magic.

THERAPY DOGS HAVE A SIXTH SENSE

Ann Cadman often tells new therapy dog handlers, "Therapy dogs are special—they have a sixth sense for recognizing where they're needed. They seem to have the wisdom of old souls when it comes to sensing people's needs and pain." Ann recalls noticing this sixth sense when making visits with a nine-year-old black Belgian Sheepdog named Glinda:

> *Glinda was veteran at making nursing home visits. One evening, we'd nearly finished when we came to our last lady, who was lying in her bed with tubes attached all over her. Glinda stood quietly next to the bed like she always did. But before I knew what was happening, my big dog jumped up onto this lady's bed. Before I could react, Glinda started methodically moving toward the head of the bed. I stared in amazement as Glinda never stepped on the woman or a single tube or wire. When Glinda reached the lady's face, she just stared at the lady. The lady reached up and grabbed Glinda's face in both of her wrinkled hands, pulling Glinda's face to her own and nuzzling and kissing Glinda. I pulled Glinda down to leave and Glinda immediately jumped back up and again returned to the lady's face. It was as though Glinda knew this lady needed her to be there—close and touching. Glinda had never before jumped on a patient's bed and never did this again. I believe Glinda had a sixth sense—she was aware of what people needed and what only she could give them. A wise handler understands the gift of pet therapy and allows the dog to give back and help.*

The Mulkerrin's Border Collie mix therapy dog Lucky D is another dog that has always had this strong sixth sense. Lucky D seems to intuitively understand what people need. When the Mulkerrins first adopted Lucky, he was a shy dog, and he typically didn't greet the many people they'd pass on their walks. On one walk, Lucky D stopped abruptly and insisted on going up to a man sitting on his front porch. The man hugged Lucky D and tearfully talked about his many years of training beagles, "My own dog just died, and I really needed this."

THERAPY DOGS CAN BECOME BREED AMBASSADORS

Therapy dog visits provide opportunities to dispel myths people may have about dogs and dog breeds. When a Rottweiler, like Dillon, or a pit bull is a therapy dog, that dog is also acting as an ambassador for the breed. Two therapy dogs who make wonderful ambassadors are American Pit Bull Terriers Haley the Comet and Cayenne Pepper. Three-year-old Haley works with children coping with cancer. Haley helps these children forget their worries, at least for a little while, by soaking up their hugs and paying them back in doggie kisses. Two-year-old Cayenne visits residents at a women's shelter. Cayenne patiently lets the kids climb all over her and give her pets and hugs. She has even been used as a model for a little girl who enjoyed dressing her up in skirts and hats, sitting patiently for each new outfit!

Another great ambassador, O'Mugzy, was a pit bull who made therapy dog visits with Ann Cadman:

> *After O'Mugzy met with a group of disabled adults, the staff ask me what kind of dog she was. When I asked them to guess, they picked breeds that most people think of as being very friendly dogs. When I told them O'Mugzy was a pit bull, they couldn't believe it. This was a great opportunity to show people that a dog's behavior is more about the training than the breed.*

WHAT DOES IT TAKE TO BE A THERAPY DOG HANDLER?

Ann Cadman understands that it takes a special person to be a therapy dog handler:

> *The handler has to be as outgoing, friendly, and social as a good therapy dog. You need to convey a positive, enthusiastic attitude, be personable, and smile, smile, smile! You'll need to engage with people with good eye contact and ready conversation. If you don't know what to say—just talk about your dog!*

Ann also understands the most important responsibility for the handler is to focus on the needs and welfare of the therapy dog. The welfare of the dog comes before convenience for the handler or the desires of the person the dog is visiting:

> *The handler's number one priority is the health, safety, and welfare of the dog. The handler must remain in control of the dog the entire time its doing therapy work—a handler must NEVER put the dog in*

someone else's care, even for just a few minutes to answer a phone, visit a bathroom, or get something from the car. The handler also needs to listen to the dog. If your dog's uncomfortable or not enjoying a visit—cut the visit short.

Ann often counsels new handlers that the dog's welfare comes before the feelings of the person you're visiting. Although patients may ask you to stay longer, when your dog has had enough, it's time to leave. Before making visits, determine how long you plan to stay and what you'll allow your dog to do when you're visiting, and then stick to those rules. My dogs aren't allowed to take food from people they visit. I like to control what they eat and make sure they're not fed anything that is harmful to dogs. Taking food can result in nipped fingers or slobbery hands. Also, taking food from sick people can spread infection. So our rule is "No eating while working." When I visit a group of older nuns, Sr. Angela always tries to sneak "people treats" to my dogs—offering them whatever's in the big pouch on her walker. This big pouch is like Mary Poppins's bag: You never know what will pop out. Sister typically pulls out bags of chocolates, popcorn, breakfast cereal, and cough drops, holding each low while eagerly calling the dogs. She gets quite annoyed when I cheerfully explain that the dogs aren't allowed to eat people food or they can get sick. When the activity director tried to explain that the dogs don't eat people food Sister replied, "They don't yet. But once you get them started they'll want more and more people food!" This is exactly what I'm trying to avoid! Sister often gets a big pout on her face when I don't let the dogs take her food, and she usually insists that "just a little popcorn or a candy bar certainly won't hurt," but I know there are good reasons for not allowing people to feed your dog on visits. Resisting the directive of a stern nun is difficult, but I need to ignore that and focus on Wheatie's and Toby's best interests. The good news is that it always takes Sister awhile before breaking out her treats, so I usually try to have the dogs say a quick hello to her first and them keep them busy with the other sisters once Sr. Angela's stash is out for the offering.

One of the treasures I've found writing this book is the amazing number and variety of people who are therapy dog handlers. Homemakers, clergy, writers, health care providers, attorneys, and every imaginable career in between can be found in folks who make terrific therapy dog handlers. Barbara Pohodich is a registered nurse, so visiting patients in nursing homes and hospices with her therapy dogs seemed very natural. When Barb asked her husband, Emil, if he'd like to join her, he was a little skeptical. As an engineer, he was more at ease with measures and calculations than sick people, and he wasn't sure he'd feel comfortable. Although initially tentative, Barb recalls that Emil soon jumped in with both feet:

> *Emil was a bit hesitant that first time he walked into the nursing home with me. But when we came out, he turned to me and said, "I'm in." And I knew, like me, he was hooked. Emil saw first hand the joy that therapy dogs bring to those who are ill. The patient reactions to the dog therapy vary. It may be a slight smile, a nod, or even a soft spoken word, but as a handler, it warms your heart to know that sharing your dog for a few moments made a positive impact on someone's life. It's a feeling you don't forget and one that brings you back week after week.*

A therapy dog handler has to improvise and adjust on the fly. You never know who your dog will meet or what that person's special requests might be. For a big dog like Bloodhound Louie, space can sometimes become an issue. Louie's handler, Anita DeBiase, remembers one visit:

> *We had a request to visit a paralyzed man in intensive care. He was seated in a special chair that was too wide for Louie to get close to from the floor and too small to have room for Louie to join him. So we improvised and pulled a small chair next to the young man. Louie got on the chair. As a big dog, Louie wasn't totally comfortable, but he's a trooper—his patients come first.*

WHY DID YOU BECOME A THERAPY DOG HANDLER?

There are many reasons people become involved in therapy dog work. Some people recognize special gifts in their dogs. Others see therapy dog work as a way to connect with people in need. And some have been on the receiving end of a therapy dog visit and decide to pursue this work when their own illnesses permit it.

Patti Shanaberg had a long, painful journey to become a therapy dog handler. Patti had been around dogs her whole life, working as a horse trainer. At age 22, her life was turned upside down when she had an accident that severed her spinal cord and put her into a wheelchair for the rest of her life. Patti still had full use of her arms and was able to continue to lead a healthy, active life, maintaining full-time professional work, swimming one to two miles a day, and participating in mono-skiing. Despite her best efforts to maintain a normal life, Patti's life continued to be affected by loss. One brother had died from a brain tumor, and another brother had been killed in a car accident. Patti also lost her dad and her long-term companion dog. With all of her loss, Patti decided she'd get a puppy to train and share her life. Although her heart had been set on selecting a pure-bred Golden Retriever, a pound puppy Golden Retriever-Border Collie-Samoyed mix Samantha won Patti's heart:

When I first got Sami, I called her "Prozac" because she made such a difference in my life as soon as I brought her home. Luckily the name didn't stick and I was soon calling her Samantha or Sami. Because I am in a wheelchair, people often incorrectly assumed that Sami was a service dog. She wasn't, and Sami's real job was giving love and getting petted. Sami was often perplexed when people were reluctant to pet her while out in public, assuming she was a service dog whose work shouldn't be interrupted.

Sami opened up a whole new side of life for me. I had been working in the entertainment industry, and during a several-month hospitalization for complications from a bone infection I decided I wanted to do something different to help make a more direct difference in other people's lives. I didn't have an idea how I would do that, but decided to keep my mind open to possibilities. At this same time, I decided that it would be better to do little things with a big heart than big things with a little heart.

When Sami turned three, Patti heard about therapy dog work and knew she'd found her calling:

Although I'd continued to enjoy an active, healthy lifestyle since my accident (including competitive mono-skiing), I've met many people with chronic conditions much more debilitating than mine. I'd seen how either prolonged or repetitious confinement to a clinical environment—dependent on others and deprived of sufficient contact with nature or animals even if only for a short time—can diminish the human spirit in profound ways that impedes the recovery process. Animals, with their complete lack of agenda, have a unique capacity to reach people on a whole new level many people underestimate.

In order to be closer to her mom, Patti relocated to Newark, Ohio, where she was disappointed to find no organizations for therapy dog work. In 2003, Patti started Angel Paws, which is now the only Delta Society Pet Partners and Reading Education Assistance Dogs affiliate organization in central Ohio. Angel Paws develops and implements therapy dog programs for a wide range of facilities, developing detailed protocols and procedures to make the therapy dog experience ideal for both the dog and the people who are visited. Angel Paws serves reading programs; residents of nursing home, psychiatric, and domestic abuse facilities; and hospital and hospice patients. Sami also helped train new dog–handler teams by serving as a role model. Each new handler would observe how Sami interacted during visits before starting to make visits independently. Sami also assisted Patti with in-service orientations, community outreach programs, and various special events.

Sami lost a battle with cancer at age thirteen and a half in February of 2010, but not before touching countless lives through her incredible therapy work. Like all the best therapy dogs, Sami had a special gift for connecting with people in a deep and meaningful way. That first connection Sami made with Patti changed Patti's life and the lives of countless other people in central Ohio who have been blessed with a visit from Sami or one of Sami's students:

I was so blessed with this special dog that had an exceptionally rare combination of intelligence and gentle yet enthusiastic sweetness. It was a privilege to be on the other end of her leash while she touched so many lives.

Do You Have What it Takes to be a Therapy Dog Handler?

Answer the following questions about yourself to see whether you are suited to be a therapy dog handler:

- Can you look out for your dog's needs to avoid overtasking him?
- Can you cheerfully accept that some people will *not* want a therapy dog visit?
- Do you enjoy being with people?
- Can you greet people with a cheerful, smiling face?
- Do you enjoy helping to make others feel like they're the center of attention?

If you can answer "yes" to each question, you will probably enjoy being a therapy dog handler.

GETTING STARTED IN PET THERAPY

The *American Journal of Infection Control* published guidelines for successful dog therapy (LeFebvre, Golab, et al., 2008). These guidelines were developed by an expert panel that included individuals with expertise in therapy dogs, infection control, public health, and veterinary medicine. Recommendations were given to provide tips for new therapy dog–handler teams getting ready to start making visits, as well as advice for both new and experienced teams to help make every visit successful.

What to Do Before You Make Your First Visit

- Make sure your dog has both the temperament and stamina to make visits. Your dog should not bothered by the following:
  — Strangers

— Loud noises or sudden movements
— Threatening voices or gestures
— Crowds
— Vigorous or clumsy petting or restraining hugs
— Small children
— Equipment that might be encountered during a visit (e.g., walkers, wheelchairs, and intravenous poles)
— Other animals

- Make sure your dog is ready for making visits.
  — Have you and your dog completed initial obedience training and passed therapy dog certification testing?
  — Will your dog consistently follow your commands?
  — Is your dog in good health, and are all of his vaccines current?
- Make sure the facility you're visiting has an approved animal visitation policy. Learn the policies for each facility you visit.
  — Are there certain locations within a facility where visits should take place?
  — Do you need to sign in or check in with a staff member each day you visit?

These recommendations can serve as a general guide when you are preparing for visits with your therapy dog. You will likely receive additional instructions from both the volunteer group organizing your visits and any facility you visit.

 ## Planning Ahead of Time Makes Visits Successful

- Make sure an experienced handler or someone from the facility you're visiting supervises your first visit to show you the ropes and explain unique aspects of the facility.

- Make sure your dog is healthy, clean, and brushed on visit days. Your dog should also complete annual health assessments by a veterinarian.
- Make sure you as the handler are healthy and free of infectious conditions on the day of your visit.
- Schedule time for your dog to relieve himself before beginning the visit. Add in additional breaks during your visit as needed by your dog.
- Wash your hands before and after seeing every patient. Carry hand sanitizer for you and the patients to use at each visit.
- Your therapy dog is your primary responsibility on visit day. Make certain you are in control of your dog throughout the entire visit. *Never* turn that care over to someone else.
- Keep your dog on a leash throughout the visit.
- Check in with the staff before beginning each visit to find out who should not be visited that day.
- Ask permission from each person you plan to visit before entering his or her room or approaching him or her with a dog. Respect people's wishes to refuse a visit, and thank them with a smile. Don't try to convince people that they'll want a visit or force a visit on them.
- Avoid visiting people when they are eating meals, having procedures done, or are being attended to by staff.

GETTING YOUR DOG CERTIFIED

As I mentioned before, every dog should be tested by an experienced expert in therapy dogs before beginning to make visits. Basic obedience training, temperament testing, and specialized therapy dog training and testing are required prior to beginning therapy dog visits. This training provides certification to a specific dog–handler team. This certification does not extend to other dogs or handlers who have not been specifically tested as a team. Basic certification can be obtained through organizations such as Therapy Dogs International and the

Delta Society. The American Kennel Club offers Canine Good Citizen certification, which is intended to demonstrate that the dog has mastered basic obedience training and shows appropriate interaction with people and other dogs. Further therapy dog testing is generally required in addition to Canine Good Citizen testing before therapy visits can be made to health care facilities.

As the dog's handler, your jobs are to drive him to visits and make sure you can tend to his needs. Therapy dog handler Pauline Glagola makes sure she always has the supplies for her therapy dogs by taking a Necessary Dog Equipment bag for every visit. Depending on where she's visiting, Pauline also sometimes brings along a camp chair that her dog can sit on when visiting.

Necessary Dog Equipment

Put together your dog's Necessary Dog Equipment bag, which will likely need to be adjusted depending on where you're going for visits. Most bags will need to include at least the following items:

- Your dog's therapy dog certificate or badge and up-to-date vaccination record
- Small towel
- Hand sanitizer
- Collapsible water dish
- Poopie bags
- Brush
- Small treats
- Small ball for playing fetch if your dog enjoys this

Routinely making visits with a Necessary Dog Equipment bag helps make certain you'll have all the supplies you need for your therapy dog. I also use a short, four-foot leash for therapy visits because it's important to keep my dogs close to me during visits. Adding a therapy dog scarf can also help remind both your dog and people you meet that your dog is serving as a therapy dog. My dogs wear their hospital identification badges, which show their photo, name, and status as a volunteer.

Neither pets nor handlers should visit patients if either the dog or handler is ill. Dogs should not make visits if they have open wounds or skin diseases. You may also worry about your dog picking up infections and spreading them to other patients or bringing them home to your family. Fortunately, this happens very rarely. The Centers for Disease Control and other agencies have published recommendations to provide guidelines to help minimize the spreading of infections between patients and therapy dogs (Sehulster & Chinn, 2003). In the next paragraphs, I provide the latest information on infection precautions with pet therapy.

Hospital patients may have difficult-to-treat infections, such as those from methicillin-resistant *Staphylococcus aureus* (MRSA) and *Clostridium difficile* infections. To determine whether dogs might be able to pick up these infections from the humans they visited, researchers at Ontario Veterinary College of the University of Guelph (Lefebvre et al., 2009) tested one hundred ninety-four therapy dogs every two months for one year and made the following observations:

- Nine dogs had a single test that showed MRSA in the dog's nose or stool. No dog had MRSA detected more than once.
- Clostridium was found in thirty-nine dogs, with repeated testing positive for eight dogs.
- None of the dogs testing positive for Clostridium had signs of an infection, such as diarrhea.

The good news was that the dogs didn't seem to typically get sick from being exposed to these human infections; the bad news was that the dog could pick up these infections and possibly carry them to others.

The researchers found that dogs that tested positive for these infections tended to be the dogs that frequently licked patients, accepted treats from patients during visits, sat directly on infected patients' beds, or shook paws with patients. Other reports have also been published describing pets contracting MRSA from infected humans with whom they have had close contact (Rutland et al., 2009). Discouraging these behaviors in your dog is important to help reduce infection risk, especially if the dog is visiting hospital patients or people living in facilities where these infections are a problem.

Tail Waggin' Tip

Therapy dogs are more likely to pick up patients' infections when they lick or accept treats from patients, sit on patients or their bedding, or shake paws. Putting a clean sheet on a patient's lap or over the patient's bedding before the dog touches it can help reduce the spread of germs.

Eating raw meat has also been linked to increased risk for infection in dogs. One study tested stool samples from two hundred healthy dogs every two months for one year (Lefebvre, Reid-Smith, et al., 2008). Dogs that ate raw meat were about twenty times more likely to have *Salmonella* or *Eschericia coli* (E. coli) bacteria in their stool samples. They were not more likely to have MRSA or Clostridium bugs. For this reason, raw meat consumption should probably be limited in therapy dogs, especially those that are allowed to visit patients with compromised immune systems and thus have a higher risk of contracting infections.

The following are some tips on reducing infection risks during therapy dog visits:

- Make visits only when both dog and handler are healthy and free of infectious symptoms or conditions.
- Make sure your dog is clean and freshly brushed before visits, to reduce dander that might cause allergic reactions in susceptible people.
- Discourage Lucky from licking or shaking paws with sick patients.
- Place fresh linen on patient beds or laps before placing Duke or his paws on the patient or the bed.
- Provide hand sanitizer for patients to use before and after each visit with your dog.
- Wash your hands before and after every patient you see.

- Wash Fluffy's feet when leaving your facility.
- Avoiding feeding your therapy dog raw meat diets.
- Don't let other people give your dog food or other treats during visits.
- Bath your dog after visits and before subsequent visits to healthcare facilities.

The best way to avoid picking up germs and spreading infections is also the easiest and cheapest: Wash your hands. According to the World Health Organization, people working around patients should wash their hands after doing the following (Pittet et al., 2009):

- Touching a patient
- Touching a patient's things (e.g., the bedding)
- Touching objects used by the patient (e.g., the bed stand, telephone, or chairs)
- Touching any medical equipment in a patient's room (e.g., moving an intravenous pole)

What's best for washing your hands? Plain old soap and water. Microbiologists at the University of North Carolina at Chapel Hill tested fourteen hand-washing products (Sickbert-Bennett et al., 2005), including regular nonantimicrobial soap, special antibacterial soaps, hand wipes, and hand rubs or hand sanitizers you use without rinsing with water. Everything was used for just ten seconds. They found that nothing, including special antibacterial soaps, worked better than regular soap and water. Other findings included the following:

- Washing with soap and water effectively kills germs.
- More costly hand wipes and sanitizers don't kill as many germs as plain soap and water.
- Soap needs water to get rid of germs. Soap lifts germs off of your skin so they can be rinsed away with water—which is why you need *both* soap *and* water.
- Washing for just ten seconds is enough to get rid of over nine in every ten germs on the hands.

So, when you're making visits with your dog, plan to wash your hands frequently to avoid catching people's germs and possibly spreading germs to others.

Tail Waggin' Tip

Washing your hands with soap and water for just ten seconds effectively gets rid of germs.

Many facilities prohibit therapy dogs from visiting patients who are critically ill. Some of these patients may have immune systems that aren't working adequately to prevent them from getting and fighting infections. This might include patients with leukemia, patients undergoing chemotherapy, and severely malnourished patients. Patients with compromised immune systems can be visited if their treatment team considers visits to be appropriate and strict precautions are followed to avoid spreading infections to these patients (Lefebvre et al., 2008). The handler will typically need to wear a gown, gloves, and/or mask. Always check with the treating nurse before seeing any immune-compromised patient to find out if you are allowed to visit and what specific precautions are needed for that patient and his or her specific condition.

Most facilities will prohibit therapy dogs from visiting patients in critical-care units or patients in isolation. Some facilities do allow visits when strict protocols are followed to ensure the safety and well-being of both the patient and the therapy dog. The value of including therapy dog visits for critically ill patients in intensive care units is being increasingly recognized by health care providers. A recent review of therapy dogs visiting critical-care patients conducted by nurses at Wright State University concluded that therapy visits from specially trained pets, such as therapy dogs, and their handlers "enables the nurse to affordably treat the patient's body in a holistic nature," filling both physical and emotional needs for many patients in intensive care (DeCourcey, Russell, & Keister, 2010). The ability of therapy dogs to provide unconditional love without expecting anything in return from the patient was seen as particularly valuable for these patients. Make sure you review your facility's policies with the facility staff before making visits to patients in intensive care units or patients placed in isolation because of infection concerns. Isolation patients can sometimes be visited when strict precautions are followed and a facility permits.

Anita DeBiase and Bloodhound therapy dog Louie received a special request to visit a young woman with a compromised immune system who needed special protection against everyday germs:

Patricia had to be gowned, gloved, masked, and wheeled outside her room before we could visit. Her nurses were a bit worried that my big dog would remove some of her protective covering, putting Patricia at risk for getting infections. On our first visit, Louie instinctively knew how to interact with Patricia. He gently laid his head in her lap. Louie either rested his head in her lap or sat quietly next to her wheelchair while she stroked him with her gloved hand. At the end of the visit, Patricia asked if I could bring her a photo of Louie to hang in her room. Patricia had worked so hard to get ready for her visit with Louie and enjoyed their time together so much that we made sure to visit Patricia regularly throughout the rest of her hospital stay. I felt so honored to take a photo of Louie and Patricia that I framed and gave to her so she'd always have a bit of Louie by her side.

In many cases, patients in isolation will be prohibited from having you come into their room for a visit. When these patients have expressed an interest in a visit, sometimes a visit can be conducted at a distance, keeping the dog outside of the patient's doorway where the patient can at least look at the dog. You might teach your dog to raise his paw in a wave when seeing these patients. You might also carry small photos of your dog or print small cards with your dog's picture that you can ask the staff to give to these patients.

Patients get to talk to people all the time—answering questions about how they're feeling and assuring visitors that they're feeling okay. When you're a patient, visits can be exhausting. People often ask me if I have a hard time starting conversations with people when making therapy dog visits and I tell them, "Most people don't want to talk to me—they really just want to spend time with the dog. So I'll introduce Wheatie, and he usually takes care of the rest!" Ann Cadman counsels new therapy dog handlers:

> *It's not what the handler says but what the dog does that's most important. Therapy dog visits are healing because a dog won't criticize a person for forgetting details or mixing up grammar tenses. The relationship matters—not the words.*

Most people feel uncomfortable visiting patients—wondering what they might say and how they might feel. Donna Kaczynski was no exception. Her grandmother entered a nursing home after suffering a stroke, and Donna knew it was important to visit: "I don't like those places, so I asked the nursing staff if I could bring my Golden Retriever, Noah, with me. I really didn't want to go alone." The nursing home staff welcomed Noah with open arms and lots of belly scratches:

> *Noah and I visited faithfully every weekend until Gram passed. After that, I knew in my heart why we had begun that journey—Noah was destined to be a therapy dog. I researched how to get Noah certified and attended a Canine Good Citizen class. Noah passed his Canine Good Citizen and Therapy Dogs International testing, and our journey as a therapy dog–handler team started.*
>
> *While I might feel uncomfortable around sick people, Noah never sees their infirmaries. He sees a hand to pet him or one to shake or one to give a kiss to. Noah teaches me how to best serve people in need. He makes me feel very proud to be his partner.*

VOLUNTEERING IS GOOD FOR A HEALTHY SOUL AND BODY

Volunteering is good for your health. Ralph Waldo Emerson seemed to understand this when he said: *"It is one of the most beautiful compensations of this life that no man can sincerely try to help another without helping himself. Serve and thou shall be served."*

In case you're skeptical of taking health advice from poets, medical researchers have proven that Emerson's sentiment is spot on: Helping others is good for your health. In a study published in the *Journal of*

Figure 3.7. Golden Retriever Noah teaches Donna the art of visiting those in need of companionship.

Urban Health, researchers followed one hundred seventy-four older adult volunteers who served at least fifteen hours per week helping children in elementary school with reading and other skills (Barron et al., 2009):

- After four to eight months of volunteering, most people reported having more strength and energy.
- How fast seniors could climb stairs improved one hundred percent in individuals who were in only fair health when they started volunteering and by fifty percent for those who were already in good health at the start of volunteering.
- Over half of the volunteers reported that they were walking more than before volunteering, from fifty to one hundred percent more than before.
- Grip strength improved by forty to seventy-five percent.

These amazing physical benefits occurred not after a few months of an exercise program at the gym but after spending time helping children with reading. And did the volunteers think it was worth the effort? Nine of every ten volunteers came back to volunteer the next year— probably the best marker of success.

Volunteering may also help you live longer. Drs. Harris and Thoresen at Stanford University published their findings of a link between volunteering and mortality in the *Journal of Health Psychology* (Harris & Thoresen, 2005). They monitored over 7,500 seniors in the United States for eight years:

- Compared with people who "never volunteered," people who "volunteered rarely" had a forty-one percent decreased risk of dying.
- People who reported that they "sometimes volunteered" reduced their risk of death by forty-two percent.
- People who reported "volunteering frequently" reduced their risk of dying by fifty-three percent.

You might wonder, did volunteering help these seniors *get* healthier, or did only more healthy people volunteer, making it seem like volunteering had health benefits? Healthier people were more likely to be volunteers, but Harris and Thoresen showed that even after taking into account people's background and their own medical conditions, the risk of dying continued to be decreased by almost twenty percent in individuals who volunteered frequently.

TIPS ON MAKING THERAPY DOG WORK A SUCCESS

Once you have decided that both you and your dog are right for therapy dog work, you'll need to figure out what type of visits work best for you and your dog. You also will need to make sure you limit visit time to avoid overstressing your dog.

Pam Gaber of Gabriel's Angels offers some specific advice on deciding whether your dog has the temperament for certain types of therapy dog work:

Your dog has a unique personality—just like you. Just because you may want to visit hospital patients doesn't mean that's a good fit for your pooch. Gabriel, the Founding Dog of Gabriel's Angels, spent his ten-year career visiting abused, neglected, and at-risk children. And he really thrived doing this work. He was amazing and connected with these kids like a champ. One day, I was asked to bring him to visit an Alzheimer's unit where my mother-in-law's friend lived. Because of Gabriel's years of successful therapy work with children, I assumed he'd be spectacular with seniors, too. Well, he wasn't spectacular that day. While no one else noticed but me, I sensed he was uncomfortable and did not understand older individuals with dementia, who sounded and acted very differently from the children he was used to. He handled it like a champ and I made sure we didn't stay very long since I could tell he was uncomfortable. During our ride home I promised him I would never ask him to do that again. He continued his career visiting children and loved every minute. This taught me an important lesson. Just like people are often more comfortable doing certain types of volunteer work and visiting some people more than others—the same is true for the therapy dog. To be an effective and successful team—the dog and handler need to find a niche that works well for both of them.

When you're trying to decide where you'd like to visit, take time to figure out what setting and group of people will be good for visiting with your dog. If you aren't comfortable sitting on the floor, getting touched with sticky fingers, and having to wipe an occasional nose—young children may not be the group you'd like to visit. Perhaps you'd feel more comfortable hanging out with a group of teens or maybe visiting seniors. When you're comfortable, you're a more effective and cheerful volunteer—your dog senses this and so do the people you visit. Be honest with yourself about what works for you and your dog. Don't just visit where you think you should go—find someplace where you and your dog will thrive. When you find a good fit—like Gabriel and I did with children in crisis—you will go on to have an amazing experience as a therapy team.

What's it like making therapy dog visits? I think the best comparison is to think of what it's like when you're hosting an important dinner party. You get cleaned up, dressed up, and cheerfully greet each guest. Your job as the host is to make sure each guest feels he's very important to you—so you show an interest, ask questions, and really listen. But while you're listening to one guest, part of your mind is focusing on what else you need to be doing for a successful party. Did you make sure you talked to everyone? Did you listen intently to their concerns and laugh in the right places at their stories? Did they get enough to eat and drink? Sure, your spouse is there to help, but really just to back you up. You're the one who needs to work the room and make sure everyone's needs are met. I think visits are like that—at least if you're the therapy dog. Being the party host is tough work; you're not just enjoying yourself socializing around a room, you're working, and working hard. The handler's really just there for backup and emotional support. Just like you need to kick back and relax after hosting a dinner party, the same will likely be true for your dog. And no one wants to host a dinner party too often, so therapy visits should also be spaced out.

Medical research bears out that therapy dog work *is* work for the dog. Maintaining a quiet and calm demeanor when confronted with new people, noises, and activity can be tiring and taxing for the therapy dog, especially when a dog is first beginning to make visits. Cortisol levels increase in dogs used for animal-assisted therapy and activities in relation to therapy visits, suggesting a possible stress response for dogs from the visits (Haubenhofer & Kirchengast, 2006).

Initially, therapy dog visits should be limited to a total of about thirty minutes per visit day. Your job is not to try to reach everyone who might benefit from a therapy dog visit but to make sure that you and your dog make whomever you visit feel special. Once your dog gains experience, if he seems eager for longer visits, the time may be extended. Any visit lasting more than thirty minutes should include frequent breaks for the dog to obtain drinks and to relieve himself, with the total visit time limited to about one hour or so.

When Wheatie finishes his "rounds," I always tell him that his work is done and give him a big drink. His whole demeanor changes after that. He no longer seems to seek out passersby for a wag and grin. It's like he says, "Okay. I'm off duty now." As a handler, I've learned to respect that.

Tail Waggin' Tip

Therapy dog work is tough, tiring work for the dog. The dog shouldn't be overscheduled or overcommitted. Limit visits to thirty minutes for new therapy dogs and up to one hour, with breaks, for experienced therapy dogs.

It's important to understand when it's time to give your dog a break from visiting. Patti Shanaberg at Angel Paws tells her volunteers they need to learn to recognize their dog's unique stress signs:

Many dogs show stress by starting to pant or showing a reluctance to make more visits. The handler has to be tuned to his or her dog and use these cues to end visits—even when you're asked, "But can't you just see one more patient?"

Some dogs—especially those that have had a lot of training in obedience or other competitions—may have a hard time telling their handlers "No." These dogs can be used to strictly obeying and following the commands of their handlers. If you have a dog who seems to want to do everything to obey and please you, you need to be especially sensitive to your dog's stress signs, which may be more subtle and less obvious.

Scheduling too many visits with your dog can be stressful for your dog and cause burnout in overcommitted handlers. Read your dog to make sure he's comfortable where you're taking him and that you're not overtaxing him on any given visit day. If Duke's having a bad day, isn't enjoying himself, or seems to be off his game—pay attention and call it quits that day.

You also need to make sure you limit your own volunteer hours and don't overextend yourself. Volunteers who try to do too much can become stressed and burn out. Just like most things in life, a little is good, but too much can be, well, too much.

Volunteers typically believe they benefit almost as much as from their volunteering as the people the visit (Selli, Garrafa, & Junges,

2008). Volunteering has consistently been shown to improve a sense of well-being in the volunteer, as well as increase life satisfaction and improve mood. Furthermore, as discussed earlier, volunteers tend to live longer (Harris & Thoresen, 2005).

People reap the greatest health benefits by volunteering about two and a half hours each week (Van Willigen, 2000). Volunteering too often, however, can become stressful and can begin to interfere with your daily routine. Volunteering for more than one organization tends to reduce health benefits in younger adults, although seniors are healthier when volunteering for more than one group.

IS YOUR DOG ALLOWED TO BE HERE?

As an active therapy dog handler, Pauline Glagola is used to getting questioning glances and comments from people unfamiliar with therapy dogs. Pauline is often asked if her dogs are really allowed to be visiting in health facilities:

> It's important to always be friendly and polite to everyone you meet—patients, family members, staff, custodians, security workers. I always quickly answer questions when asked, and try to remember that they're probably asking because they want to make sure everything is safe and secure for those under their care. It's important to let them know that a therapy dog has been specially trained for this work and undergone careful testing and certification before being allowed to visit. This helps to explain why family members may not be allowed to bring a pet into a facility, but my dog is allowed.

HOW WILL I KNOW IF MY VISITS ARE REALLY HELPING PEOPLE?

Sometimes the smallest response to the therapy dog can be the most powerful. When Anita DeBiase was visiting patients with her bloodhound Louie, they stopped in a room where two solemn-looking young women were quietly seated at their elderly mother's bedside:

> *I asked if Louie could visit and they agreed, although they warned me that their mother wasn't fully conscious. Shoulders straightened and faces brightened as the sisters enjoyed visiting with Louie. I then asked Louie to rest his head near the mother's hand on the bed. The eager daughters tried to wake up their mother without success—or so we thought. After a few minutes, Louie and I turned to leave and the patient gave a brief smile and patted her hand on the bed for Louie to return. The sisters were so excited to realize that their mother was still with them. And of course, Louie turned back to the bed to continue to weave his magic!*

Ann Cadman remembers another brief but profoundly special moment with her dog, Beethoven:

> *Beethoven was a deaf, ten-year-old Husky mix with a gentle temperament. I always called him my dog-without-bones, because he was so floppy. Even though Beethoven was a very big dog, he'd just droop over your lap like he was a rag doll. I took Beethoven to visit disabled children at the Western Pennsylvania School for the Blind—these children have vision loss along with multiple other severe handicaps. Beethoven walked up to a girl named Cheryl who was sitting alone in her wheelchair with her eyes closed. Naturally, he just flopped across her lap. Immediately, Cheryl's eyes opened, she smiled, and she began slowly kneading his fur between her fingers. After about fifteen seconds, Cheryl stopped and Beethoven moved off of her lap. Almost instantly, she seemed to withdraw, again closing her eyes and appearing to be lost in her own world. The staff said to me, "You don't need to visit Cheryl again. She'll never remember having the dog come by." But I responded, "It doesn't matter if she remembers or not. For those few, precious seconds, Cheryl knew what was going on and reveled in her experience with Beethoven." It really doesn't matter what happened in the past or what will happen in the future. When you're with a therapy dog, you have a moment. Sometimes a moment is all you get. Sometimes a moment is all you need.*

SETTING UP A THERAPY DOG PROGRAM

Starting a therapy dog program takes commitment, organization, and good information. Before therapy dog–handler teams can begin making visits to a facility, it's important that the same procedures for visits have been approved and accepted by the volunteer organization, therapy dog–handler teams, and the facility.

The following are recommendations for an effective therapy dog volunteer program:

- Select dogs with proper temperaments for patient visits.
- Train handlers and their dogs before they start to make visits.
- Before any visits are scheduled, the dog–handler team should be tested and certified through a recognized credentialing organization, such as Therapy Dogs International, the Delta Society, or Therapy Dogs Incorporated.
- Encourage handlers to continue the training process after successfully completing therapy dog certification. A well-trained and consistently obedient dog makes a reliable therapy dog.
- Write down easy-to-understand policies for dog visits and share these with every handler and facility staff and administrators.
- Require annual health and temperament assessments to make certain dogs continue to be appropriate for making visits; health problems or changes due to aging may make your dog no longer suitable for making visits.
- Include a veterinary consultant on your team to review and approve visit policies, and provide consultation when questions or concerns arise.

Boys and girls, men and women, dog people and cat people can all benefit from therapy dog visits (Braun et al., 2009). You don't have to be a dog owner or dog lover to enjoy the healing touch of a therapy dog. Visits should be limited to people who have expressed an interest in a visit from a therapy dog and those who are well enough to participate in a visit.

 The following are some suggestions for when you are selecting people to visit (Coakley & Mahoney, 2009):

- Only make visits to people who express an interest in a visit from a therapy dog.
- Avoid patients with
  — a fear of dogs
  — an allergy to dogs
  — open, uncovered wounds
  — a contagious illness

DOGS AS HEALERS

4

Napoleon and Nikita as Nurses: Caring for and Comforting People With Illness

N urses help people get better. According the American Nurses Association, *what nursing is* was best described by two famous nurses. Florence Nightingale described the nurse's role as having "charge for the personal health of somebody." Nurse educator Virginia Henderson later explained that "Nurses help people, sick or well, to do those things needed for health...that people would do on their own if they had the strength, will, or knowledge" (http://www.nursingworld.org).

In 2010, the American Nurses Association published an updated description of nursing: "The aims of nursing...are to protect, promote, and optimize health; to prevent illness and injury; to alleviate suffering; and to advocate for individuals, families, communities, and populations" (p. 10). The American Nurses Association said it best when they stated that "It is often said that physicians cure, and nurses care" (http://www.nursingworld.org). Although doctors can't cure many diseases, nurses always care.

As a doctor, I understand what nurses do: They make sure patients get the treatments they need and make lifestyle changes that are important for better health. In the hospital and in nursing homes, the doctor may come by for a short visit, but it's the nurses who are there caring for the patients hour by hour, helping them with their therapies and providing needed support, reassurance, and care. Nurses make sure that what needs to be done gets done. They also provide comfort to people who are anxious or frightened by their sickness.

If you're having an examination or procedure performed, it's always comforting to have a nurse at your side, speaking to you in soothing tones and giving you a hand to hold. Everyone feels better when a nurse is nearby. Research shows that dogs can help give some of this same comfort that we would normally get from a nurse. In one study, the effect of having a dog nearby was tested in children ages seven to eleven years going to the dentist for a procedure (Havener et al., 2001). Half of the children waited for the dentist in the dental chair alone and then had the procedure with just the dentist present. The other children had an eight-year-old Golden Retriever therapy dog sitting next to their dental chair while they waited for the dentist and during the procedure. The dog was close enough for the children to pet. In order to see whether having the dog next to them made the children feel less stress, the researchers measured skin temperature. Have you ever noticed that your hands can feel cold when you get scared and stressed? When you are anxious or frightened, your body pulls blood from the skin to get it to the muscles in preparation for fighting or running away. When you're relaxed, on the other hand, your skin temperature gets warmer. This is the same principle used in biofeedback: Warm skin temperatures are used to determine when you have achieved a proper, calming relaxation response. This change from stressed to relaxed usually causes a few degrees warming change in skin temperature. This study yielded the following observations:

- When the children got more scared and anxious, their skin temperature dropped a few degrees, to colder levels.
- When the children felt calm and reassured, their skin temperature grew a few degrees warmer.
- Children who reported being afraid of the dentist visit and who saw the dentist without the dog had their skin temperature drop by almost 2° Fahrenheit while they waited for the dentist. After their dental procedure was done, their skin temperature was over 3.5° colder.
- The kids who were afraid of the dentist but were allowed to pet the dog grew calmer and more relaxed while waiting, with their skin

temperature increasing by over 2°. Also, after their procedures were finished, their stress had increased less than the kids without the dog, with temperatures dropping only about 1.5°.

Tail Waggin' Tip

Petting a dog can offer some of the support and caring usually given by a helpful nurse.

Another study showed similar results, with increasing calmness in children three to six years old seeing a doctor for a physical examination when a dog was with them in the room (Nagengast et al., 1997). In this study, children had two 10-minute physical examinations, with their parents in the room for both exams. During one of the examinations, a Beagle was placed on the examination table next to the child. Researchers made the following observations:

- Children found the physical examination stressful, and their blood pressure and heart rates increased while the doctor was checking them over when there was no dog with them.
- When the dog was present, however, heart rate and blood pressures dropped, showing a calming effect.
- Distress levels were also measured in the children on the basis of their behaviors, with scores twice as high during an examination when the Beagle wasn't with the child.

These studies show that simply having a dog by one's side offers support and a calming presence that has reassuring powers you often see from a caring nurse.

Mary Ann Hirt has been a nurse for over thirty years, working in the hospital, operating room, and doctors' offices over the course of her career. She currently works at Allegheny General Hospital in Pittsburgh, Pennsylvania, a teaching hospital that helps train new health care providers through Drexel University. Recognizing the amazing power of dogs to give patients some of the same support they might get from caring nurses, Mary Ann worked with her hospital's volunteer department to develop a formal hospital therapy dog program. Her interest in the caring gift of dogs started when she watched her own German Shepherd caringly tend to her disabled nephew:

> *One day, I was visiting my nephew Johnny, who was severely hand-icapped from cerebral palsy. My brother was not a dog person, but I had my 130-pound German Shepherd Baron with me, and my brother graciously let us both in. My brother didn't dislike Baron— but he was concerned that Baron might inadvertently step on Johnny and hurt him. So when I waltzed in with Baron, turned him loose, and Baron started his rapid-fire investigation of the house, my brother thought for sure that the dog would trample Johnny. I can't explain why I didn't have that same fear—I just knew Baron would be okay. You can imagine my brother's surprise when Baron, who had been leaping over furniture at 110 miles per hour, barreled into the living room where Johnny was lying on the floor and abruptly stopped in his tracks. Baron walked ever so gently over to Johnny, sniffed him a little, and softly lowered himself to the floor, lying quietly next to my nephew. It was amazing to see this usually boisterous dog in such a caring and tender posture. It was as though Baron knew—here was someone in need of care. Care that he could unselfishly give.*

SOME DOGS SEEM DESTINED TO BE OUR NURSES

Just like some people have a knack for nurturing others, the same is true for certain dogs. When my mom died, my dad felt very alone and wanted to fill a bit of the void in his life with a dog. My dad had raised and trained hunting dogs while I was growing up and had always had a dog in the house until he and my mom grew older. When an active Cocker Spaniel named Buddy took up residence with Dad, we in the family were a little concerned that the dog might accidentally knock my dad down or pull him over when they were walking on the leash. Amazingly, although Buddy could be very exuberant with the rest of us in the family, he seemed to understand that my dad needed a quieter and more subdued Buddy. At the time, my dad was walking very slowly, with frequent stops. When he'd hook Buddy to the leash, Buddy would patiently move at my dad's crawling pace, never pulling or rushing him ahead.

After my dad died, Buddy attached himself to my sister-in-law, Sue. Living with Sue, Buddy always wanted to be in the center of the action, eager to play with everyone around him. When Sue fell and dislocated her shoulder, she needed to rest her shoulder and take time to heal. Somehow, Buddy again sensed that it was time to don his nurse's cap, moving more gingerly around Sue and protecting her from getting bumped or jostled:

> *After I hurt my shoulder and was recovering, Buddy wouldn't leave my side. He'd stay right with me until I needed to get up to move. Then he'd make sure to stay out of my way while he'd follow me to wherever I would go and quietly wait for me to get up and move again. Having him by my side was really a tremendous comfort and reminded me so much of how he'd cared for my father-in-law when Dad needed special gentleness, too.*

DJ Goodell has been around animals her whole life—she grew up on a farm, took in injured animals from state game lands to rehabilitate when she was a teen, and worked in animal rescue for thirty years as an adult. While working with animal rescue, she even helped prison inmates learn to work with seizure-alert dogs. DJ is now the product manager for Dogwise Publishing:

> *Kelly was one of my first dogs, and he really had a knack for taking care of others—animal or human. When the ranger called me about a fawn in the state game lands that had lost its mother, I brought it home. And Kelly was always there by its side, nursing it along. My cat really took advantage of Kelly's nursing instincts. When she had kittens and wanted breaks to leave her nest, she'd get Kelly to come over to sit with the kittens and tend to them until she would return.*
>
> *One of the most incredible duties Kelly filled was to help a chicken with her eggs. When I'd feed the horses each morning, Kelly would come along, steering clear of the hay bales where the chickens often roosted. He knew there was nothing worse than an irritated mother hen. One morning, I noticed Kelly was walking very slowly, and he had something in his mouth. I was alarmed to see he'd snatched*

an egg. On a farm, there's nothing worse than stealing eggs. So I chastised him and thought that was the end of it. Two days later, I spotted him again doing his slow walk across the yard. His head was lowered and he was walking so carefully, I was afraid he'd grabbed another egg. He seemed to be intent on reaching the garden at the front of the house. I raced down the stairs, dashed outside, and by the time I reached Kelly and was about to scold him, he carefully lowered an egg to the ground. Imagine my surprise when I saw a chicken's head pop out from under a nearby juniper bush, grab the egg, and nudge it gently under the brush and into her nest. When I looked at the nest, there were already twelve eggs there. Since Kelly seemed to be helping rather than stealing eggs, I let this continue and by the end of her roosting, that chicken had twenty eggs in her nest, with sixteen hatching into lovely chicks. It was amazing to watch Kelly make his slow deliberate march with her eggs each day. It was a full acre from the barn to the front yard garden. And not once did Kelly abandon his mission along the way.

Kelly's nursing skills weren't just applied to animals; he also took his family nursing duties very seriously:

At night, Kelly would sleep in the hallway outside of everyone's bedrooms. The only time this pattern changed was when someone was sick—then Kelly slept in the ill person's bedroom. He was so consistent about this that it became the family joke. If Kelly was in your room in the morning—everyone knew you were really sick! When one of us kids would announce we weren't feeling well and needed to stay home to avoid school, Mom would simply say, "I didn't see Kelly in your room last night." We all knew—if Kelly didn't say you were sick, you probably weren't really sick! One time I lured Kelly to sleep in my bed so I could miss a test the next day at school. He stayed awhile until the treats ran out and left before "giving testimony" to Mom.

DJ had another dog who similarly took her nursing role seriously. Gracie was a Tricolor Bull Terrier:

Like Kelly, Gracie slept in the hallway until you were sick and then she held a vigil with you—lying beside your bed or next to your feet if you were in a chair or on the sofa. She really seemed to sympathize with you and wanted to offer comfort. We always called Kelly and Gracie our family nurses.

As an adult, DJ's Wirehaired German Pointer mix, Baylor, would be the one to sit with you when you were feeling bad:

Not every dog seems to have an inclination for caring for the sick— but those who do, like Kelly, Gracie, and Baylor, really take their duties seriously. I have no doubt that they view themselves as our nurses. It's like they're saying, "You're a part of our pack and we're here to make sure you get better." They can really tell you a lot about yourself, if you'll just open up to listen to what they're saying.

DOGS SENSE OUR DISCOMFORT AND THE NEED TO BE NURSED

As a nurse, Sherry Meininghaus spent the beginning of her career caring for critically ill patients in intensive care units. About a year after completing nursing school, Sherry started a new challenge: She began breeding and handling her champion Ashberry line of Bearded Collie show dogs. Sherry had been raising her Beardies for two years when she learned she was pregnant with her first child. At the time, her house was filled with dogs—Beardies Duffy and Chrissy, Apricot Miniature Poodle mix Max, Yorkie Freeway, and nine Beardie puppies from a new litter.

Like many first-time mothers-to-be, Sherry had nausea and vomiting with her pregnancy. But this wasn't the everyday nausea of morning sickness that many women experience. Sherry had *hyperemesis gravidarum*—a combination of Greek and Latin words that literally means lots of vomiting during pregnancy. Only about one in every 100 pregnant women develops hyperemesis, which can cause life-threatening dehydration and weight loss. Sherry recalls how her Bearded Collie took on a role nursing her:

Normally, my Beardies were big, active, rambunctious dogs with a tendency to jump. Once I became pregnant, their whole demeanor changed around me. They seemed to sense a need for calmness. It was as though they understood that I couldn't have them bumping and bouncing into me.

The hyperemesis was terrible, and I was in the hospital for a month getting intravenous fluids to stay hydrated. Once I went home, I spent a lot of time resting on the couch. It was kind of funny that instead of me being the nurse, my show dog Beardies became my big, bearded caregivers. They'd patiently sit next to me when I was lying down, rest their heads on my chest, and give me great comfort. They helped show me how a good nurse can bring tremendous assurance, relief, and support to a patient.

The Beardies continued to tend to Sherry throughout her pregnancy. Instead of the usual weight gain most women expect during a healthy pregnancy, Sherry lost thirty-six pounds. However, under the watchful eyes of her Beardie nurses, Sherry rested and kept up her fluid intake. After nine months, she gave birth to a healthy baby boy, who was excitedly welcomed home by this band of Beardies who carried on their caring work with this newest member of their pack.

Figure 4.1. Pregnant Sherry gets a caring smooch from a brown Beardie puppy.

Tail Waggin' Tip

Dogs with a nose for nursing can sense our need for them to take on this important role.

DOGS ARE A COMFORT IF WE NEED CHRONIC THERAPY

One of the toughest things about being sick is doing what you need to do to get healthier. Following healthy habits is hard work, and tiring, and if you have a chronic illness that's not going to go away, it can be especially hard to stick with your treatment recommendations. For example, if you have diabetes you need to carefully watch what you eat and how much you exercise, and know what your blood sugars are every single day. If you miss days here and there, your blood sugar levels can quickly get out of control and you can get very sick. Everyone with diabetes knows this. But knowing something and doing what's needed don't always go together. In one study, researchers asked people with diabetes how often during a seven-day week they followed their treatment plan. On average, people with diabetes ate a healthy diet four and a half days each week, checked their blood sugar levels four days each week, and exercised only two days each week (Shigaki et al., 2010). A study of patients with heart disease similarly found that most people do not regularly follow their treatment plan (Heo et al., 2008).

This is where a nurse is often extremely valuable; he or she can provide practical tips on how to successfully follow your therapy recommendations and encouragement to keep up your treatments. Experts argue that nurses can play a critical role in helping patients stick with their medical therapies (Goode et al., 2004). Unfortunately, most of us talk to a nurse only now and then. We really need someone to motivate and encourage us every day.

Tail Waggin' Tip

Like a good nurse, a dog in our lives can help keep us motivated to take better care of ourselves—even when we take care of ourselves only to make sure we'll be well enough to care for our dog.

A recent issue of the medical journal *Chronic Illness* was entirely devoted to the idea that patients with chronic illness often can't be expected to manage their treatment plans on their own at home; they frequently need help and support from their family to stick with disease management recommendations (Piette, 2010). In this case, family members can take on some of the traditional role of the nurse, helping people follow through with the treatments.

As a doctor, I've learned that people often ignore my best advice and recommendations, even when their family is encouraging them to continue their treatments at home. It's easy to find excuses for eating what you shouldn't, forgetting to take pills, and skipping exercises. And people can begin to resent family members "nagging" them. This is where a canine "nurse's" gentle touch, soft eyes, and unconditional acceptance can provide the motivation to stick with a daily treatment routine.

Olivia Brendel is an adorably bubbly, petite fourteen-year-old with a passion for dance. She is articulate, with an infectious smile and ready sense of humor that instantly draws you to her. Olivia also has cystic fibrosis, an inherited disease that causes thick, sticky mucus to build up in the lungs and digestive system. This results in serious breathing and nutrition problems. Cystic fibrosis limits the body's ability to absorb food and can cause wheezing, shortness of breath, and recurring serious lung infections. According to the Cystic Fibrosis Foundation (http://www.cff.org), about 30,000 Americans have cystic fibrosis. Over seventy percent of those affected are diagnosed by the time they turn two years old. Olivia was diagnosed when she was just a baby.

Being a normal, active teen and having cystic fibrosis is tough. Olivia has to do about three hours of breathing treatments each day, using an inhaler and wearing a compressive vest that "shakes up" her chest to help loosen thick mucus. She also needs to make sure she gets a handful of enzyme pills before eating, so she'll be able to digest her food. When I asked Olivia what happens when she skips her treatment, she shot me a horrified look, "I've *never* missed a treatment!" Olivia's mom, Janet, concurred; Olivia has been getting her daily treatments every day of her life, never missing even a single treatment:

> *The treatments are really very time consuming and it can be difficult fitting them into an already-busy routine. I hate having to get her up so early each morning so she can get her treatments done before school. And after-school activities may also be limited because of her treatments.*

So whether Olivia's at home, out with friends, or on vacation, she always has to break from what she's doing to get her twice-daily breathing treatments and pills. Unlike other teens, Olivia often has to come home in the middle of activities or earlier than her friends to make sure she has enough time to get in her breathing treatment before bed.

Into this challenging life walked—or rather, waddled—Chloe, an eight-year-old, chubby Pug. During the summer of 2007, Olivia had been searching Pugs on the Internet to gather information to help convince her parents that their family *needed* a Pug. "I've always liked Pugs," giggles Olivia. "They're just so cute." Her parents, however, insisted that a dog "would just add complications to our already very complicated life." When they attended a family reunion, however, Janet's Pug-owning cousin heard about Olivia's interest and thought that Olivia and her senior Pug, Chloe, would be a perfect match. Olivia was thrilled by the offer, but Janet remained skeptical, "I didn't even *want* a dog—and now I have this thing that snorts, grunts, and snores." Within weeks, however, Chloe won over the whole family.

Although unfamiliar with the complex breathing machines and equipment Olivia uses each day, Chloe soon became an important part of the daily therapy routine. Janet was amazed that Chloe instinctively took on the role of nurse during Olivia's daily therapy sessions:

> *Whenever Chloe heard Olivia's machines starting up, she'd head to the sofa for therapeutic cuddling time! Without prompting, Chloe would hop up on the couch, find the nearest available leg, snuggle up, and let the comfort flow. This is one of the most endearing things*

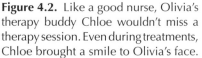

Figure 4.2. Like a good nurse, Olivia's therapy buddy Chloe wouldn't miss a therapy session. Even during treatments, Chloe brought a smile to Olivia's face.

> *about Chloe—she was just so affectionate and seemed to understand when you needed her the most. Chloe brought an element of silliness to our household. She helped make us laugh more. The children have said she was the best thing that has ever happened to us. She exuded positive energy and a kind of serenity that made each treatment a little more bearable.*

Three years after Chloe entered the Brendels's lives, she went to the vet for what should have been the simple removal of some fatty tumors. Two hours after dropping Chloe off, Janet got a phone call that everyone dreads, "There was a problem with the anesthetic. I'm very sorry, but Chloe didn't make it." Suddenly, Janet, who had never wanted a dog in the first place, felt a hole ripped in her heart. They had lost not just a dog but a family member who had added peace, companionship, and laughter to a household shadowed by chronic illness and the drudgery of daily breathing treatments:

> *Several weeks after Chloe died, Olivia started complaining about having to do her treatments. At first, I was a little taken aback because Olivia rarely complained about having to go through her treatments—she's had to do them her whole life. And then I made the connection. Her therapy buddy, Chloe, was missing and now she had to go through her treatments alone.*

Ten months after losing Chloe, the Brendels brought a new nurse into their home—a Pug puppy named Lacey. Lacey has a big collar to fill—and I bet it'll be a bright pink, jeweled collar like Chloe's.

DOGS PROVIDE COMFORT DURING OUR FINAL DAYS

Therapy dogs visiting hospice patients during their terminal stages of illness have been shown to improve interactions between patients and staff and boost morale of both patients and their caregivers (Chinner & Daizel, 1991). Becky Kikukawa and Shih Tzu Mattie found the value of a therapy dog nursing patients during their final days through their visits to eighty-seven-year-old Anthony:

During our first visit with Anthony, Anthony explained to Mattie that he'd decided to withdraw from his medications and knew that his end was near, saying, "Dog, I've seen a lot and I've lived my mission in this life, so it is time to go on to the next." Over three more visits, Anthony shared a life's worth of lessons with us, always talking to Mattie, "Mattie, you have to have a mission in life. You just can't go through life willy-nilly." Mattie and I spent the last days of Anthony's life with him, listening to his stories, with Mattie licking his hand and gently cuddling with him.

I didn't comprehend what a deep comfort Mattie had been for Anthony during his final days until I received a card in the mail that Anthony had written, saying "Mattie, you know your mission in life, and for this I am grateful. Your friend, Anthony." Anthony understood the therapy dog's mission of spreading love, joy, and peace. As Mattie's handler, I have the responsibility of helping Mattie fulfill this important work.

5

Duke and Daisy as Doctors: Sniffing Out Disease

We often define a *doctor* as someone who understands and recognizes disease—and then knows what to do about it. Doctors can't always fix or cure all of our health problems, but we do expect them to know when something's wrong. And then we'd like our doctor to help correct the problem or at least point us in the direction of someone who can help.

Have you ever said, "My dog knows me better than my doctor. When something's not right, my dog acts funny to let me know." Well, your doctors have actually been listening to you and, in some cases, wondering if you may be right: Perhaps a dog *can* be a doctor's assistant.

SNIFFING OUT CANCER

Scientists are using dogs' amazing power of analyzing scents to literally sniff out disease. Wonder if you might have cancer? Most of the time your doctor will recommend screening tests, which can sometimes be unpleasant and expensive. These can include blood tests, biopsies, and x-rays—like computed axial tomography testing, usually dubbed *CAT scans*. Some researchers are suggesting that, for some cancers, it may be better to turn to the "DOG scan"—a sniffing dog, that is.

How does sniffing out cancer work? Cancer cells produce proteins and chemicals that are different from those made by normal cells in the body. Although we may not notice tiny differences from these chemical changes, sniff expert dogs can. Most scientists have relied on testing chemical odors collected in people's urine or breath. For example, everyone breathes out gases like isoprene, acetone, and methanol; however, the concentration of these gases is slightly lower in people who have lung cancer (Bajtarevic et al., 2009).

Tail Waggin' Tip

The chemicals released by our bodies can change when we have certain cancers. In some cases, dogs can detect these abnormal scents that we humans miss.

So does sniffing out cancer really work? Yes—and no. In 2005, doctors from the University of Wisconsin Cancer Center reported a case of breast cancer detected by a Dachshund puppy in the journal *Community Oncology* (Welsh, Barton, & Ahuja, 2005). In this report, a forty-four-year-old woman's puppy persistently sniffed and poked at one of her armpits. After a month of this annoying behavior, the woman found a lump in her armpit that turned out to be breast cancer.

By far the largest and most highly publicized work in this area came from researchers at the Pine Street Foundation in California. In 2006, they published findings of a study in which they had trained ordinary household dogs to identify differences in exhaled breath from people with lung and breast cancer (McCulloch et al., 2006):

- In almost all cases, the dogs correctly identified whether breath samples came from people with or without cancer.
- Dogs who indicated that a person's breath "smelled like" cancer were right about ninety-eight percent of the time.

Another study, conducted at Amersham Hospital in the United Kingdom, had dogs sniff urine from people with and without bladder cancer (Willis et al., 2004). In this case, the dogs correctly selected urine as coming from patients with bladder cancer in twenty-two of fifty-four tests, so they were forty-one percent accurate. A later study, however, conducted at Scripps Clinic in La Jolla, California (Gordon et al., 2008), found that trained dogs correctly identified urine from breast or prostate cancer patients at a rate no better than would be found by chance. The most recent report on cancer-sniffing dogs was a study presented at the June 2010 meeting of the American Urological Association in San Francisco. Dr. Jean-Nicolas Cornu and colleagues from Tenon Hospital in Paris reported on a Belgian Malinois dog they had trained to identify prostate cancer odors in urine. This dog was administered eleven tests. In each test, he was given six samples of urine: one sample came from a man with prostate cancer and the other five were from men who were cancer free. In his sixty-six tries to identify whether cancer was present or not, the dog was right sixty-three times. Perhaps most amazingly, there was one time the dog "incorrectly" identified a urine sample as having come from a man with prostate cancer, but the man did not have cancer—or so he thought. After the study, this man had another prostate biopsy, and the dog was right: The man did indeed have prostate cancer that was previously undetected by his human doctors.

Tail Waggin' Tip

Most studies suggest that dogs can be trained to correctly identify certain cancers by smell, although the dogs aren't right every time.

SNIFFING OUT SKIN CANCER

Studies in which dogs are trained to sniff cancer odors are fairly new, but dogs have understood there's something different and disturbing about cancer long before researchers started thinking about this. In 1989, Drs. Williams and Pembroke wrote an article in the medical journal *The Lancet* describing a patient whose Border Collie–Doberman mix began constantly sniffing a spot on her leg. She had a number of moles, but only one interested her dog. Because the dog was like— well, a dog with a bone with the constant sniffing—the lady asked her doctor to check out the mole. Sure enough, it turned out to be a skin cancer called *malignant melanoma*. Because of the early detection and treatment, she did well. In 2001, another group of doctors reported a similar case in this same journal. Their patient had had an itchy spot of eczema on his leg that grew slowly over eighteen years (Church & Williams, 2001). At some point, the man's pet Labrador Retriever began persistently nudging the spot under his owner's trousers. The constant attention by the dog prompted the man to have his doctors take another look, and a biopsy showed cancer. This man also did well after surgery.

Inspired by Williams and Pembroke's (1989) report, a Florida dermatologist, Dr. Cognetta, teamed up with a retired police dog handler to train George, a Standard Schnauzer who had originally been trained to sniff out bombs, to recognize skin cancer (Church & Williams, 2001). After months of training and sniffing, George became pretty good at correctly distinguishing melanoma from normal skin. When George sniffed a man with several moles that the skin doctor thought were benign, George honed in on one particular mole that turned out to be an early case of malignant melanoma.

Tail Waggin' Tip

Several doctors have reported cases in which skin cancers were first detected in patients by a sniffing dog.

Are you skeptical that a dog could *really* sniff out early skin cancer? If you are, then DJ Goodell's story will probably convince you. DJ works at Dogwise Publishing and knows a lot about dogs. She'd noticed that when one of her dogs had a minor injury, another would often tend to it, licking the damaged area for the other dog. When her English Bull Terrier Poly started nosing at a small spot on the back of her leg, however, DJ initially brushed off the attention.

When I looked at my leg, I just saw a small freckle that didn't look like it would be a problem. I figured it was just a little age spot or something. But every time I'd sit or lie down near Poly, she'd hone in on that spot, licking it and grooming it. It was like she was trying to get rid of it.

Although I figured it was nothing, to satisfy Poly, I went to see my doctor. She assured me the spot was nothing to worry about, "There's less than a 15 percent chance this is anything serious." So I went home and tried to ignore it. Poly, however, had other ideas. Poly's relentless attention to this spot continued, and I thought, "My tracking classes always teach us—trust your dog," so I went back to the doctor.

I was pretty sure my doctor thought I was crazy when I told her my dog insisted something was wrong with that spot on my leg. Although my doctor again reassured me nothing was wrong, I asked for a dermatology referral. The dermatologist told me the same thing—less than 15 percent chance of something serious. The dermatologist told me not to worry and I surprised myself by explaining to the dermatologist that my dog told me something was wrong and I wanted a biopsy. I couldn't believe I actually asked for a biopsy and again thought this doctor must think I was a nut. She agreed to do the biopsy and ten days later I got a phone call that the spot was indeed a basal cell cancer and I needed to return for more complete removal.

Since then, I've been fine. The spot didn't come back and Poly no longer focuses on my leg. Thanks to Poly, I got this taken care of when I did. Since then, I've heard about dogs trained to sniff out cancer. While some people are skeptical about a dog's ability to sniff out disease, I have no doubt that Poly knew my spot was something more serious, and if she couldn't take care of it, she wanted to make sure I found someone who would.

SNIFFING OUT DEATH

In 2007, Dr. David Dosa amazed the medical community with his publication in the *New England Journal of Medicine*, titled "A Day in the Life of Oscar the Cat." Dosa specializes in the care of elderly patients. Part of his practice involves a nursing home with a resident cat, named

Oscar. Although not a particularly friendly and outgoing cat, Oscar had an uncanny ability to know when death was approaching. In some cases, even before the staff knew the patient had taken a turn for the worse, Oscar would perch on the patient's bed to start his vigil, which soon became recognized as a signal that the end was near by both staff and patients' family members. Dosa (2010) later expanded his writings on Oscar's experiences and the peace that Oscar brought to patients and families through his vigils in the book *Making Rounds with Oscar: The Extraordinary Gift of an Ordinary Cat*.

Oscar's ability, however, is not unique. Danielle Di Bona trained her 50-lb (23-kg) therapy dog Naomi to approach elderly patients with gentleness to avoid injuring these frail folks. Danielle and Naomi had

Figure 5.1. The Rev. Danielle Di Bona has learned to trust Soft-Coated Wheaten Terrier Naomi's ability to sense changes in people's health.

often visited Judy, although always when Judy was in her wheelchair. Naomi knew she needed to wait until Danielle got patients positioned before carefully jumping up on the bed. One day, Judy was too ill to get into her chair and was lying quietly in her bed. Naomi immediately recognized that something was different and, instead of waiting for permission to jump on the bed, simply gently crawled onto the bed and rested her head on Judy's chest. Judy placed her hand on Naomi and spent an hour holding and gently stroking Naomi. Later that night, Judy died. Naomi understood that something was different and that that difference required her action.

THERAPY DOGS ARE GOOD ROLE MODELS OF BEDSIDE MANNER

When you go to the doctor, you'd like to have your problem diagnosed and then receive something that's going to make you feel a lot better. In medical school, doctors learn that it takes more than just a pill to make people better. Doctors need to let their patients know they have been listening to them and that they understand their problems.

The soft word, gentle touch, and sympathetic gaze of the doctor are sometimes called *bedside manner*. For those medical personnel who think simple bedside manner may be too old-fashioned for today's high-tech hospital rooms, most patients will tell you good bedside manner is an important part of hospital treatment. Fletcher, Rankey, and Stern (2005) reported the following observations:

- Eighty-four percent of hospital patients rated that seeing their hospital doctors as caring is very important.
- Patients believe their doctors are caring when they:
  — show concern
  — seem to understand how the patient feels
  — demonstrate warmth

Another article listed poor bedside manner as a reason patients leave the hospital without completing their treatment (Onukwugha et al., 2010).

Doctors could learn a lot of good bedside manner skills by watching patient interactions with a therapy dog. The soft brown eyes, eager face, and gentle nuzzle are often the prescription that's needed.

Tail Waggin' Tip

Trained therapy dogs model ideal bedside manner that can serve as an example for health care providers.

Mary Ann Hirt had worked for many years as a nurse and understood the power of good sincere bedside manner. Mary Ann's first visit as a therapy dog handler was with her 90-lb (41-kg) black Labrador, Sam. On this visit she learned that therapy dogs have an amazing power to understand their patients and show that they care, just like doctors with the best bedside manner:

We went to see Kelly, a young girl who had been treated for a tumor involving blood vessels in her jaw. Her recovery had been slow following some procedures done in a desperate attempt to help her. Because of her procedures, her lips and chin had been damaged and Kelly could barely speak in anything more than a whisper. Sam looked right past her surgeries, seeing only the eyes of a new friend.

Sam sat with Kelly on her bed and she gently stroked him and whispered softly to him. When it was time to go, I told Sam to say good-bye and gave him his signal to speak. Kelly was impressed, and I asked if she'd like to ask Sam to talk to her. I told her, "Hold this treat for Sam and say 'speak.'" Kelly held the treat and, in a barely audible whisper, asked Sam to speak. Incredibly, Sam responded with the softest "Woof" I had ever heard him utter—it was as though he understood and mirrored Kelly's speech. This simple, pure display of acceptance and love was followed by tears down both parents' cheeks. Since then, Sam has "spoken" to many people and answered requests from others to give his woof to command. But he has never again answered in the soft whisper he used for Kelly—that was his special bond—just for her.

Figure 5.2. Black Labrador Retriever therapy dog Sam shows handler Mary Ann the best in bedside manner.

Five-year-old Bloodhound Louie and his handler Anita DeBiase have visited many patients, but one visit that stands out was when Louie helped jump-start a man's recovery by being "just what the doctor ordered." Richard was a depressed, quadriplegic gentleman in intensive care:

Because the intensive care beds were too high for Richard to be able to see Louie on the floor, I asked the nurses if I could put Louie on the bed. They agreed, and Louie gently positioned himself next to the Richard's head—within kissing distance. During what seemed to me like a typical visit with Louie and his patient enjoying each other's company, the patient's doctor came by on rounds. I told him Louie and I would go so the doctor could see his patient, but the doctor insisted we stay and said he'd come back after we were done.

Little did I know, but the doctor realized that Louie was the medicine his patient needed most. I found out days later that before Louie's visit this gentleman had been unresponsive to his nurses and doctors.

Figure 5.3. Handler Anita learns that a dose of Bloodhound therapy dog Louie is strong medicine.

After visiting Louie, the nurses noticed a marked improvement in this man's attitude and spirit. He started engaging with the staff and was soon interacting with nurses and doctors—and smiling. His nurse sent a letter to the Volunteer Office detailing the success of Louie's visit. We visited the man two more times while he was still in intensive care. And both times Louie snuggled next to him. Louie was truly the medicine this man needed.

WHEATIE THE WONDER DOG SAVES A LIFE

One of the greatest joys you can have as a doctor is to know that what you have done has saved someone's life. We've all read stories in the newspaper about dogs that have saved drowning children or woken their sleeping owners to permit escape from burning homes. Dogs are often proud heroes, sometimes putting themselves in harm's way to save one of their human pack members. Well, my therapy dog also helped save a life on one of his routine hospital visits.

My husband, Richard (Richie), trains young doctors, helping to turn them into specialists. Because Wheatie was Richie's first dog, this proud new doggie dad would often share tales of Wheatie's progress with his students at work. Daily training rounds with young doctors would often be spiced up by stories of Wheatie's latest achievements: graduating from puppy class, earning his Canine Good Citizen award, receiving his Therapy Dogs International certification. The young doctors, a bit sarcastically, dubbed my little terrier "Wheatie the Wonder Dog." Once Wheatie started making therapy dog visits, one of the boldest students would jokingly begin rounds asking, "So, has Wheatie saved any one's life yet?"

It wasn't long before Richie had a great story to tell. On one of our hospital visits, I was asked to bring Wheatie to see an elderly man in the cardiac intensive care unit. A special note was added to this patient's name on my list of requests: "Please make sure you see Mr. Reinhold. He just *loves* dogs." When Wheatie and I arrived outside Mr. Reinhold's room in intensive care, Mr. Reinhold appeared to be asleep. Not wanting to interrupt what likely was needed rest, I turned to the nurse sitting outside of his room and told her Wheatie and I could come back another day for a visit. The nurses insisted, "Oh no—he's been asking for the dog and has been sleeping all afternoon anyway."

Not wanting to have Mr. Reinhold startled when he woke by being greeted with an unexpected doggie nose in his face, I asked the nurse if she could wake Mr. Reinhold for us as I lifted Wheatie up and carried him into the room so he'd be eye level with the elevated unit bed. Cheerfully, the nurse began calling Mr. Reinhold's name—at first softly, then more loudly, and finally accompanied by some gentle and then a bit more frantic shaking. Within seconds, we both realized that Mr. Reinhold was no longer "asleep"—he'd become dangerously unresponsive. The nurse called a code to bring the resuscitation team to the bedside, and Wheatie and I left to finish our rounds elsewhere.

A few days later, Wheatie and I couldn't help but wonder what had happened to poor Mr. Reinhold, and we made the trip back to the cardiac care unit—even though Mr. Reinhold was no longer on the "to see" list. We were delighted to see that Mr. Reinhold had been revived and was now sitting up in bed. I couldn't wait to introduce him to Wheatie. Beaming, I walked into the room, casually asking if he'd like a visit from a dog and knowing that I'd hear the usual response about how much he loved dogs and had been eagerly anticipating our visit. Instead, Mr. Reinhold gave Wheatie a cursory glance and gruffly snorted, "Nah. I hate dogs!"

Mr. Reinhold may not have realized it, but after that day, I began telling my husband's students that Wheatie insisted they change his moniker from "Wheatie the Wonder Dog" to "Doctor Wheatie." So, has Wheatie saved any one's life yet? Without a doubt. And although Mr. Reinhold will never know the role a scruffy little terrier played in his hospital stay, Dr. Wheatie was confident in his knowledge that his visit to this gentleman fulfilled its purpose.

6

Dogs as Therapists

Working with therapists helps people get healthier quicker. But does spending time with a therapy dog *really* affect your health? In an interesting study conducted by Dr. Carl Charnetski of Wilkes University and his colleagues, fifty-five college students were asked to sit on a sofa for eighteen minutes (Charnetski, Riggers, & Brennan, 2004). One group sat next to a 20-lb (9-kg) Sheltie mix that they were told to pet. The second group sat petting a stuffed dog that looked like the Sheltie. A third group sat quietly on the sofa. Health improvement was measured by testing levels of a major immunoglobulin called *immunoglobulin A* (IgA). (Immunoglobulins are proteins in our blood that help the immune system fight off disease.) IgA levels were measured before and after spending time on the sofa:

- The only group with a significant increase in protective IgA was the group petting the real Sheltie mix dog.

- Petting the Sheltie increased this immune factor by thirty-three percent.

Interestingly, it didn't matter whether the people had a positive attitude about petting the dog or not. The immune system was strengthened by spending time with the dog regardless of whether the participant was a dog lover. This study confirmed what therapy dog handlers have known all along: Spending time with a therapy dog is therapeutic and good for your health.

Therapy dogs can inspire patients to do more than everyone thinks they can. Therapy dog–handler team Barbara Pohodich and Janet Malinsky have seen their dogs help people start moving again:

Sometimes when we come to visit patients in a nursing home, the staff will tell us, "Don't bother going to see Martha. She has terrible arthritis and can't use her hands. So she'll never be able to pet your dogs." But you'd be surprised what happens when a soft dog is placed in someone's lap. Suddenly fingers that are horribly deformed begin to slowly stretch and move as they gently stroke a dog's coat. It's really rewarding to see that!

Another time, Janet and Barb's dogs went to visit a lady whose daughter said, "I don't know if you want to visit Mom. She doesn't talk." Barb placed Maltese Sadie in the lady's lap, and the lady slowly started petting Sadie. As the woman's fingers stroked the soft white fluff, she smiled and said, "Pretty. Pretty." Her daughter began to cry tears of joy, "I haven't heard Mom say a word in over a month."

THERAPY DOGS HAVE AN INSTINCT FOR SNIFFING OUT WHAT PEOPLE NEED

Like any good therapist, therapy dog coordinator Ann Cadman will tell you that therapy dogs seem to have an intuition that allows them to instinctively know when they're needed and how patients need them. Although I was skeptical about this when I first heard it during a volunteer orientation session, a few months of seeing patients with Wheatie told me that Ann was right. When we're in the hospital, people often comment how well behaved, quiet, and calm Wheatie and Toby are. "It must be nice to have such mellow dogs. I guess Wheatens are known for being sedate and calm." Anyone with a Wheaten will tell you—these high-energy, enthusiastic dogs need lots of training to keep their energy in check. Although more exuberant at home or when touring the pet stores, my Wheatens seem to know that it's work time when their therapy tags are clipped on and their short hospital leashes come out.

Wheatie has always seemed to also have an uncanny ability to "sniff out" the patient in the room, bypassing the often more outgoing visitors and family members who reach out to pet him to preferentially give "first dibs" to the patient. "Look Dad—he *knew* you were the one who needed therapy" are words we often hear during visits.

Tail Waggin' Tip

Like any good therapist, therapy dogs have an uncanny instinct for recognizing how to best approach people who most need their healing touch, often to the surprise and amazement of their handlers.

Anita DeBiase has also noticed that her Bloodhound, Louie, instinctively recognizes which patients are in special need of his therapeutic touch and how to best deliver his help:

> *Louie is enthusiastic to visit every patient on his list, but he seems to have more empathy for special patients, like those patients asking for a therapy dog visit in the intensive care unit or patients with special visit requests. He just knows how to act and respond to them. On our first visit to the intensive care unit, Louie jumped in bed with the patient and carefully snuggled him without me asking him to. That was exactly what that patient needed. Louie has also sat quietly and patiently with a special needs patient for forty-five minutes just letting the patient pet him.*
>
> *Louie even judges how to conduct himself with children during reading programs. One student came into a session and looked a little panicked when she saw Louie's size. She sat down on the floor and Louie gently laid his head on her leg. He never moved the whole time. With other children who are more comfortable with him, he'll sit right on a big bean bag chair with them.*

Louie's gift for reading people and understanding their needs is shared by the best therapy dogs.

You may have heard about Sadie, a Bouvier des Flandres rescued by writer Jane Miller. Jane wrote about Sadie in the book *What I Learned from the Dog*, a 2009 *Chicken Soup for the Soul* book. Jane described how Sadie provided comfort and strength for their family as they tended to her dad through his final days after suffering a massive stroke.

Sadie is also well known in her community for bringing needed joy, comfort, and peace throughout the neighborhood:

Figure 6.1. Bouvier des Flandres therapy dog Sadie's a big part of the conversation as she sits with Wil and Rick.

Sadie has a gift for sensing sadness and possibly illness, too. We first noticed this after my dad died when my elderly neighbor, Wil, strolled by the week before he and his wife were scheduled to move to New Hope Assisted Living. Wil came over and sat with my husband, Rick. As expected, Sadie came right over, but surprisingly ignored Rick and sat with her paws wrapped around Wil's legs. A few days later, Wil's wife, Barbara, was diagnosed with cancer. It was as though Sadie knew Wil would need extra support.

About this same time, Sister Alice, the hospice chaplain who'd helped with my dad, asked if Sadie might like making visits at New Hope. I'd planned to visit residents individually, but Sister Alice insisted, "I know Sadie and I'm not missing out on Sadie visits." So we did our visits with groups of residents and Sister Alice in a community room. Every week, Sadie makes her rounds from resident to resident, getting butt scratches at each stop. Every once in awhile,

Sadie breaks from her usual circuit, selects specific individuals, and strides over to put her head in their laps, wet chin and all, or lays on their feet (a Bouvier trait, we have learned). Almost every time this happens, the person says something like, "How did you know I needed that" or "I was sitting here feeling so sad. Sadie, how did you know?"

On our first visit after Wil's dear wife Barbara had died, Sadie picked Wil out in the room of more than twenty people, and although I was about to lead her to go around a circle of seniors, she pulled on her leash and turned to face Wil. Sadie just looked into his eyes, with her chin on his lap, and he stroked her face and wet beard. Guess she understood that he still needed extra support.

THERAPY DOGS FOR PATIENTS WITH MENTAL ILLNESS

People with serious mental illness have an extra burden, making everyday tasks more challenging. In an interesting study published in the *American Journal of Occupational Therapy*, Drs. Zimolag and Krupa from Queen's University in Ontario reported on the impact of pet ownership among adults with serious mental illness (Zimolag & Krupa, 2009). The most common reasons cited for not owning a pet were cost, living in a place that didn't permit pets, or not having room for a pet. In their sample, pet owners were more socially integrated in the community and participated in more meaningful activities compared with people who did not own a pet. Zimolag and Krupa also observed the following:

- One in five pet owners was employed compared with less than one in ten people who did not own pet.
- Over half of the participants in this study listed the same reasons for having a pet that most people cite: companionship, stress relief, social support, sense of purpose, helping to establish a routine, and exercise.
- Three out of every five people reported having a pet because it improved their mental health.

Researchers at Tzu Chi University in Taiwan looked at the impact of weekly therapy dog visits for patients with schizophrenia (Chu et al., 2009). Compared with patients who did not receive the therapy visits, patients who received weekly therapy dog visits developed better self-esteem and self-determination and had fewer psychiatric symptoms after having therapy dog visits for eight weeks. The following observations also were made:

- Self-esteem improved by sixty-two percent and self-determination by fifty-nine percent for patients who received therapy dog visits. Both measures worsened slightly in patients with schizophrenia who did not see the therapy dogs.
- Psychiatric symptoms commonly seen in schizophrenia were reduced by twenty-four to forty-three percent in patients who visited with the therapy dogs.
- There was a slight worsening of psychiatric symptoms in patients who did not receive therapy dog visits.

Another interesting study of seniors with schizophrenia, this one conducted in Israel, included weekly visits from therapeutic pets during psychiatric treatment sessions for half of the patients in the study (Barak et al., 2001). Therapy dogs and cats were used to help model normal daily activities by letting the patients pet, feed, and groom them. Working with the therapy pet was also designed to improve patient walking and socialization. Patients whose sessions included a therapy pet showed significantly more improvement in overall functioning, with marked improvement in socialization.

Tail Waggin' Tip

Therapy dog visits can help boost therapy of patients with mental illness by helping to improve activity, socialization, and mood. Interacting with a therapy dog brings healthy, normal, everyday activities into the lives of people with serious mental illness who brush, pet, and walk with them.

Patti Shanaberg recalls that her therapy dog, Sami, had a special gift for connecting with a patient struggling at a psychiatric facility:

We think Sami was a Golden Retriever–Border Collie–Samoyed mix. And I think she got the best characteristics of each of those breeds, being particularly smart and sensitive. One day, we were getting ready to make visits at a psychiatric facility and were on our way into the building to sign in. A male patient was in front of us, angrily yelling at a nurse. He was very agitated and upset and I wondered if Sami and I should just discreetly walk on by unnoticed or try to intervene. As I was pondering whether to walk by or not, Sami surprised me by looking at the yelling man, waving her tail, and pulling me over toward the angry man. She appeared so eager to meet this man, I decided to follow her lead and just pretend everything was okay. "Do you like dogs?" I asked, interrupting the man's tirade. He looked surprised by my question and still seemed quite agitated as he stumbled to find the right answer. Soon, I noticed he was petting Sami and his entire demeanor changed. Sami seemed to defuse the negative energy that had filled the air, and the man was now calm. We left this man, started our visits, and didn't think much about this encounter.

When we returned for a visit on another day, I was stopped by the nurse, who explained that the man Sami had calmed had been a patient in the facility for twenty-four hours when we'd come in. And during that time, he'd been continuously hostile and disruptive. After Sami's visit, the man seemed transformed. He had even returned to the nurse at the front desk and apologized for his earlier behavior, which absolutely stunned the nurse. It's not every dog who would be eager to greet someone who was so upset and yelling, but Sami seemed to understand that the man needed her and that she had something special to share that only she could give.

Sami's experience shows us that therapy dogs can effectively connect with patients in many different settings, including patients struggling with psychiatric illness. Sami's ability to accept, understand, and bond with this patient provided an effective therapeutic intervention that had eluded human efforts. Those brief moments connecting with Sami released pent up anger, fear, and hostility that allowed this man to start connecting with the human staff there to help him.

THERAPY DOGS CAN HELP A WIDE RANGE OF THERAPISTS

Dr. Beth Macauley works in the Department of Communicative Disorders at the University of Alabama. She investigated what happened when she added therapy dog visits to her speech therapy sessions with three stroke victims who were experiencing speech problems (Macauley, 2006). She compared what happened during traditional therapy and when that same therapy was provided with the addition of the therapy dog. Patients showed improvements in their speech with both treatment sessions, but patients noted that having the therapy dog made them feel more motivated and less stressed, and they enjoyed the therapy sessions more.

Canadian investigators likewise added therapy dog visits to speech therapy for a sixty-one-year-old man who had lost his speaking skills after a stroke (LaFrance, Garcia, & Labreche, 2007). The man was treated with speech therapy over the course of eleven weeks. For some sessions, the patient worked just with the speech therapist and was accompanied back to his room at the end of the sessions by a porter; for other sessions, a dog handler was included in the sessions and walked the patient back to his room; and some sessions included a therapy dog with the handler during the sessions, with the therapy dog and handler accompanying the patient to his room at the conclusion to encourage spontaneous conversation between the patient and others seeing the dog. The patient spoke an average of once every four minutes during the two weeks before the therapy dog visits started. His talking increased once the therapy dog visits began, and he spoke the most when the dog was present. The researchers also noted the following:

- When sessions included no dog or the dog handler without the dog, the man spoke 1.3 times each minute.
- When the dog was present, he spoke 3.3 times per minute.
- Having the dog for the walk back to the room also resulted in increased social verbal and nonverbal behaviors and improved the man's cheerfulness.

THERAPY DOGS MAKE GREAT PHYSICAL
THERAPY BUDDIES

Rehabilitation is tough work, and physical and occupational thera-pists often have to find unique solutions to the challenges presented by their patients. For some patients, motivation is a major problem after an illness or injury that has led to disability. The staff at a facil-ity in Boston have a magic weapon: Naomi the therapy dog. Bill had suffered a major stroke that left him paralyzed on one side of his body and unable to walk unassisted. To help him regain his mobility, his physical therapists urged him to begin walking between a set of par-allel bars. Bill was having none of it, and each session became a strug-gle of wills. Into this situation strutted a little Wheaten terrier, Naomi. Naomi's handler, Danielle Di Bona, let Bill hold onto Naomi's leash so he could "walk her" down the parallel bars. Danielle enjoyed seeing Naomi help motivate Bill to work hard in his program:

> *It wasn't easy for Bill, and he really needed a lot of assistance from the therapists to make that first trip. But having my smiling Wheaten at his side gave Bill the drive to take those first few difficult steps in his recovery. After that, we frequently joined Bill for his therapy ses-sions, my little terrier coaxing him back to independence.*

Bloodhound Louie also is a hit in a physical therapy department for seniors. His handler, Anita DeBiase, enjoys watching her Bloodhound work as an enthusiastic physical therapy aide:

> *Louie really lights up when he goes into the physical therapy suite— everyone makes such a fuss over him there. The therapists let their patients take a short break while Louie goes from wheelchair to wheel-chair, visiting. And Louie has found a fun way to motivate these patients to work hard during the rest of their therapy sessions. Before we leave, Louie shows off his own "exercise routine" by doing puppy push-ups—quickly alternating between sitting and lying down posi-tions. This always brings smiles, cheers, and claps and, hopefully, brightens the day for patients to inspire them to stick with their own exercise programs. I bet the therapists remind their patients, "Now you saw Louie doing his exercise—so let's get to work so you can show him yours."*

Tail Waggin' Tip

Therapy dogs are sometimes used to help people who need to practice range-of-motion exercises in their hands and arms. Stroking the dog or brushing the dog's hair can produce good exercise for arms and hands. Range of motion can be increased by encouraging people to pet or brush along the dog's whole body.

Sandy Grentz also discovered that her seven-year-old Whippet-Wire Hair Fox Terrier mix therapy dog, Callie, makes a great therapy aide. One day, she and Callie were visiting a little boy named Johnny who needed to get rehabilitation for his arm. The parents had been instructed to encourage Johnny to use his arm throughout the day, although he generally refused to move it:

When Callie came in for a visit, the mother was telling Johnny to move his arm. When he saw Callie, Johnny rested his arm on her back. The mom chatted with me for about ten minutes while Johnny's arm just rested on Callie. A nurse then came to the room to take Johnny for physical therapy and we noticed he'd started moving his arm back and forth across her back as he stroked her soft fur. I told the nurse we would go so she could take Johnny and she replied, "Absolutely not. Callie's the best therapy he can get."

Coping with the effects of trauma is tough for everyone, and perhaps toughest for children who have suffered injuries and lost family. This was the case for five-year-old Ian, a typical boy who loved sports and especially surfing with his daddy. In July 2008, Ian was riding in the car with his parents when a tragic accident left Ian with severe brain injuries and no parents. After four months, Ian left the hospital in a wheelchair and was being fed through a tube. His long rehab and recovery were just beginning.

Part of Ian's rehabilitation involved ocean therapy. Exercising in water is often soothing, and salt water provides extra buoyancy and healing minerals. The benefits of ocean therapy have even been recognized by the U.S. military, who provide ocean therapy sessions for wounded Marines at Camp Pendleton; the physical therapy occurs while these Marines learn to surf in the ocean.

Ocean therapy was important for Ian's physical training and, perhaps more so, because the ocean and surfing provided needed connections to Ian's lost daddy. This emotion-packed bond with the ocean made ocean training especially challenging for Ian, and this was where Ian's therapists called upon a silky Golden Retriever to join the therapy team.

Ricochet is a two-and-a-half-year-old Golden Retriever who started life as part of Judy Fridono's service dog program in San Diego. Like many dogs, Ricochet was a whiz at learning skills to help disabled people, but she was too easily distracted by birds and small animals to successfully complete her service dog training. What Ricochet did have was incredible balance and coordination, which made her a natural on a surf board. Today, Ricochet's a certified goal-directed therapy dog, although most of her therapeutic activities don't take place in typical therapy dog locations such as schools, nursing homes, or hospitals. Being a goal-directed therapy dog means that Ricochet and Judy work closely with therapists to identify activities for which Ricochet can aid in someone's therapy. Ricochet can usually be found fulfilling her unique niche on the beach, working with adaptive surfers. One life Ricochet has touched is Ian's.

Judy recalls that before Ian started working with Ricochet, Ian's therapists would spend one or two hours coaxing Ian to get into the water and onto a surfboard:

> *Ricochet started working with Ian in January. Initially, they'd just socialize and bond, sharing lots of kisses. Ian then started playing with Ricochet, throwing a ball to help exercise his arms, and soon we'd moved to hanging out together on the beach. In May, Ian was ready to hit the water. Ian lives with his aunt, and she was amazed at how excited Ian grew to surf with Ricochet. The morning of their first scheduled surf together, instead of the usual hesitation, Ian demanded to go to the beach, "I want to surf today with Ricochet!"*

Ian and Ricochet started therapeutic surfing together, with Ricochet helping to lick away Ian's fear and insecurities with her kisses:

> *With Ricochet at his side, Ian could get onto his surfboard right away, forgetting the doubt and apprehension that previously made*

Figure 6.2. Ricochet hangs 20 as she gives Ian support and courage to hit the waves. Photo courtesy of Tamandra Michaels from Heart Dog Studios.

this journey too hard to make alone. Ricochet inspires people like Ian to let go of their fears and expectations—to look beyond disabilities and see possibilities. Ricochet teaches people to shift their focus from regretting what they can't do to seeing what amazing things they can do. After all, if a dog can "hang 20," then anything's possible!

CANINE COURAGE

Sandy Grentz and Callie were the first dog–handler team to work with a therapist at an animal shelter to help children overcome severe fear of dogs:

When we first met the therapist, mom, and the two girls, nine-year-old Lisa and seven-year-old Maria, Lisa was terrified of Callie and didn't want to be anywhere near her. We met at the shelter for about seven weekends in a row. At first, Callie had to wait outside of the room Lisa was in, but soon Lisa was able to read to Callie when she was sitting on the other side of the room. Lisa later touched Callie's leash and finally brushed and walked Callie. By the end of our sessions, Lisa would even let Callie give her a kiss on the cheek.

Once the sessions were over, Sandy was surprised to hear that Lisa had asked her mom if she could have her birthday party at the shelter—with Callie as her special party friend. Callie was really the star of the party as Lisa's friends and grandparents all wanted to see "the amazing dog we've been hearing so much about!" Several months later, summer vacation had started from school, and Lisa's and Maria's parents told them they could pick three special activities to do over the summer. Their first pick was a visit from Callie!

We met them at a park where dogs can go off-leash. Lisa's and Maria's faces just beamed as they spotted Callie across a field, called her, and then ran together for a sweet embrace. When I heard Lisa arguing with her sister about how much time they could each spend holding Callie's leash, I knew the program had been a success.

Figure 6.3. Sandy and Whippet–Wire Hair Fox Terrier mix Callie help children overcome fears.

Because of the success from including Callie in the therapist's work with Lisa, the animal shelter where they volunteer decided to offer this type of program to other children afraid of dogs, and the "Canine Courage" class was born.

Tail Waggin' Tip

Therapy dogs can reach people's hearts and help them do the therapy they need. A gentle nudge from a therapy dog can jump start many types of therapy programs.

UNLOCKING DOORS IN AUTISM AND OTHER DEVELOPMENT DISABILITIES

Service dogs may be used for autistic children to help improve safe behaviors on the part of the child to permit more independence (Burrows, Adams, & Spiers, 2008). Research shows benefits to autistic children from therapeutic activities with dolphins (Lukina, 1999) and horses (Wuang et al., 2010) to improve motor skills and interpreting sensations. Special education specialist and certified dog trainer Merope Pavlides wrote the book *Animal Assisted Interventions For Individuals with Autism* (2008), detailing how the healing power of animals can help individuals with autism develop both physical and social skills.

When she was first starting to treat patients, speech and language pathologist Patricia A. Bednarik discovered the healing power of therapy dogs for children with autism:

> *In a school program, an occupational therapist and I were working together to help a young boy with autism who was minimally responsive, named Timmy. The therapist was also a therapy dog handler and she decided to bring her dog to our sessions with Timmy. While we'd been unsuccessful in getting Timmy to follow directions for us, he'd readily throw a ball for the dog and watch as the dog returned it. When the dog joined our sessions, Timmy became more focused and attentive. Timmy seemed to share a relatedness with the dog that he*

didn't feel with us or other people. Through the dog, we were able to begin to reach Timmy and provide therapy that he could relate to and benefit from.

Jacque Speed and her seven-and-a-half-year-old Golden Retriever, Reilly, are a therapy dog–handler team who visits autistic children each Friday during the school year. These visits give the children an opportunity to interact with Reilly and improve their focus:

Brushing Reilly helps one boy stay calm and attentive while his teacher works with him on his school lessons. Reilly also provides a role model for behavior control. On one occasion an autistic boy sat down next to Reilly and kept poking him. I had asked the boy to stop several times, with no luck. Reilly helped me out because she stood up, turned around and sat down with her back to him. The boy was so offended and wanted to know why my dog did that to him, because he was expecting Reilly to react by barking or biting. This simple behavior by Reilly provided a springboard for talking about understanding boundaries, personal space, and appropriate reactions.

Kerri Stamas loves having her therapy dog, Dillon, spend time with Hayden, a six-year-old boy with autism: "One of the few times you see Hayden smile or laugh is when he's with Dillon." Hayden's mother, Nancy Torres, agrees that Dillon is the perfect therapy for Hayden:

Both my boys love being with Dillon. For them, Dillon's just another playmate. Hayden is especially bonded with Dillon. Hayden has autism, which gives him trouble with his speech, motor skills, and learning. Hayden also has a problem socializing and has difficulty being comfortable with groups of people. If several children come around Hayden to play, he'll retreat away by himself. That is, unless Dillon is around! When Dillon is there, Hayden doesn't want to leave Dillon's side. Dillon just draws children to him and he's usually surrounded by a big group of kids.

Even though Hayden would normally avoid a group, when Dillon's there, Hayden's right in the mix playing with everyone else. Dillon also helps Hayden use his voice. I couldn't ask for better therapy than time spent with Dillon. When Hayden's with Dillon, you'd never know Hayden has autism.

Therapy dogs can help people with developmental disabilities open up when human efforts have been unsuccessful. Debbie Brown and her Standard Poodle, Natalie, started visiting a fifty-year-old woman, Betty, who tended to stay isolated, didn't speak, and had problems interacting with others:

> *The staff asked me to visit Betty with Natalie, hoping that some sort of communication would happen with Betty through our visits. For five months, Natalie and I visited Betty every week, rain or shine, with no change in Betty. Natalie and I would simply sit on the floor, hoping Natty would draw Betty's interest. After months of what seemed like no impact, Betty reached down and tried to take Natty's leash. On the next visit, I brought two leashes—one for me and one for Betty to hold. Betty took the leash and together, each holding our own leash, we walked Natty around the facility. Over the next several weeks, Betty continued to enjoy her walks with Natty and began giving Natty treats I brought and even brushing Natty. I was also able to teach Betty hand signals she could use for Natty. Through Natty, Betty and I were successfully communicating—just not with words.*

READING WITH ROVER

Kids who struggle with reading can find reading to even the kindest adults intimidating and frustrating. Reading to an eager dog who never minds pauses to sound out words or going back to read something again can make reading practice more enjoyable for many kids. My Wheaten Terrier Wheatie's first therapy dog job was with a reading program called "Reading with Rover." Our volunteer coordinator taught us to talk to the children through the dog. If the child skipped a sentence or made a number of errors, we might ask the child to read it again because "Wheatie wasn't sure he understood that part" or "Wheatie wanted to hear something again." And when words were too tough and couldn't be sounded out, we'd check to see if Wheatie knew that big word. Invariably he did not and I could say, "Let me tell you and Wheatie both what that says." Wheatie's periodic nudges and kisses, his wagging tail and eager smile would all encourage a hesitant reader to stick with the story because I'd tell the child how much

Wheatie was enjoying the story and how eager Wheatie was to hear what would happen next.

Our first Reading with Rover student was a boy named Kenny. Kenny was in elementary school, struggling with reading, and full of energy. My oldest son was a very "energetic" boy through elementary school before he finally settled down in fifth grade. So when I saw the frustrated and exhausted look on Kenny's mom's face when she brought Kenny for the first reading session, with pre-emptive apologies for his unbridled energy, I had fond memories of my own struggles with my boy.

Kenny's first book was filled with words too challenging for him and difficult to sound out. After trying to skip ahead a few pages and jump over difficult sections, he finally realized that Wheatie would "insist" he return to read the uncompleted parts every time. On every page, there'd be a word or two Kenny didn't know, and we'd have to ask Wheatie if he was familiar with the word, which he never was, so I told them both. When we reached the final page of the book, another big word jumped out at Kenny. With a big sigh he said, "I don't know that word. Does Wheatie know it?" Naturally, Wheatie was equally stumped, and when I told Kenny Wheatie also didn't know the word, Kenny's face beamed with a huge smile of relief. "Oh, if he doesn't know it either, that's OK!"

Several weeks after completing the reading program, I saw Kenny and his mom. When I told Kenny how much Wheatie had enjoyed reading with him, Kenny beamed and announced, "I can't read to Wheatie anymore. I have my *own* dog!" His much-less-frustrated mother then related how Kenny enjoyed reading so much to the dog that they'd decided to select a mature dog for Kenny at the shelter and said that Kenny now reads to him every night. This is a story of success for Kenny, the shelter, and a loving dog in need of a home.

Lisa Saroyan, cousin to famous author William Saroyan, brings the gift of reading to many children—with a bit of help from a four-pound Pomeranian, Minnie. Minnie didn't begin her life as an educator; she spent her first five years confined to a small cage as part of a puppy mill breeding program. Thus confined, Minnie missed out on important lessons in socialization, had an untreated thyroid condition, and ended up losing many of her teeth from poor nutrition. But Lisa saw great opportunities for Minnie:

Minnie was looking for someone to be in charge of her—to care for her. And she found that in me. She will do anything for me and also seems to have a sixth sense for detecting distress in others. When she's with children, she gauges their personalities and seems to understand when she should look away or become more engaged quicker than we humans do.

Lisa recognized Minnie's special gifts as an opportunity to help children struggling to read. When Lisa initially approached the Fresno (California) United School District about using Minnie to help children with speech and learning disabilities improve their reading, district officials were skeptical. However, watching Minnie work as a reading therapist changed everyone's mind. Most dogs participating in reading programs are trained to sit or lie quietly while a child reads. Lisa had trained Minnie to intently watch the reading child. Through subtle commands few observers might detect, Lisa guides Minnie to not only stare attentively at her reader and the book but to also move her head as the reader moves from page to page. Children really get a sense that Minnie is completely absorbed in the story, which helps their confidence and motivates them to keep working hard:

When kids first start reading to Minnie, they'll sometimes look over their shoulder at me or get distracted by others. By the second or third session with Minnie, however, the children only have eyes

Figure 6.4. Reading specialist Minnie hangs on every word.

for Minnie. She gives them her undivided attention and kids really respond to that positive energy.

Today, Minnie has her own second-grade reading class and also works with first- and third-graders: "Minnie has her own classroom *and* her own teacher's aide." And the proof of Minnie's success is the new-found confidence and joy of reading in her charges, along with boosts in their reading scores.

Bouvier des Flandres therapy dog Sadie, her owner Jane Miller, and Jane's eleven-year-old daughter Beth unintentionally started a reading program when they decided to leave children's books at an assisted living center they visited so the seniors would have stories to read to visiting grandchildren. Soon, the seniors and grandchildren convinced Beth to read the stories to them. Jane is impressed that Beth's friends will sometimes join her on her visits to the seniors:

The girls will read aloud to the group together. It's amazing when children who would otherwise feel uncomfortable reading aloud in school can get up in front of a room full of people and enjoy reading

Figure 6.5. Therapy dog Sami looks especially literate when sporting her reading glasses.

out loud with lots of emotion and dramatic facial expressions. Both seniors and the girls benefit from these sessions, supervised by wise Sadie.

Before long, Beth and her mom had developed a successful reading program and created the Ruff Writers Web site that recommends nine children's picture books each year to be shared at libraries, schools, home, and senior residences to share the joy of reading.

One of Patti Shanaberg's favorite photos of her therapy dog Sami is one where Sami's getting ready for a reading session, wearing a big pair of glasses:

Sami really made a big impact when children would read to her. Parents would often tell me about the difference sessions with Sami made for their children's interest in reading. Children would come to our reading programs, eager to read to Sami, saying "I want to read to the dog with the glasses!" When children would meet Sami and ask me where her glasses were, I'd simply respond, "Oh, Sami's wearing her contact lenses today!"

A DOCTOR'S VIEW OF HEALING DOGS HELPING MEDICAL ILLNESS

7

Let Shadow and Sammy Ease an Ailing Psyche

Dogs can reduce psychological distress, isolation, and grief. Doctors at St. Michael's Hospital in Toronto, Ontario, Canada, reported the results of using therapy dog visits for a forty-three-year-old man with bipolar disorder who needed to be hospitalized for severe depression and anxiety after being assaulted (Sockalingam et al., 2008). Bipolar disorder is a condition in which patients have marked swings in their mood from excessive activity and euphoria to intense depression. After this man had not responded to the usual medication treatments, the staff decided to add a new member to the treatment team: a Golden Retriever therapy dog that made daily visits. Adding the therapy dog resulted in marked improvements in this man's symptoms:

- His mood improved.
- His anxiety decreased.
- The dog attracted other people, who would come over to see the dog and then talk with the man, helping the man become more at ease with other people.
- His self-esteem improved, which the man attributed to knowing that the staff had entrusted him with the dog as a visitor.
- The man became more active, spending time walking the dog during visits rather than isolating himself in his room.

This man knew he had to keep good control on his emotions for the dog to be able to visit, and this gave him the motivation he needed to work hard with his other treatments.

When you're having problems with your mood, it's often hard to share your distress with other people and easy to bottle up problem feelings inside. When therapy dog handlers Barbara Pohodich and Janet Malinsky ask patients how they're feeling, they've come to expect that they may not get much of a response—until those patients begin sharing with their dogs:

> *People will share things with our dogs that they'd never share with us or the staff. When we say, "Sadie and Courtney wonder how you're doing," floodgates can open and people will share their deepest fears*

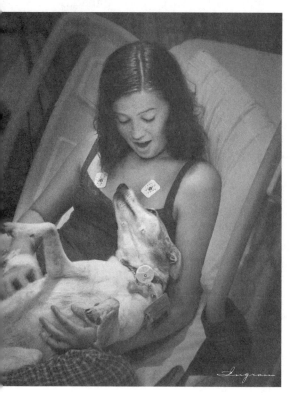

Figure 7.1. Jack Russell Terrier Moe's knowing gaze and charming spirit help patients replace fear, anxiety, and sadness with joy and hope. Photo courtesy of Patricia A. M. Ingram of Ingram Portrait Design.

and concerns with these thoughtful-looking dogs. Sometimes they tell our dogs important problems that they're having that the nurses need to know. The dogs can reach people and help them open up and, hopefully, start getting better.

Psychiatrists have studied the role of therapy dogs for boosting the benefits of treatment for a number of serious psychiatric conditions. For example, researchers at the Brain Behavior Laboratory in Haifa, Israel, showed that there was greater improvement and motivation in patients with schizophrenia when their treatment sessions were conducted with a therapy dog present (Nathans-Barel et al., 2005). Other studies have likewise shown improvement in independence, socialization, and overall well-being in patients with schizophrenia when therapy dogs were added to their long-term treatment (Kovács et al., 2004; Barak et al., 2001):

- Therapy dogs encouraged increased activity among patients with schizophrenia.
- Therapy dogs increased patient's interpersonal contacts and communication.
- The researchers called the therapy dogs "modeling companions," because patients with schizophrenia learned how to improve their own behaviors by watching how the dog responded to others, interacted, and stayed active.

Therapy dogs have also been shown to help people with depression, phobias, and addiction problems, prompting Dr. Ivan Dimitrijević to write a review article in 2009 titled "Animal-Assisted Therapy—A New Trend in the Treatment of Children and Adults" for a psychiatric medical journal.

Tail Waggin' Tip

Therapy dogs have been used to help patients with mood disorders, schizophrenia, phobias, and addiction.

THERE'S SOMETHING ABOUT A DOG IN THE ROOM

Rose Mary Mulkerrin has been therapy dog Lucky D's handler for a couple of years:

> *The patients we visit form a bond with Lucky D that's special to see. One day when Lucky D was visiting patients at a rehabilitation facility, a woman asked me, "Please come back again. There's something about a dog in the room."*

That lady was right: Special things happen when a therapy dog enters the room.

Rose Mary discovered just how special Lucky D's visits could be when they met three children who had lost their mother to cancer. The nine-year-old twins and twelve-year-old could not or would not talk to the counselor assigned to help them. In came Lucky D:

> *We met with the kids four times. At first, they ignored Lucky D, but soon they were brushing and hugging him. They seemed to relate to Lucky D in a way they couldn't to the adults who were so eager to help them. As a handler, I've learned that my job is just to stay in the background—Lucky D's the one doing all the work. And his work with the children was like a miracle. He seemed to be able to look into their souls and recognize what they needed. With the active boy, Lucky D would race around outside, while he'd sit solemnly with the little girl as she gently brushed him. He instinctively understood what each child needed and adapted for their needs. After spending time with Lucky D, the children were ready to open up to the therapist.*

Lucky D didn't do any counseling, but he sure paved the way for the children's therapy to start.

Sometimes a dog can reach people in a way that another person cannot. Sigmund Freud, the father of psychoanalysis, had an important colleague to assist him during his sessions—his Chow, Jofi. Freud described a calming influence that Jofi had on his clients. He further insisted that Jofi's reactions to patients helped Freud understand the patients better.

Tail Waggin' Tip

Famous psychiatrist Sigmund Freud included his dog during therapy sessions to bring calm to patients in distress.

Kad Favorite didn't need Freud to tell her that a dog can be the calm in a storm. Kad makes nursing home visits with her three-year-old Golden Doodle, Lucy.

Usually when we visit, a group of residents congregate in a circle in the large activity room. One day as Lucy and I came into a room, we could hear an elderly man in his room, yelling, screaming, and verbalizing extreme frustration and anger. Several of the residents in the circle looked mortified, embarrassed at the behavior of their fellow resident.

The staff brought the angry man to the circle where he sat with a huff until he spotted Lucy. Suddenly, all the hostility melted away and a giant smile replaced the earlier scowl on his face. He began singing funny songs including the words, "I love Lucy!" and soon had the whole group in stitches. It was amazing to see how the simple presence of a therapy dog could defuse emotions and turn irritation to joy.

Other therapy dog handlers have similarly seen how having a dog in the room can add an aura of calm. Part of hospice chaplain the Rev. Danielle Di Bona's work includes serving on church committees. Not wanting to be left out, therapy dog Naomi usually accompanied Danielle, retiring unobtrusively under a big table while the committee members hashed out details for their work. As with most groups and committees, decisions were sometimes greeted with disagreements in the group, and things could occasionally get a bit heated. As tempers would begin to flare, Naomi would stir from her position under the table and move to sit next to one committee member or the next. On several occasions, Danielle

Figure 7.2. Kad appreciates Golden Doodle therapy dog Lucy's ability to bring peace and serenity to those she visits.

was stopped after the meeting broke up, with words of thanks for bringing Naomi:

> *Several times someone would tell me, "I was just about to lose it in there, when Naomi came and sat next to me. Having her there and giving her some pats really helped calm me down so I could be productive and not say hurtful things I would have regretted." Naomi really had an uncanny gift for recognizing when her calming and healing presence was most needed. Naomi would often sense tension in people long before the rest of us humans might recognize it.*

Therapy dog Reilly and his handler, Jacque Speed, attend therapy sessions with children who live in a group home:

> *During the sessions, therapists talk to the children about their problems and how to handle frustrations and feelings. I tell them all about Reilly and what she does when she's happy, sad, angry, scared, or lonely. The therapist asks each child to tell Reilly how they react to their emotions. The therapists are always amazed about how the kids feel so much freer to share with Reilly. They share things with Reilly*

that the therapists have never heard during their individual sessions. One boy told Reilly that he just punches people when he gets angry. The therapist was able to get this boy to understand why that was inappropriate by asking about what might happen to Reilly if she bit people when she got upset. These revelations open important doors so the therapists can most effectively deal with each child's problems.

KEEPING A POSITIVE ATTITUDE

You've probably heard Sue London on her radio show or seen her on television's Pet Network, talking about turning your life around with a positive approach to challenges both big and small. But did you know that Sue learned some of her first lessons from a cuddly Shih-Tzu named Rocky?

Sue has been no stranger to bad news herself. At age twenty-six, then a young wife and new mother, Sue was diagnosed with Crohn's disease, a chronic digestive disorder that causes severe abdominal pain, cramping, fatigue, diarrhea, and often, as was the case for Sue, bowel surgery. Because of Crohn's complications, Sue's doctors didn't think she'd be able to have another child—but she now has two beautiful daughters after a difficult second pregnancy at age thirty that required her to be hospitalized on intravenous therapy. Three years later, an abscess ruptured her intestine, resulting in emergency surgery that Sue wasn't expected to survive, but thankfully did.

As Sue struggled through one prediction of bad news after another, Rocky was her constant companion, modeling a positive attitude that Sue then adopted for herself:

Through everything that happened, Rocky was always with me. When I'd feel frustrated or lonely, Rocky would somehow remind me that I was not alone. During tough times, Rocky would stick by me, giving me kisses and showing me he understood my pain. When my Crohn's pain would get too severe, Rocky would move toward me and breathe very heavily into my ear. It was as if he wanted me to focus on his breathing and not my pain. Just having Rocky near was so therapeutic.

At the end of 2001, Rocky left Sue as he breathed his last breaths. But Rocky's memory continues to strengthen Sue and others through

Figure 7.3. Sue and Shih-Tzu therapy dog Willy share *Rocky's Trip to the Hospital* with Ryan.

Sue's children's book series, *"Rocky's Journey,"* the tale of a magical dog named Rocky that helps people with illnesses, just like Sue was helped by her Rocky.

> *My first book,* Rocky's Trip to the Hospital, *is based on my own story of triumphing over sickness—aided by my own Rocky. I take this book and my two certified therapy dogs, Willy and Molly, into children's hospitals. I read Rocky's book and then let the dogs work their magic.*
>
> *Willy always gets a laugh. Willy becomes very relaxed as children pet him. And the more relaxed Willy becomes, the louder he snores. Even the sickest children will laugh at this comical snore—taking their focus off their pain. Molly has developed a technique to help children who don't want to take their medicine. For every sip of medicine swallowed, Molly will do a trick and accept a treat from the child. The more medicine in the child—the more tricks and treats for Molly. We haven't found a child yet who can resist Molly's charm.*
>
> *Many of the children I visit have been hospitalized for weeks. They are depressed, missing their normal life at home, missing their friends, and, if they have one, missing their pet. When children see my dogs and their wagging tails, they brighten right up. You can see the life literally coming back into these children. Laughter fills their eyes, huge smiles appear on their tiny faces, and positive energy fills*

the room. Some of the children will even share their fears with the dogs—telling the dogs things they haven't told others. Every child tells me how the dog visits help, and the parents get comfort from Willy and Molly, too. Willy and Molly give unconditional love—a love that you can't and don't want to resist.

LIFTING DEPRESSED MOODS

Depression affects about eight to ten percent of adults in the United States and Canada (Vasiliadis et al., 2007). Seniors are more likely to have mood problems, with depressive symptoms reported in up to one in five seniors overall (Hamer, Bates, & Mishra, 2011) and about one in three seniors living in nursing homes (Seitz, Purandare, & Conn, 2010). Seniors with depression have more than a fifty percent increased risk for developing dementia (Saczynski et al., 2010) and a twenty-four percent increased risk of dying (Hamer et al., 2010).

Dr. Cline at the University of Missouri—Columbia completed a national survey evaluating the impact of dog ownership on depression (Cline, 2010). Although dog ownership did not affect mood overall, there were positive effects for certain groups. Owning a dog reduced depression in women and people who were single.

Tail Waggin' Tip

Mood is improved in women and unmarried people when they share their lives with a dog.

Patti Shanaberg routinely saw people's moods brighten when she visited with her therapy dog, Sami:

One day, I was with a therapy dog–handler team, visiting an older man we saw regularly in a nursing home. While we were enjoying our visit, the man's son entered the room and started to cry, saying, "I haven't seen my father laugh like this in years!" We weren't sure what to say—we were used to seeing this man laughing during our routine visits and chats. That's how he always was during our visits. Before his son visited, I had no idea how much the therapy dog visits lifted this man's spirits.

Other times, we wouldn't think our visits were making much of a difference for nursing home residents who didn't seem to respond while we were with them. Later, we'd sometimes have family members of these same residents tell us how their loved one had eagerly talked to them about the wonderful visit from a therapy dog. One family member even invited Sami to attend the visiting hours for one of the residents after she had died because Sami's visits had been so important in bringing her cheer.

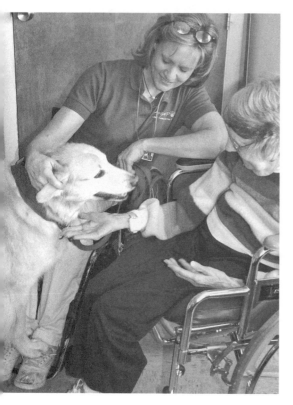

Figure 7.4. Sami would often stand on Patti's toes to reach those she was visiting, like this woman, for whom Sami made such an impact that the family invited her to pay her respects with loved ones after the lady had died.

Once, Sami visited in bed with a hospice patient near death, and both family members and staff had tears in their eyes during her visit with him. The man was nearly unresponsive, but he made the effort to pet Sami after Sami gently licked his hand. This was more of a response and engagement than the family or staff had seen in awhile and they were very excited to see it.

Sami also had a special gift for easing burdens in children:

Often when we'd visit terminally ill patients, Sami and I would take a visiting child into a separate room to read or visit so adults could have conversations they might not want to have in front of the child or just to give the child a break from all the tension in the room of a hospice patient near death.

Sami was also a big help to children at the Hospice Bereavement Camp for children who had recently lost a loved one. I would explain how I often didn't feel comfortable sharing my grief with family or friends for various reasons after I lost my brothers and father. But Sami helped me through my own grief because I could tell her anything and she didn't mind or get upset or depressed the way family or friends might. The kids would line up and I'd take Sami around so the children could share their own secrets one by one. Often the children would be reluctant at first. But when they saw others lifting up her soft furry ear so they could share their secrets and could see how receptive Sami was, they'd change their minds and want to share—and some children would want to share again. It was very moving.

Being depressed saps your energy and strength and tears away at the motivation you need to follow through with all of the doctor's recommendations. It's hard to eat, it's hard to sleep, and it's hard to get better. Breaking through depression can be very hard. There are often no words to heal the pain and despair that often led to depression, but a dog's gentle presence can sometimes open a hole to let a bit of light begin to shine over the darkness of depressive gloom.

During his long-term hospital stay, Robert became depressed, and no one had been able to reach him. For three weeks, he hadn't responded to any of the hospital staffs' efforts to improve his mood.

Robert's social worker knew he'd left two beloved dogs at home with his family and thought a therapy dog was just what the doctor ordered. Jacque Speed recalls how Robert's visits with her therapy dog, Reilly, helped Robert turn a corner away from his depression:

> *When Robert's social worker saw me and my Golden Retriever, Reilly, coming down the hall in the hospital, she sort of kidnapped us! She explained that her patient was so depressed and had stopped talking much to his visitors. Reilly and I went to the man's room and weren't greeted with the usual smiles and beaming faces that we typically see when patients discover they're being visited by a gorgeous Golden. Instead, Robert quietly reached down for Reilly and began gently rubbing her face and ears. After a few minutes, I started talking to Robert and the more he petted Reilly, the more he'd talk to me. During the visit, his daughter stopped by, watching and listening quietly from the hallway. As we left, she turned to me with teary eyes, thanking me for helping to bring her father back. Robert was discharged before our next hospital visit, so we never saw him again, but I'd like to think that Reilly's visit opened a door for him to start getting better.*

Patients going through illnesses and recovery can become discouraged and despondent. This was true for a patient visited by Shelley Bates and her Beagle–Coon Hound mix therapy dog, Bentley.

> *The young man was in a rehabilitation hospital, surrounded by patients who were mostly much older than him. He was depressed at being injured, depressed at being apart from his family and friends, and depressed at being in an unfamiliar environment. He had been unresponsive to everyone and everything—until Bentley arrived. Bentley is the MOST laid-back dog you will ever meet in your life— guaranteed. I've even nicknamed him "Eeyore" after the Winnie-the-Pooh character. Bentley's calm temperament and acceptance of everyone, however, make him a wonderful snuggle companion and the perfect therapy dog.*
>
> *Our young man immediately asked for Bentley to be put on his bed, and Bentley happily complied by snuggling lengthwise along the man's body. Eventually, both man and dog closed their eyes in contentment. You would have thought they were sleeping, except*

for the smile that formed on the man's face—and I swear there was one on Bentley's face, too. This young man's whole demeanor changed—all from a bit of snuggle time with little Bentley. While I was watching the pair, I heard a shuffle by the door and saw the entire staff admiring Bentley's work—each one sharing a grin that mirrored the new-found blissful expression on their patient.

Marlene Miller and her Keeshonden, Zeus and Mitsu, visit a lot of folks at MacKenzie Place, a long-term care facility in Newmarket, Ontario, Canada, where many residents have no family to visit them. Loneliness is common in people with health problems, especially seniors who may have lost lifelong companions and peers. Loneliness is serious business, and reducing loneliness is medically important because loneliness has actually been linked to an increased risk for developing serious memory problems in seniors (Conroy et al., 2010). Loneliness is also linked to an increased risk of dying younger (Patterson & Veenstra, 2010; Shiovitz-Ezra & Ayalon, 2010).

 Loneliness increases your risk of dying. Shiovitz-Ezra and Ayalon (2010) followed a sample of adults ages fifty and older for eight years and noted the following:

- Risk of dying during the study was fifty-six percent higher for people who were lonely for less than two years up to two years.
- Risk of dying increased eighty-three percent for people who were chronically lonely throughout the study.

Staying socially connected is an important way to stave off the effects of loneliness (Drageset, 2004). When family members and frequent visitors are sparse, visits from a therapy dog can effectively reduce loneliness in seniors (Banks & Banks, 2002). As a therapy dog handler, it is important for you to understand that those few minutes a lonely senior spends with your dog is doing more than just providing a few moments of joy—your dog is probably helping that person maintain a happier, healthier, longer, and fuller life.

EASING BURDENS DURING TIMES OF GRIEF

Loss and the grief that comes with it are a part of every life. Dogs can provide important unconditional, nonjudgmental support during times of grieving. Dr. Karen Allen (1995) described how five widows gave her similar descriptions of how their dogs had helped them after losing their husbands:

> *Each widow said that while she appreciated the consolation efforts of family and friends, she really wanted to be alone with her dog, especially immediately following her husband's death. Part of the reason was that the dog had been shared by the husband, but more important was the feeling that, with the dog, no social pretenses were necessary, and no one was judging her ability to "bear up." These women all said that the dog provided the desirable qualities of a best friend (e.g., listening, physical contact, empathy) without any undesirable evaluative ones. They also all reported that to help get through times during the funeral proceedings when it was socially inappropriate to have the dog present, they thought about the dog and carried something related to the dog in a pocket (e.g., a dog toy, a collar, etc.). That these widows behaved in such similar ways impressed me immensely. (p. 6)*

Mary Ann Hirt learned about the healing power of a therapy dog for grieving people when she thought she would just be making a routine hospital visit with her Great Dane, Cooper:

> *Our last stop was one of the critical-care waiting rooms. As we walked in, I noticed a husband, wife, and grandfather sitting off to the side, huddled together, sobbing. I wasn't sure if I should approach them or not, so I opted to leave them be and went to the other side of the room—to a family who couldn't resist the charms of Cooper, my real life Marmaduke.*
>
> *As these family members were petting him and talking to me, I noticed a person standing next to me. When I looked, I realized it was someone from the distraught family. The wife asked if they could meet my dog, and of course, Cooper obliged. Great Danes have this need to stand up with their paws on your shoulders, and Cooper immediately did that to the husband, who was bald and*

shorter than him. And then Cooper started licking the man's head. All three of the members of that distraught family plus most of the waiting room burst out laughing. Cooper provided a welcome little respite to a family who needed a distraction from their grief.

People often say that having pets teaches children about life and death, learning how to let go of loved ones as pets pass too soon from our lives. Rita Reynolds's 2001 book *Blessing the Bridge: What Animals Teach Us About Death, Dying, and Beyond* is a great example of learning lessons from our pets about accepting loss.

Our pets can also help us as we struggle through the grieving process. They are by our sides as we need comfort and understanding, reflecting our emotions with their knowing eyes and giving needed licks and opportunities for comfort petting. Emotions can flow between you and the dog without words that never truly capture your feelings and with a freedom that can be initially uncomfortable with other humans. Dogs also teach us that one can't wallow in misery. With their continued needs for food, play, and walks to go potty, dogs show us that we too need to care for basic needs for others and for ourselves and, as we do, saying goodbye becomes a natural part of life.

Saying a final goodbye to loved ones at funeral homes can be especially emotionally charged. In some cases, having a gentle, quiet therapy dog can help ease the burdens of those in mourning. Some funeral homes even keep grief therapy dogs on staff.

The Rev. Danielle Di Bona has also found the value of dogs during times of grief:

As a minister, I'm there for my parishioners in times of great joy and great sorrow. One time, I was conducting a funeral service for a family for whom my therapy dog Naomi and I had visited the loved one many times. Naomi had been to work with me earlier that day, and I hated to leave her in the car when I drove up to the funeral, so I brought her inside with me. During the service, Naomi sat earnestly next to the pulpit. As the service concluded, I invited the family and friends to come up to pay their final respects to their loved one. As each person passed the casket, they passed me and stopped in front of Naomi to give her a pet. No one passed her by. Naomi didn't have to say a word—through her simple presence and gentleness she gave incredible comfort.

Marie and Loren were a special couple. Pauline Glagola met them when they arrived at the Residence at Hilltop, an assisted-living facility, with her therapy dogs, Rocky and Chip.

Marie had end-stage cancer and her husband Loren had early Alzheimer's disease. But with Marie and Loren you didn't see disease—you saw devotion. All of the ladies would comment they had never seen a husband dote on his wife like Loren did to Marie. He pushed her wheelchair to dinner, fed her, and attended to her personal needs. Their fifty-year marriage was clearly one of devotion and joy.

Although Rocky would usually visit his ladies in a common room, he made an exception for Marie, visiting her in her room. Rocky would just put his head in her hands and stare deeply into

Figure 7.5. Marie and Australian Shepherd–Bernese Mountain Dog mix therapy dog Rocky have eyes only for each other. Photo courtesy of Ron Paglia.

Marie's eyes, which was something he only did with Marie. Chip was a bit bolder with Marie, heading straight to her bed to jump up and lie down with her. When I'd instruct Chip to get off the bed, Marie would insist, "No—leave him here. You know who loves you, don't you Chip?!"

On Chip's final visit to Marie, she couldn't open her eyes:

"Wake up! Chip's here to see you," a distressed Loren hopefully told Marie. This time, however, instead of jumping on the bed, Chip just laid his head on Marie's hand and stood for a few seconds staring solemnly at Marie before leaving the room. I was so surprised that Chip had cut his usual visit so short, but decided he must know what he was doing. The next day, I learned that Marie had died about forty-five minutes after Chip's visit. Looking back, it was almost as if Chip wanted Loren to have Marie's last moments for himself.

Pauline knew how important Chip was to Marie and Loren and called the funeral home to ask if Chip could pay his respects to the family during the scheduled visitation. This out-of-the-ordinary request was met with shock by the funeral director:

You would've thought I asked the director to raise Marie from the dead. So I did what I thought was right—my husband and I got dressed up, put Chip in the car, and drove to the visitation. When the family found out that Chip was in the car, they insisted he be allowed inside. The family ushered Chip smack dab in the middle of the room. Chip looked around for a minute, saw Loren, and made a beeline for the man Chip sensed so needed his special brand of comfort. Loren reached out to Chip, "There's my little friend. I'm so glad to see you." Chip sat with Loren for fifteen minutes, Loren's hands never leaving Chip's fur as people came over to offer their condolences. As I got ready to take Chip out, I saw we had to stay—the entire family was waiting to see this little dog Marie loved so much and talked about all the time. Loren reflected, "Marie would have just loved knowing Chip was here." And I suspect what would have made Marie smile the widest was knowing that she was leaving her beloved Loren in the paws of those same therapy dogs who eased her burdens and made her smile—even when life was the most hard.

You know who loves you, don't you, Chip? Chip surely knows who loves him—and he most certainly loved them back.

STAYING SOCIALLY CONNECTED IS IMPORTANT FOR YOUR EMOTIONAL AND PHYSICAL HEALTH

Being socially engaged in your community and with family and friends will also improve your physical health. A lot of medical research has investigated the health impact of social involvement. A lack of friends is linked to poor health, whereas health improves for people who are socially involved and, among older adults, general health continues to improve as the number of social activities increases (Zunzunegui et al., 2004). Interestingly, older adults need more than simply involvement with family. In a large study of over 3,000 seniors, being involved with networks of friends provided more health benefits than networks of only family and children (Zunzunegui et al., 2004). It's pretty amazing that doing something as simple as checking in with friends, greeting your neighbors, and taking an interest in others can substantially improve your own well-being and help you live a longer, healthier life (Barefoot et al., 2005; Giles et al., 2005).

 Researchers at Duke University reported their findings of social involvement and health in a large survey of almost 10,000 people (Barefoot et al., 2005). More frequent interactions with family and friends resulted in about a twenty-five percent reduced risk for heart disease and death.

Older people who are more socially engaged also develop fewer memory problems. Reduced involvement with relatives and friends has been linked to having worsened memory (Zunzunegui et al., 2003). Fortunately, more social involvement has similarly been linked to a reduced rate of developing memory problems. A study that followed over 6,000 seniors across a span of about five and a half years found that those who had frequent social engagement had a slower decline in intellectual and memory abilities (Barnes et al., 2004). Good mental capacity was maintained best in the people who were the most socially active. So, chatting with neighbors and friends today may help keep the brain sharp for years to come.

When people are younger, eating is often an important social occasion, and eating is always more enjoyable if you share a meal. As people age, their diets often become more limited, and many seniors lose an interest in eating. Having meals can become a chore rather than an occasion. Researchers at the University of Maryland proved that seniors with more social contacts ate better (Sahyoun & Zhang, 2005):

- Seniors who stayed socially connected ate better.
- Socially active seniors' diets were healthier and contained more nutritious calories.
- Socially active seniors ate more fruits and vegetables compared with seniors who had few social contacts.

So, whether you're able to eat with others or need to eat alone, having a strong network of friends and acquaintances results in healthier eating habits, at least in the elderly.

Social connections are also important for living longer. Researchers in Australia followed senior citizens for 10 years (Giles et al., 2005) and made the following observations:

- The risk of dying over the course of the ten-year study decreased by twenty percent in seniors at least seventy years old when they had a strong network of friends.
- Social interactions with friends had a greater effect on this risk reduction than interactions with family members.

Therefore, although we children may think that we and the grandkids should be enough to keep Grandpa engaged, it's essential that seniors develop relationships outside of their family. Visiting with and walking a quiet, well-behaved dog can be a great way to help seniors shift their focus from their own concerns onto those of other two- and four-legged friends.

Researchers in the United Kingdom decided to ask dog owners what benefits they got from their dogs by surveying people taking their dogs to a dog park (Knight & Edwards, 2008). In addition to the physical benefits from exercising with their dogs, the dog owners discussed social and emotional benefits, such as making new friends through their dog and using their dog as a conversation starter. These dog owners "talked about their dog as their companion, their friend, even their therapist" (Knight & Edwards, 2008, p. 443).

What Dog Owners Say About Their Dogs (Knight & Edwards, 2008)

- Physical benefits
  - Dogs give them motivation to exercise each day.
  - If they felt lonely or depressed before a dog walk, dog owners feel both physically and mentally better afterward.
  - Exercising with dogs keeps seniors active and healthy.
- Emotional benefits
  - Dogs cheer people up when they feel blue.
  - Dogs give unconditional companionship, comfort, and love.
  - Dogs understand their owners' moods and act as their therapists, listening to their troubles and providing nonjudgmental comfort.
  - Dogs provide a sense of confidence, safety, and security when out walking.
  - Dogs keep people from feeling alone, lonely, and isolated.

8

Connecting With Bailey Is Heart Healthy

Heart disease can include a number of health problems. Damage to blood vessels from high blood pressure and high cholesterol can restrict the flow of blood to the heart, causing chest pain or heart attacks. When blood flow to the brain is limited, you can develop a stroke. Heart damage can also lead to irregular heart beats, called arrhythmias.

Heart disease is unfortunately very common. One in every three adults has heart disease (Zhang, 2010). Heart disease is the number one cause of death for both men and women. One in every three deaths around the world is caused by heart disease (Bitton & Gaziano, 2010).

 Heart disease is not just a man's problem.
It is an equal-opportunity disease—affecting one in every three men *and* women.
Heart disease is the number one killer of men and women—killing more people than cancer.

Cardiopulmonary resuscitation (CPR) saves the lives of people having a heart attack. CPR can help keep people alive while they're waiting for help from emergency personnel, like paramedics and emergency medical technicians. CJ Anderson is committed to teaching people how to react when someone has a heart problem and thus teaches classes in CPR. CJ also has a passion for dogs in general and therapy dogs in particular. CJ volunteers with children in crisis through Gabriel's Angels, an organization that provides pet therapy for abused, neglected, and at-risk children (see Chapter 3), and with people at the end of their illnesses at Hospice of the Valley in Phoenix, Arizona.

As an instructor of first aid and CPR for humans, CJ was inspired to start a first aid class for pet owners. After CJ taught CPR to a veterinarian and his employees, the vet told CJ that pet owners also needed to learn CPR, asking, "Do you know how many animals die just as we are putting them on my table to help? If only their owners knew first aid to buy just a few more precious minutes—it would make such a difference." So CJ developed and taught a pet first aid class—long before the Red Cross began offering similar classes.

Tail Waggin' Tip

The American Red Cross offers first aid and CPR classes to teach you how to care for fellow humans and your dog.

CJ is someone who likes to identify problems and then fix them. Sometimes, though, getting people motivated to do what they need to do to help themselves can be a challenge—and this is where CJ has seen that pets can make a big difference:

I cannot begin to tell you how I have seen people do things for their animals that they wouldn't do to help themselves. When we started the Pet First Aid class, many people taking the class came up to me and said, "This was great learning CPR for my dog. You know, my husband (father, brother, or sister) has a heart condition. I wonder if I should learn CPR for him, too?" My mom would have been one of these people—sooner to take care of the dog than her own heart condition.

My mom was a diabetic with bad heart disease. Unfortunately, she wasn't a good friend to herself when she needed to take care of her health problems. Her idea of watching her diet was to take an extra insulin shot before having a bowl of ice cream as her lunch.

As Mom's heart disease worsened, she grew more and more fearful of leaving the house—fearing that she'd develop a health crisis away from home. What really kept her going and from become a recluse was having her Chihuahuas. She took her Chihuahuas to American Kennel Club shows and even became club treasurer. Even though she was never more than a hobby breeder, her dogs won ribbons, and that gave her needed motivation to keep herself as healthy and active as possible. For her dogs, she stayed connected to the world, took care of herself, interacted with people, and I am absolutely convinced lived longer then she would have without them.

When I remember Mom, I think of her surrounded by dogs. And the dogs became guardians for Mom. If she was getting sick, we'd know because the dogs would come together and form a pile in the bed around her. She and her Chihuahuas really took care of each other.

CJ's mom is a terrific example of owners and their dogs caring for each other. Feeling needed for the well-being of her tiny dogs gave CJ's mom the strength, desire, and motivation to take care of herself and her heart disease. As a doctor, I've learned that sometimes sharing all the scientific evidence in the world, and nagging from me and a patient's family, is much less effective than the power from a pair of thoughtful brown eyes on a doggie's face saying, "I'm helpless without you. You are my strength. Take care of yourself so you can take care of me!"

FLUFFY CAN HELP REDUCE YOUR HEART DISEASE RISK FACTORS

Unless you have a parent or sibling with heart problems, you may not really worry that you're at risk for developing heart disease. A national survey of young adults in the United States, however, showed that three in every five people have at least one of the following risk factors for developing heart disease (Kuklina, Yoon, & Keenan, 2010):

- High blood pressure
- Obesity

- Smoking
- Someone in the immediate family who had repeated chest pains or a heart attack when that person was younger than fifty years old

Unfortunately, many people are unaware of what factors increase your risk for developing a heart problem. On average, adults can list only two lifestyle risk factors, most commonly identifying (a) poor eating habits and (b) smoking (Sanderson et al., 2009). People often forget other important lifestyle changes that they might make to reduce their heart disease risk.

How to Improve Your Heart Disease Risk Factors

- Be physically active every day. Add in daily aerobic exercise, walk when you can instead of driving, and take the stairs instead of elevators.
- Maintain a healthy weight by eating right and exercising regularly.
- Check your blood pressure and ask your doctor how to keep it normal. You may need to change your diet and exercise more. You may need medication.
- If you have diabetes, keep your blood sugars controlled.
- Learn how to cope with stress.
- If you smoke, quit.
- Check your cholesterol and work to correct abnormal levels. You may need to change your diet and exercise more. You may need medication.
- Eat a diet rich in healthy, unprocessed foods (e.g., fresh fruits, vegetables, whole grains, fish, and nuts).
- Don't drink too much alcohol. Limit yourself to no more than one mixed drink or two glasses of wine on a given day.

You can't change some risk factors—like having a dad or brother who had a heart attack when he was forty-five years old. Certain ethnic and racial groups, such as African Americans, Native Americans, and Mexican Americans, are at higher risk for developing heart problems. There are, however, a number of risk factors you can reduce. You can quit smoking and, if you have diabetes, make sure your blood sugars are controlled. Eating right and exercising regularly are essential to lowering your heart disease risk, especially if you're overweight, physically inactive, or have high blood pressure, high cholesterol, or diabetes.

Walking is great exercise for your heart. Cardiac exercise physiologist Dr. Gordon Blackburn from the Cleveland Clinic encouraged more people to exercise by walking in his article, "Exercise for Women Who Hate to Exercise" (Blackburn, 2007). What's Dr. Blackburn's number one tip to make exercise more appealing? "Walk your dog, or walk your neighbor's dog" (p. 6).

Walking is the easiest exercise for people who don't normally workout. Walking is something almost everyone can do—with no special equipment or facilities required.

Tail Waggin' Tip

Daily dog walks are good for your heart. Heart specialists recommend walking for a total of at least thirty minutes a day (Tudor-Locke, 2010). You still get good heart benefits if you take several ten-minute walks rather than one thirty-minute walk.

Although any regular walking is helpful, walking for a longer time and at a brisker pace gives you greater heart protection benefits. The following are the findings from several studies that have linked simple walking with reduced heart disease benefits:

- Normal walking for a total of just thirty minutes, five days each week, reduces your risk of heart disease by nineteen percent (Zheng et al., 2009).

- Studies of healthy women have shown that walking as little as one hour each week reduces risk for heart disease by forty percent and stroke by over twenty percent (Oguna & Shinoda-Tagawa, 2004).

- Another study similarly showed that regularly walking at least an hour per week reduced heart disease risk by about thirty percent in both men and women (Hamer & Chida, 2008).

Tail Waggin' Tip

Simply walking reduces your risk for heart disease. Adding thirty minutes of walking into your daily routine typically reduces your risk of developing heart problems by almost twenty percent. Increasing your walking time or picking up the pace gives you added heart disease prevention benefits.

Sticking with a walking program can be tough. It's easy to find excuses to skip a day's walking exercise. Medical research, however, consistently finds that having a dog provides a great motivator to stick with an exercise program (Cutt, Giles-Corti, et al., 2008). Like CJ's mom, many people won't feel guilty about not taking care of themselves, but they won't want to let their dog down by missing daily walks. A research study published in the *International Journal of Behavioral Nutrition and Physical Activity* monitored activity in people without dogs who moved into a new home (Cutt, Knuiman, & Giles-Corti, 2008):

- A year after moving to a new neighborhood, people walked more.
- People without dogs walked in the neighborhood twelve minutes more each week.
- Dog owners walked four times as long: forty-eight more minutes each week.

What if your friend with a heart problem doesn't have a dog for motivation? Share your dog with her. Knowing that having your own dog will motivate you to stick with a walking program, researchers from the University of Missouri—Columbia decided to test whether having a "loaner" dog would also make a difference (Johnson & Meadows, 2010). In this study, people without dogs were paired up with a therapy dog–handler team to walk with for twenty minutes on five days each week. After a year, people were consistently completing about three out of four scheduled walks and had lost an average of over 14 lbs (6 kg). What motivated them to stick with the walking program? The most common reason was that the dog "needed me to walk him—the dog's counting on me."

What Motivates People to Stick With a Dog Walking Program? (Johnson & Meadows, 2010)

- They feel responsible for walking the dog.
- Knowing the dog needs a walk gets them moving in the morning.
- Being with the dog cheers people up and improves their mood.
- They feel that spending time with the dog "makes me a better person."
- Walking a dog makes them feel better.
- Doing a walking program helps reduce pain problems that might limit exercise.

In my book, *Fit As Fido: Follow Your Dog to Better Health* (Marcus, 2008), I argue that "eating like a dog" can improve your health habits. Most of us follow these simple rules when feeding our dog:

- Your dog will be fed on a regular schedule.
- Your dog will be given nutritious food.
- You'll probably measure the dog's food to make sure the portion size is right.
- You'll make sure the dog has a full water bowl.
- You'll probably limit extra treats.

If you apply these same common-sense rules to your eating habits, you'll also be eating healthier.

CJ's mom showed that feeling responsible for a pet can help encourage people to eat better. An interesting study published in the *Journal of Nutrition for the Elderly* (Dembicki & Anderson, 1996) investigated the impact of pet ownership on the health of seniors. The researchers found that seniors with pets consumed significantly more servings of milk and vegetables compared with seniors without pets. They attributed this better eating to companionship provided to seniors by their pets during meals, because eating alone has been shown to be a major factor leading to poor nutrition in seniors.

Fit As Fido (Marcus, 2008)
Heart-Healthy Eating Tips

- Don't skip meals.
- Choose nutrition-packed foods instead of high-calorie, nutrient-poor junk food.
- Limit your portion sizes.
- Drink about ten 8-oz (240-mL) glasses of water each day *plus* extra water before and after exercising.
- Limit snacks to healthy fruits and vegetables or snack-sized treats.

High blood pressure is a major risk factor for developing more serious heart problems. Blood pressure readings are given as a higher top number over a lower bottom number:

- The top blood pressure number is the *systolic* blood pressure, the force on the walls of your blood vessels when your heart is pumping.
- The bottom blood pressure number is the *diastolic* pressure, the force on the vessels between beats when your heart is resting.

In general, most people recommend that your blood pressure should be below 140 over 90 mm Hg to be considered to be normal (Quinn et al., 2010). Your ideal blood pressure may be different, depending on your age and health problems.

General Blood Pressure Targets (Volpe & Tocci, 2010)

- Below a reading of 140 systolic over 90 diastolic, for most people
- Below 150 over 90, for seniors over sixty-five years old
- Below 130 over 90, for people with diabetes or kidney disease

Be sure to ask your doctor what *your* blood pressure target should be.

To see whether having a dog in your life really can reduce your blood pressure, researchers at the State University of New York at Buffalo evaluated patients with high blood pressure who had high-stress jobs (Allen, Shykoff, & Izzo, 2001). All of the patients were treated with blood pressure medication, and half had an additional prescription: Get a pet. Doctors then tested heart rate and blood pressure six months later:

- Resting blood pressure dropped in both groups treated with the blood pressure medication.
- Blood pressure response to mental stress, however, was significantly lower in the patients who got a pet.
- Heart rate and systolic and diastolic blood pressures were each about ten points lower in the pet owners.

One of the stress situations used in the study was making the people do math problems. Pet owners were allowed to have their new pet with them during the test. The pet owners felt calmer and less stressed doing the calculations with their pets in the room. They also made fewer errors than they had when they had been tested at the start of the study, before getting their pet.

DON'T SMOKE

If your dog comes upon cigarette butts during your walks, he probably sniffs them with a bit of disgust and leaves them alone. We could all take a lesson from Fido and stay away from cigarettes. Unless you've been living under a rock for the last few decades, you surely know that cigarette smoking is bad for your health. According to the American Cancer Society publication, *The Tobacco Atlas*, tobacco kills about six million people a year, with the average smoker dying fifteen years earlier than people who don't smoke (Shafey et al., 2009).

The American Heart Association reported that about one in every three cases of heart disease can be attributed to smoking (Ockene & Miller, 1997). Smoking affects the heart by changing a lot of chemicals in the body (Unverdorben, von Holt, & Winkelmann, 2009):

- Tobacco increases inflammation of blood vessels.
- Tobacco makes the blood thicker and more prone to clotting.
- Tobacco affects how the body metabolizes sugars for energy.

If you need helping quitting smoking, check out the 1–800-QUIT-NOW program developed by the U.S. Department of Health and Human Services, the National Institutes of Health, and the National Cancer Institute. Smokers can receive a free helpful smoking cessation plan and coach.

Tail Waggin' Tip

After quitting smoking for at least five years, your risk of dying from heart disease or a stroke decreases by up to sixty-one percent. Your risk of dying from other problems will be reduced by twenty-five percent (Kenfield et al., 2010).

BAILEY CAN ALSO HELP IF YOU HAVE HEART DISEASE

Spending time with a dog—even limited time from a therapy dog visit—has been medically proven to reduce stress on your heart when you have heart problems. The cardiac care staff at the University of California in Los Angeles tested whether a twelve-minute visit with a therapy dog would produce measurable improvements in patients admitted to a heart unit with advanced heart failure (Cole et al., 2007). In this study, researchers compared pressures measured inside the heart and the blood vessels leaving the heart, levels of stress chemicals in the blood (epinephrine and norepinephrine), and anxiety scores for patients who had the normal care in the unit and those who had an additional twelve-minute visit from a volunteer or from a therapy dog:

- Improvements were best in patients who received the therapy dog visit.
- Heart patients who met with a therapy dog had healthier lower heart pressures.
- Heart patients who met with a therapy dog had lower levels of stress chemicals in the blood.
- Anxiety levels were lowest after the dog visit.

This study suggests that therapy dog visits help reduced stress on the heart.

Learn Healthy Ways to Cope With Stress

- Add aerobic exercise, such as regularly scheduled walks with Fido, to your routine each day. When you're feeling extra stressed, add in an extra walk, increase your walking pace, or add extra exercises (see Chapter 12 for suggestions) to spice up your routine.
- Don't over-schedule yourself.
  — Set realistic goals for each day.
  — Schedule adequate time for exercise, meals, and sleep. Don't skip meals, and don't short-change yourself on sleep.
  — Delegate chores to family members.
  — Remember that it's more important to have a happy home than a spotless house.
  — Limit volunteer commitments and your children's after-school activities.

— Schedule down time every day for reading, reflection, or a fun family activity.
- Spot your "stress buttons." Do you feel stressed after meeting with your boss, helping with a school project, or talking with your mother-in-law? When you know stress is likely to occur that day, practice relaxing habits before your buttons get pushed.
  — Anticipate when your stress buttons will be pushed, take deep breaths, and tell yourself positive messages beforehand.
  — Stretch muscles when they first become tense.
  — Play a game of fetch with Fido, or sing him a silly song.
  — Look at your dog and laugh at her silliness.

Medical research has consistently shown that having a companion pet reduces the body's negative physiological reactions to stress and lowers the risk for heart disease (Virués-Ortega & Buela-Casal, 2006). Heart disease risk is particularly lowered with long-term pet interaction, suggesting that having a companion dog in the home would be heart healthy. Researchers at Brooklyn College showed the benefit gained from companion dogs by studying ninety-two patients during their first year after having a heart attack (Friedmann et al., 1980). This study showed that six percent of pet owners died during the following year, compared with twenty-eight percent of those who did not own pets. This study was subsequently repeated with a larger group of three hundred sixty-nine people during the first year after they had a heart attack (Friedmann & Thomas, 1995). Among the heart attack victims with no dog in the household, seven percent died during the first year. This number was dramatically dropped to only one percent dying when there was a dog at home.

Researchers have speculated that dogs help reduce death after heart attacks in two ways (Giaquinto & Valentini, 2009). First, having a dog in the house makes adding a new walking routine to a heart rehabilitation program easier: You already have an eager walking partner in the house who will encourage you to walk each day. Second, being with a dog reduces stress. Stress causes lots of health problems and, when you have a heart condition, stress can be dangerous. Stress can cause people with heart disease to have dangerous abnormal heart rhythms and even heart attacks (Brunckhorst et al., 2003). It has been estimated that reacting to emotional stress is the fatal trigger for one or two of every five people who experience a sudden death from heart disease (Vlastelica, 2008).

A recent study that examined four hundred twenty-four patients admitted to the hospital for a heart problem failed to show that pet ownership was protective for the combination of having to go back to the hospital or dying within the following year (Parker et al., 2010). This study was different from the earlier reports showing a protective effect from dog ownership in that it did not include deaths or repeat hospitalizations that occurred during the first month after the initial hospital stay and instead looked at the combination of deaths *plus* repeat hospital stay rather than just death.

When Mary Ann Hirt developed *atrial fibrillation*—an abnormal heart rhythm—her dogs were there to help. The heart is made up of four chambers; the top two are called *atria,* and the bottom two are called *ventricles.* Normally, the chambers of the heart beat in a synchronized rhythm. The beating makes one chamber squeeze, pushing blood into the next. The muscles in each heart chamber have to work together so that they're all squeezing at the same time. With atrial fibrillation, the muscles in the atria stop working as a team, so the blood is not effectively moved into the ventricles. The heartbeat becomes irregular, the blood is not effectively pushed out into the rest of the body, and the person can experience heart fluttering, shortness of breath, and weakness. Mary Ann had just returned from walking her dogs when she felt severe chest pain:

> It felt like I was shot in my chest. I just doubled over and dropped to the floor. The dogs knew something was wrong and wouldn't leave my side, even when I tried to get them to go away. They stayed right with me until the ambulance came.

Today, Mary Ann's heart rhythm has been corrected with medications, and her dogs are still steadfastly at her side.

Joseph Dunn, Jr., also suffered from a serious heart rhythm problem, called *ventricular tachycardia*, a rapid heartbeat caused by problems with the heart's ventricles. When the ventricles don't pump normally, they can't get enough blood to all the organs in the body. Ventricular tachycardia can cause chest pain, dizziness, shortness of breath, and fainting spells. Joe would also get an irregular, chaotic beating of the lower chambers of the heart, called *ventricular fibrillation*, which is life threatening.

Years ago, ventricular fibrillation was routinely treated with a small blow delivered to the heart, called a *precordial thump*. This thump gave the heart a bit of a shock that sometimes could stop the abnormal rhythm. Today, a more effective shock is delivered to the heart using electric defibrillators. Because Joe's rhythm problem kept coming back, he was actually treated with a mini-defibrillator implanted into his chest to give small shocks when abnormal rhythms would start. Joe's sister Sherry Meininghaus remembers how his Golden Retriever, Louie, used to help:

> *Joe and Louie were certified as a therapy dog–handler team. Before Joe became sick, he and Louie made visits to help other people. When Joe developed his heart problems, he'd get runs of ventricular tachycardia and ventricular fibrillation and would pass out. When this happened, Louie would paw at Joe and even shake Joe to get him to wake up. Sometimes, Louie would even seem to pounce on Joe's chest like he was trying to shock the heart out of its problem rhythm. Louie really understood something was wrong and Joe needed immediate attention.*
>
> *Toward the end, when Joe was very sick, Louie became Joe's constant companion. This normally rambunctious dog would just sit or lie patiently next to Joe, resting his head gently near Joe. When we couldn't be there for Joe, we knew Louie would be at Joe's side for comfort.*

Thom Harding's dogs provided comfort during his convalescence from heart surgery and an inspiration for a new heart-healthy hobby. Thom was having some problems that took him to see a heart doctor, who ordered an ultrasound test of the heart called an *echocardiogram*. As the doctor viewed the images from the test, he could see that the walls of the major blood vessel that leaves the heart—the *aorta*—were tearing. This tearing is called a *dissection*. A dissection is a medical emergency, and the doctor told Thom he needed surgery. Thom agreed and asked when he should return to schedule surgery, only to hear the doctor tell him he was going in for surgery immediately.

Thom's surgery was a success: The doctors fixed the tear and replaced a leaky valve in his heart. When Thom got home, he couldn't do much:

> *I was off of work for six months after my surgery. It took a long time to get back to myself. So I spent my days with my dogs. At first, all I could do was lie on the sofa and sleep. My German Shepherd Hobie and Black Lab Holly really seemed to understand that I was very sick. Holly would just lie on my feet, which kept me warm. And Hobie would come over and nudge me about every half hour, not stopping until I'd look up at him and tell him I was okay.*

After his recovery, Thom stayed active with the dogs and followed his doctor's heart-healthy advice. Then his sister-in-law sent him a wine making kit. Research has shown that drinking wine in moderate amounts—no more than one or two glasses per day—can actually reduce your risk for heart disease (Beulens et al., 2007, 2010; Bos et al., 2010). So Thom started making wines—designing labels around his favorite dogs. He dubbed his wines *Fattoria Due Cane*—Italian for "Two Dog Farm"—in honor of Hobie and Holly. Today, he has wines named for each of his dogs.

DJ Goodell's grandmother, affectionately dubbed "Rosebud," was in her late 80s and suffering from *congestive heart failure*, a condition in which the heart is not strong enough to pump enough blood to the rest of the body. This causes people to be weak, tired, and short of breath. Although rest is necessary for these patients, staying as active as possible is also important. DJ remembers that Rosebud had had enough and was ready to throw in the towel:

> *Rosebud was ready to die. She stopped leaving her house. She stopped cleaning the house. She stopped paying her taxes. She was just waiting for death to come for her—that is, until a Spaniel mix from the pound named Roy entered her life.*
>
> *Roy was a sweet dog, and the change that came over Rosebud was almost immediate. She may not have wanted to get up in the morning, get breakfast, and go out for a walk—but she had to, for*

Figure 8.1. Thom with 2009 "Shelter Dog" Shiraz.

Roy. They began a daily walking program together and Rosebud dusted off her knitting needles so she could make sweaters for Roy to keep him warm in the cooler weather. It was amazing. This little dog brought meaning to Rosebud's life—he gave her a reason to live. With Roy, someone needed Rosebud—Roy needed her to live, to get up in the morning, to stay out of bed, and to remain busy and active during the day.

Rosebud continued to enjoy a happy, fulfilling, active life—living to be over 100 years old. The congestive heart failure weakened her heart, but Roy strengthened it more.

In one study, hospital patients with heart failure were four times more likely to participate in walking therapy and walked twice as long when a therapy dog joined the walk (Abate et al., in press).

STROKE: ANOTHER DEVASTATING HEART DISEASE

Stroke is a leading cause of serious, long-term disability, affecting about two and a half percent of all adults in the United States (Centers for Disease Control and Prevention, 2009). According to the American Heart Association (2010), nearly 800,000 Americans have a stroke each year:

- One person has a stroke about every forty seconds.
- After having a stroke, about one in three people need help to walk.
- After a stroke, one in four people will need help with daily activities.

The best defense against strokes is prevention.

A new study released in the journal *The Lancet* evaluated people who had had a single stroke and healthy individuals of the same age and sex in twenty-two countries (O'Donnell et al., 2010). By comparing what was different in those who had had a stroke and those who had not, they were able to develop a list of top risk factors for having a stroke. These risk factors accounted for almost ninety percent of the risk for having a stroke.

 The Top Risk Factors for Stroke (O'Donnell et al., 2010)

- High blood pressure
- Current smoking
- Increased belly fat
- Poor diet

- Low physical activity
- Diabetes
- Drinking more than thirty drinks per month
- High stress level
- Depression
- Heart disease
- Abnormal cholesterol

Experts believe that efforts to encourage people to increase exercise, eat right, quit smoking, and correct high blood pressure would substantially reduce the world's burden from stroke. Simply adding daily dog walks to your routine is a fun and easy way to substantially lower your stroke risk.

Still not convinced? The Women's Health Study was a large research project that followed almost 40,000 healthy women in their forties for an average of almost twelve years (Goldstein, 2010; Sattelmair et al., 2010). The results showed that increasing leisure time walking reduced stroke risk. Picking up the walking pace added additional risk-reducing benefits.

 Women's Health Study Highlights on Walking and Stroke Risk (Sattelmair et al., 2010)

- Walking at least two hours weekly reduced stroke risk by thirty percent.
- Walking briskly—more than three miles (4.8 kilometers) per hour—reduced stroke risk by thirty-seven percent.

SOMETIMES HEART DISEASE GETS COMPLICATED

People with one heart problem often develop other heart conditions. Research shows that having high blood pressure, for example, increases your risk of dying from other heart problems, such as heart attacks, heart failure, or strokes (Miura et al., 2001). Out of every ten people who go to the hospital with heart failure, one will die in one month, four will die in one year, and six will die after five years (Curtis et al., 2008; Rusinaru et al., 2009). Marion Francis's mom, Norine Isacco, is one of those who was hospitalized with serious heart failure at age eighty-three. Norine beat the odds by living to be over ninety years old—thanks to a little help from an Airedale mix named Reina.

Marion and Rod Francis knew Reina would be a special dog when they adopted her from a shelter in Pittsburgh. At three years old, Reina was invited to be part of David Letterman's Stupid Pet Trick segment, during which she would show off her ability to catch oyster crackers faster than you could flick them off your fingers. Unfortunately, while Reina and her family were waiting offstage for Reina to amaze the audience with her rapid-fire trick, Dave was too long-winded in his monologue and Reina's segment was cut.

One of the most endearing memories that Marion remembers about Reina, though, was her relationship with Marion's mom, Norine:

My mom had lived in Florida and didn't return to Pittsburgh until Reina was about four years old. But once they met, they really bonded. Mom was clearly Reina's favorite person. We knew Reina liked me and Rod, but when my mom would come to the house, Reina would greet her with more enthusiasm than anyone else. When Mom visited, Reina would just want to sit by her side the whole time she was here. Mom also loved Reina, and my sister used to joke that Reina was Mom's favorite grandchild.

When my mom developed heart problems with atrial fibrillation and congestive heart failure, she had to go to the hospital. After a few days, Mom just seemed to be languishing—she wasn't getting better and the doctors seemed to have run out of ideas. Although Reina wasn't allowed in the hospital, Rod brought her to the front of the building so my mom could look out and see her. This really seemed to perk up Mom and two days later she was well enough to come home. Mom came back to our house and Reina seemed to immediately understand that Mom was more fragile now. Reina never jumped on Mom, but instead greeted her with a gentleness that showed she really understood Mom needed to be taken care of.

A few years later, my mom had a stroke and was in a rehabilitation facility for ten weeks. We were allowed to bring Reina there to visit

Figure 8.2. Norine and Airedale mix Reina—a couple of older gals taking care of each other.

Mom and I was amazed to see that everybody wanted to see Reina. Reina had a beautiful face that was irresistible and drew people to her. But I was still surprised to find patients seem to come to life when Reina came into the room—they just gravitated to her. We also noticed that Mom's condition seemed to improve after each of Reina's visits. I think having Reina there brightened Mom's mood and gave her renewed strength and motivation to work a bit harder at physical therapy and her other rehab.

And Mom returned the favor later when Reina developed a stomach problem where she couldn't eat and had to get her nutrition through intravenous fluids. Poor Reina was just miserable and would spend each day lying on the floor. My mom came to visit Reina and before I could tell her Reina wasn't feeling well, Reina surprised me by getting up, coming over to Mom, and wagging her tail. Mom had made Reina better, too.

The last few times my mom and Reina were together, both were quite old with lots of health problems. We even had to lift Reina into a chair so she could sit next to my mom. But once they were together, you could see how happy they were—Mom scratching Reina's head and Reina with a contented grin on her face. It was like they knew they both had lots of aches and pains and couldn't do much, but they could still enjoy their friendship, company, and special bond.

My mom is now ninety years old, and I know Reina helped her live this long. Did Reina cure her heart problems? No. But Reina made my mom feel better. They understood each other and Reina's devoted love for my mom helped pull Mom through rough times and I'm convinced helped Mom live longer.

9

I Have Cancer:
How Can a Dog Help Me?

"*You've got cancer*" are probably the three most dreaded words in medicine. According to the American Cancer Society (http://www.cancer.org), over eleven million people in the United States have cancer. Probably all of us know someone with cancer. Nothing makes your heart sink worse than a call from a friend who tells you, for example, "My doctor thinks I have breast cancer." At those times, words are so inadequate and can't convey our fear, hope, and support in the same way as a hug or sitting down to just listen. A dog can become an unwavering, unconditional, nonjudgmental source of support throughout one's struggle with cancer. Bottled-up fear and frustration can become unleashed by the simple act of a dog offering his head for a pet or paw for a shake, which soon leads to hugs and a release of needed tears.

Rose Mary Mulkerrin heard these words when her daughter was diagnosed with cancer. As the family rallied around her daughter, so did their Border Collie, Lucky D. Rose Mary discovered that Lucky D had a knack for recognizing when someone was upset, distraught, or in need of comfort:

> *When you're troubled or worried, Lucky D will bring you some-*
> *thing—usually one of his toys. He loves chewing the squeakers and*
> *stuffing out of toys, so his favorite treasures often look like slobbery,*
> *dirty rags instead of playthings. So on a bad day, you can be sure to*
> *look down and see Lucky D holding his latest precious bit of fabric,*

covered in doggie drool and love. He brings you what he has to give—his prized toy, his comfort, and his love.

When Rose Mary's daughter was struggling with cancer, Lucky D was sometimes her greatest comfort:

When my daughter was first diagnosed, she was understandably upset. Lucky D came over and sat next to her. After a few minutes, he went to get her one of his toys. He gave her one toy and then returned to his stash for another and then another. Soon, my daughter was loaded down with every toy Lucky D had, and he jumped up on the sofa to sit next to her. My daughter just sat there quietly, tears streaming down her face. And before you knew it, Lucky D reached up and started licking the tears from off of her face. His simple, unselfish acts of love and devotion were a bigger comfort to her than all the words anyone might have said.

WHAT DOES MEDICAL RESEARCH SAY ABOUT DOGS AND PATIENTS WITH CANCER?

In a small, but important study, Dr. Rebecca A. Johnson and colleagues at the University of Missouri—Columbia and the Ellis Fischel Cancer Center studied what cancer patients thought about therapy dog visits (Johnson et al., 2003). In the study, thirty hospitalized patients were randomly assigned to receive one of three 15-minute interventions in addition to their usual cancer therapy. One group had a visit from a therapy dog, with the handler instructed to introduce the dog but to otherwise avoid chatting with the patient. Another group received a visit from a friendly volunteer who was instructed to engage in light, cheerful conversation. The third group was given material to read. Cancer patients appreciated and benefited from each of the interventions—but they benefited the most from the therapy dog visits.

So don't underestimate the impact of those fifteen minutes a cancer patient spends with your dog—and don't feel like you have to make conversation. Cancer patients appreciate visits from therapy dogs, probably more than you would have imagined.

What Did Cancer Patients Feel About Their Extra Treatment?

	Extra treatment		
	Therapy dog	Friendly visitor	Reading material
The extra treatment made my therapy easier	7 in 10 patients	5 in 10 patients	2 in 10 patients
I looked forward to my extra treatment	9 in 10	5 in 10	3 in 10
The extra treatment gave me energy	6 in 10	4 in 10	1 in 10
I wish I could have this extra treatment when I go home	6 in 10	1 in 10	3 in 10
I will remember this extra treatment after I leave the hospital	10 in 10	6 in 10	3 in 10

Note. Source: Johnson et al. (2003).

How Did the Therapy Dog Visit Compare With the Friendly Visitor?

	Extra treatment	
	Therapy dog	Friendly visitor
I confided in the dog or visitor	7 in 10 patients	4 in 10 patients
The dog or visitor is my friend	8 in 10	4 in 10
I told others about the dog or visitor	9 in 10	1 in 10
The dog or visitor knew when I was happy	6 in10	5 in 10
I feel attached to the dog or visitor	8 in 10	2 in 10

Note. Source: Johnson et al. (2003).

Dr. Orlandi and colleagues in Italy published a study on therapy dog visits during chemotherapy in the journal *Anticancer Research* (Orlandi et al., 2007). During a chemotherapy visit, cancer patients were offered to have their treatment in a room with or without a therapy dog. Patients in the dog room received twenty-minute therapy dog visits. The researchers noted the following observations:

- Patients who chose to have the therapy dog visit during chemotherapy experienced a thirty-three percent drop in their feelings of depression.
- Mood didn't change for patients who received their chemotherapy treatment in the room with no dog.
- Patients who received chemotherapy in the non-dog room had a thirty-one percent increase in aggravation scores.
- Aggravation remained unchanged for cancer patients who had the dog visit during chemotherapy.
- The amount of healthy oxygen in the blood increased by six percent for patients who received the dog visit.
- Blood oxygen dropped by four percent in patients in the non-dog room.

So, adding a therapy dog visit to chemotherapy was good for cancer patients.

Therapy dog Mitsu and Marlene Miller were honored to serve Helen when Helen was diagnosed with terminal cancer. During Helen's treatments, her immune system became compromised, which prevented her from visiting her elderly mother in a nursing home. Mitsu became Helen's ambassador, making visits to Mom: "We'd take messages of love back and forth between mother and daughter—with Mitsu acting as the special courier. Mitsu carried their love in her knowing eyes that conveyed much deeper feelings than my mere words might have done."

As Helen approached the end of her own fight with cancer, she asked for Mitsu. "It was an honor to again tend to the needs of this dear lady. And I know Mitsu carried for her the message from her mom that she'd be waiting for Helen to come home."

Mariann Murrin and her husband Jim can usually be found with their agility dogs Rocky and Sammie. Rocky is a German Shepherd–Husky mix who, at fourteen and a half years old, is retired from competition. The United States Dog Agility Association recognizes three levels in agility competition: Starters, Advanced, and Masters. Rocky

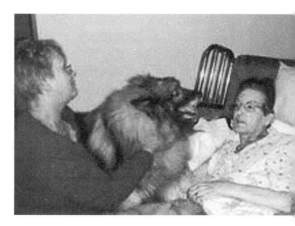

Figure 9.1. Keeshond therapy dog Mitsu visits Helen as she nears the end of her battle with cancer, just like Mitsu was there for Helen's mom.

earned his Master Jumper title. Sammie, a five-year-old Border Collie, started agility work when he was three years old. Sammie is playing at United States Dog Agility Association Master's level and is currently working on his Canine Performance Event Level 5. Canine Performance Events offer titles in agility from Levels 1 through 5.

Mariann and Jim's world was turned upside down in July 2003 when Mariann was diagnosed with breast cancer and treated with a radical mastectomy:

> *It was so terrifying. The cancer just came out of nowhere. I was lucky, though, I only had to have surgery. Then I started a program of healthy eating and exercise, lost thirty-five pounds, and started to feel fantastic! I was really enjoying life again!*

Mariann's doctor told her that if she remained cancer free for five years, she'd have her breast cancer licked. Everything seemed to be going well until she started to feel a bit tired in July 2009, which Mariann attributed to "working too hard." A month later, she stepped out of the shower and heard a cracking sound in her left shoulder. The emergency department didn't find anything to explain her pain, so they sent her to see an orthopedic doctor the next day for a magnetic resonance scan. "The doctor came in and looked very sad. He told me, 'I am so sorry to have to tell you that the cancer is back. You need to go back to your cancer doctor.' I just burst into tears."

Mariann's news was worse than she had expected: The cancer had spread to bones throughout her body. Her doctor told her she might need to have surgery on the cancer that had spread to her hips before they could start chemotherapy. Mariann asked her doctor if she should take a leave from work. "He just looked at me and told me to quit work. Everything sounded so final that I thought I only had a couple months to live."

Back at home, Jim found Mariann petting Sammie. Mariann was already so tired before treatments had even started, and she tearfully explained to Sammie that she'd never be able to "play" with him again. For Mariann "playing with Sammie" means working him through his paces for agility trials. Jim helpfully chimed in, "Don't worry—I can start playing with Sammie. I'll take over the handling duties for you until you're feeling up to it." Jim was struck that Mariann stopped crying, looked up at him, and was suddenly very serious. Mariann stuck out her chin and said, "Oh no you won't. You'll ruin my dog!" Whereas some husbands may have taken offense at this jab, Jim beamed. He knew the cancer had worn Mariann down, but it hadn't broken her spirit. Mariann recalls,

> I wanted to get better for Sammie. I know it sounds funny and I suspect people wonder what my priorities are. Jim is my wonderful support and I know he'll always be there for me. But Sammie's a sensitive dog who was very difficult to train. Ongoing training is essential to maintain the terrific dog he has become. I just couldn't let Sammie lose that.

Mariann's new doctor encouraged her desire to continue dog training. "My doctor told us, 'Part of cancer treatment is maintaining your lifestyle. The cancer should be just a nuisance.'" Although Mariann says that she "wasn't able to do very much" over the next few months while getting chemotherapy, she continued to work four days a week, go for regular walks with the dogs, and do some dog training. "Wasn't able to do much" really meant there were no agility trials— but both Mariann and Sammie understood that competition was just on hold. The daily loving, training, and bonding were going to continue. Mariann no longer felt like she was dying from cancer; instead, she and Sammie were *living* with cancer.

Now, a year after finding out her cancer had recurred, Mariann states, "I'll battle this for the rest of my life." She finished chemotherapy three months ago and started more training with Sammie. They did attend one agility trial, which was great fun for both of them. In a recent class, teams were working on increasing their speed for agility commands, and one quick turn caused Mariann to catch her foot, fall, and break her arm, only this time, there was thankfully no tumor responsible for the break. Jim smiles, "This was just a clumsy break!" And what was Mariann's first concern: Sammie, of course:

> *We were scheduled for a team competition where Sammie was working with two Dalmatians. They were going to run agility courses with Sammie sandwiched in the middle, so we'd dubbed the team the*

Figure 9.2. The strong bond between Mariann and Sammie helps her cope with cancer treatments and setbacks.

"Dalmatian Samm-ich." When I saw my arm was broken, I turned to Sammie, "Now I can't play with you!"

But don't worry, the cancer may have beaten Mariann back a little, but it won't hold her down. And when Sammie gazes into her eyes he knows it, too: It would take more than cancer to break up this team.

A GOOD DOG PROVIDES UNCONDITIONAL ACCEPTANCE AND UNDERSTANDING DURING TREATMENT

Everyone says the same thing when they first meet Diana Hare: "What a great laugh!" You always know when this bubbly mom with sparkly eyes and an infectious chuckle is around—her laugh's contagious.

Once you get to know Diana, you're amazed at her ability to laugh at a life that has often been so tough. When she was only sixteen years old, Diana said her final goodbyes when her mother lost her battle with breast cancer. As Diana grew into an independent woman and mother herself, she watched as two aunts, two cousins, and even her older sister were diagnosed with breast and ovarian cancer. Diana held her breath as she reached her fortieth birthday cancer free. "I never thought I'd make it to forty, and once I did, I thought I was home free." Two years later, Diana's routine annual mammogram turned out to be anything but routine—they'd found a lump. And after a biopsy, she heard those words she'd been dreading since she was a teen: "You've got breast cancer."

Despite her doctor's prediction of a smooth course after surgery, Diana's recovery was complicated by the development of a blood clot in her leg. While hospitalized for the blood clot, her doctor had more bad news: She needed more surgery. Her first surgery had failed to get out all of the tumor. And now she'd have to wait until her blood clot was treated before she could have her second surgery and finally start radiation.

One of Diana's biggest supporters through her complications, treatments, and recovery was a smiling brindle Labrador Retriever mix named Sonia. While Diana has the laugh, Sonia was the dog with the smile. Diana would laugh, and Sonia would gaze up at her adoringly, with a huge grin on her face that seemed to say, "You're the greatest. I'd do anything for you!" Through the dark days of her early cancer treatments and the many weeks of radiation, Sonia became a lifeline for Diana.

Sonia was more than a pet, more than a child—she was like a best friend. I was very lucky to have a devoted family and thoughtful friends to help me through my cancer. But when everyone else was busy with other things, Sonia was always there to give me comfort and make me laugh. If anything was wrong, Sonia just understood. She seemed to know what I needed and selflessly gave her love and devotion when I needed it most. When I needed to rest, Sonia would lie next to my bed, so I could reach down and pet her. Just petting her and hearing her snoring gave me such comfort. And if I'd sit in a chair, she'd sit right on my feet, letting me know she was always there.

During her radiation treatments, Diana would leave an hour early each morning so she could get to the hospital to have her treatments before she had to be at work. By the time she'd come home at the end of the work day, she was exhausted. Although Sonia had been cooped up in the house all of this time and would normally have wanted to dash outside, instead she'd wait for Diana to come in and then stick to her like glue:

Sonia knew how hard it was for me to be alone and would stay with me and make me laugh! Her face was so expressive. She'd look at you with those big brown eyes and you really knew she understood. She was devoted to caring for me, and she'd never let me down. I'd ask, "Do you want to go out?" and she'd just smile at me as though saying, "No need for that now. I need to be here with you." Through all my treatments, Sonia never let me down.

Although Diana always seemed to put a brave face forward for her family and friends, she felt that she could really let her guard down with Sonia:

I always felt that Sonia was so nonjudgmental. When you have cancer, after a time you begin to feel sorry for yourself and people around you often try to cheer you up, telling you how you're going to get better and be fine and that you should focus on positive thoughts. Especially during the night, even when I knew I was going to make it, I'd start crying—after all, my mom did die from this same thing. My husband would just hate to see me cry and I'd feel bad making him feel sad, so I'd seek out Sonia. Sonia would just BE there for me—no comforting words, no suggestions about how to keep a positive attitude—just a shoulder to cry on. During my cancer treatment, I think I loved her for that more than anything else. She let me have the cries I needed, and being able to cry on someone who didn't feel the need to make it better really made all the difference.

Four years later, the doctors declared Diana to be cancer free. A few months later, Sonia grew what was first called a "hot spot,"

Figure 9.3. The ever-smiling Sonia knew her place was always by Diana's side. Although her mother was a Labrador, Sonia was not a water dog— never going for a swim until one day when Diana and her husband Tim went out in a canoe. Horrified to see Diana drift away, Sonia braved the terrifying water, frantically doggie paddling to the boat to get pulled in by Tim so she could remain where she knew she belonged—right next to Diana.

blossoming into an angry tumor that eventually took away Sonia's joy in life. "When we had to put her down, I needed to be there with Sonia. She had been with me every step of my journey through my cancer recovery. I owed her to be there for her journey, too." The ever-smiling Sonia finally had to leave her Diana's side, knowing that she had completed her mission to help Diana find her way to recovery.

Dogs have also been a foundation of support for Dave Mitchell, a youthful seventy-year-old who was diagnosed with prostate cancer sixteen years ago. He has undergone numerous treatments and tests, and the results always come back the same: He still has cancer, and it's slowly progressing.

When Dave gets a bad report from his doctor, he turns to his two Labrador Retrievers, three-year-old littermates Ricky and Lucy:

> *Cancer is an island on which we survivors frequently find ourselves if we're not careful. We speak a different language there—where simple words like "mets" and "nodes" can strike terror, and time is measured in checkups and treatment cycles. It is a strange place where things that can kill you, like radiation and poisons, are used as cures. And the cures each come with side effects that, in turn, require their own treatments.*
>
> *Ricky and Lucy keep me off this island by helping to keep me grounded in the here and now rather than focusing on worries for the future. I quickly learned a lesson from my little charges— there is joy in every life experience. You can sit around and mope about all that is going wrong, or you can look at the world like a Lab—like it has just been created and created just for your amusement. When you look at life that way, there is no room for anger. Frustration is reduced to what it should be—solving the problems of the moment, not worrying about what life has in store for you six months, or a year, or five years from now. I learned from my Labs to do the best I can, to see the good in all people and all events, and to savor each moment of life. I have my wonderful dogs—I've got a great life—and it really doesn't get much better than that!*

About two years ago, Dave decided to train Ricky and Lucy to be therapy dogs, eager for new training challenges. Ricky and Lucy sailed through their testing and were soon visiting patients with terminal diseases and children with severe disabilities at a school for the blind:

> *Visiting patients—especially those with end-stage diseases—really takes a lot out of me. It's hard to overcome the initial blow you feel when meeting someone so close to death or a child with severe birth defects. Ricky and Lucy, however, just look past all of that. They see an opportunity to make a difference and plow forward, gazing beyond outward appearances and seeing the person's need.*
>
> *It's a privilege seeing the amazing work that Ricky and Lucy do. At the blind school, Ricky visited a boy named Sammy who would always clutch a balloon for comfort, only relinquishing the balloon*

Figure 9.4. Dave has learned to approach life with the joy, excitement, and optimism of a Labrador Retriever.

to the staff at the end of each school day. When Ricky visits, Sammy gives up his balloon so he can hold Ricky's leash in one hand and pet Ricky with the other. The staff also introduced Ricky to Lisa, with whom the staff was working to have Lisa start talking with them. Although Lisa had been asked repeatedly to greet different staff members, she never would. But when Ricky visits, the staff is amazed to hear her cheerfully saying, "Hi Ricky!" when we come in and "Bye Ricky!" as we leave.

Lucy also understands when people need her. Lucy knows she's not allowed on furniture, so I was taken aback when we visited a nursing home and, when a woman in a bed reached out for Lucy, Lucy immediately jumped up on the bed to lie down next to the woman. Lucy was instantly surrounded by the woman's embrace. Lucy hasn't jumped up with a person since—she understood that this lady, however, craved that closeness.

Ricky and Lucy haven't cured my cancer. It is still there. And in the end, it is very likely to win the battle between us. What they have done is to give me a "cure" for living with cancer. They have taught me to forget about it for awhile. To remember how much I love my family, helping others, and just being outside enjoying nature. They've taught me to find joy in each moment—like they do.

LET YOUR FIDO HELP REDUCE YOUR RISK OF CANCER

Exercise, including a regular walking program, can help reduce your risk for developing several common cancers, including colon and breast cancer.

About five percent of adults in the United States will develop colon cancer (http://www.cancer.org). Colon cancer is the third leading cancer killer in the United States, after lung, prostate, and breast cancer. Colon cancer most commonly affects people after age fifty, with an increased risk in men, African Americans, and people with a family history of colon cancer. Regular screening is recommended after age fifty. Screening should start sooner if you have a family history of colon or rectal polyps or cancer, or if you have inflammatory bowel disease.

What can you do to reduce your risk of developing colon cancer? Exercise is well known to reduce your risk for getting colon cancer. A study published in the German journal *Deutsches Ärzteblatt International* linked regular exercise with reduced colon cancer risk (Halle & Schoenberg, 2009).

 Research Has Shown that Exercise Cuts Colon Cancer Risk (Halle & Schoenberg, 2009)

- Brisk walking decreased colon cancer risk.
- Walking a total of about seven hours weekly decreased the risk of developing colon cancer by forty percent.
- Among people who already had colon cancer, walking about four hours per week increased survival rates.

Another research study, published in the journal *Archives of Internal Medicine*, similarly showed that men who were more active had better outcomes after they were diagnosed with colon cancer (Meyerhardt et al., 2009). Compared with men who were relatively sedentary, risk for colon cancer death was cut by half in men who were physically active.

A number of studies have convincingly linked physical activity with a decreased risk of breast cancer. An article in the journal *Seminars in Oncology* reviewed data from seventy-three published articles looking at a link between breast cancer and exercise (Friedenrich, 2010). Researchers concluded that the average reduction in breast cancer risk for the most physically active women was twenty-five percent less than for the least physically active women. Links between physical exercise and reduced breast cancer risk as well as increased survival have been found in a number of studies:

- A study in the journal *Cancer Detection and Prevention* showed that breast cancer risk was reduced by forty percent among women with moderate physical activity and fifty-seven percent among those with vigorous activity (Kruk, 2007).

- An article in the *Journal of Sports Sciences* reported a forty-four percent reduction in breast cancer risk with moderate or vigorous exercise (Kruk, 2009).
- Researchers published data in *Cancer Epidemiology* that showed a sixty percent reduction in breast cancer risk about diabetic women who exercised (Sanderson et al., 2010).
- A study published in the *International Journal of Cancer* linked increased physical activity with a decreased risk of death with breast cancer (Friedenrich et al., 2009). Furthermore, moderate-intensity exercise decreased the risk of breast cancer recurrence, progression, or the development of a new cancer.

Researchers at Colorado State University have suggested that physical activity decreases breast cancer risk by muscular, hormonal, and metabolic mechanisms (Thompson, Jiang, & Zhu, 2009). Furthermore, because obesity is linked to increased breast cancer risk, activity that reduces obesity will also likely reduce cancer risk (Pollán, 2010).

Tail Waggin' Tip

Being physically active reduces your risk for developing breast cancer. If you have breast cancer, physical exercise helps increase your survival.

Although medical research has shown a link between exercise and better survival from breast cancer, nearly half of breast cancer survivors are unaware of this link (Weiner et al., 2010). In addition to staying physically active, other healthy lifestyle behaviors, such as eating more fruits and vegetables, further improves survival from breast cancer (Pierce et al., 2007).

10

Pain and Pet Therapy

Almost everyone can say they know about pain. You sprain your ankle, hit your finger with a hammer, touch a hot stove—you get pain! Most of the time, the pain doesn't last too long. Sometimes, however, we'll have an injury or develop a problem, such as arthritis, and the pain lasts for months or even years. This is chronic pain.

Most of my career has focused on caring for patients with chronic pain. Having chronic pain is no picnic. Chronic pain can affect many aspects of daily life (Brevik et al., 2006):

- Half of people with a chronically painful condition will have problems doing household chores.
- Half will also miss out on important social activities—like watching your child's soccer game, going to a concert, or having dinner out with friends.
- One in three people with persistent pain problems actually has to change jobs because of pain.

There is good news for people with pain problems: There are lots of effective treatments. Different medications, exercises, relaxation skills and biofeedback, and even some nutritional supplements can help. And research has also shown that dogs are also pain relievers.

When people get a visit from a dog, therapy dog handlers Barbara Pohodich and Janet Malinsky have seen their pain washed away—at least for a moment:

For that moment, the person is transported to a different place where they don't have to think about their pain—where they forget about their illness. For those moments, pain is replaced with joy. It may be just a moment—but that moment can be worth it. And those small moments are what we cherish as therapy dog handlers—that's why we do it.

DOGS CAN BE PAIN RELIEVERS FOR CHILDREN

Your doctor is unlikely to replace the old expression "Take two aspirin and call me in the morning" with "Snuggle two Yorkies and call me tomorrow." Interestingly, however, dogs are actually pain relievers. An article in the journal *Complementary Therapies in Clinical Practice* described research in which children in the hospital who were reporting pain were studied (Braun et al., 2009). The average age of the children studied was twelve years. The children were asked to either sit quietly by themselves or with a therapy dog. After fifteen minutes, the children were asked to report their pain severity:

- Pain levels dropped thirty-four percent after spending time with the therapy dog.
- Pain dropped only six percent when sitting quietly alone.
- Breathing became calmer with the dog, dropping by over two breaths each minute after seeing the dog.
- Breathing was essentially unchanged with sitting quietly alone, with no calming reduction.

The researchers noted that the level of pain reduction achieved by having a dog at the children's sides was similar to pain relief that would be achieved from taking the painkiller acetaminophen with codeine.

In another study, Dr. Elisa Sobo and colleagues at San Diego State University measured pain in children after surgery, comparing pain levels before and after a visit from a therapy dog (Sobo, Eng, & Kassity-Krich, 2006). In most cases, the visits lasted eleven to twenty minutes. About one quarter of the visits lasted ten minutes or less, and a few visits lasted more than twenty minutes. Dr. Sobo and her colleagues noted the following:

- After these brief visits, pain dropped by more than half.
- Physical pain decreased by fifty-seven percent.
- Emotional pain decreased by sixty-eight percent.

Dropping that much pain is better than the expected response from most pain-relieving medications.

Tail Waggin' Tip

In one study (Sobo et al., 2006), a therapy visit lasting ten to fifteen minutes decreased pain in children by at least one third, sometimes by up to two thirds.

DOGS ARE PAIN RELIEVERS FOR ADULTS

Therapy dogs can also reduce pain in adults. Dr. Elaine Lust and associates monitored medication usage in adults aged twenty-four to sixty years living at a rehabilitation facility for patients with brain or spinal cord injuries, degenerative diseases, or severe physical disabilities (Lust et al., 2007). Patients noted that the facility's therapy dog—eighteen-month-old therapy dog Blue Merle Collie, Neil—gave them a positive distraction from their own problems and worries. Although the comments about Neil the researchers recorded didn't specifically address an effect of Neil on patients' pain, the amount of painkillers patients used dropped by forty-eight percent after Neil joined the facility.

Here's What Patients Said About Therapy Dog Neil (Lust et al., 2007)

- "He makes me feel better."
- "He comforts me."

- "He gives me a warm feeling in my heart."
- "He helps me not to think about bad things in my day."
- "He understands tears and fears."

Spending time with therapy dog Neil also reduced the amount of pain medications used by these patients with neurological injuries by about half.

CHRONIC PAIN

Jodi Tuckett learned first hand that a furry pooch with a wagging tail can be a great pain reliever when you have a serious chronic pain condition:

My life was turned upside down when I was T-boned by a dump truck on July 13, 2005. They said I was lucky to be alive—I'd suffered a skull fracture and brain injury, broken neck, broken collarbone, and broken arm. My carotid artery was cut, and the skin was literally ripped off my left arm. I lost a lot of blood and needed several transfusions. I was alive—but I wasn't convinced about the "lucky" part.

After my initial treatments, I spent two months in hospital doing intense rehab and then moved home with my parents for a year. As a twenty-six-year-old woman, I resented feeling parented so much. And, proving I really needed to be parented, I decided to do a silly thing and moved out of their house. I knew it was a bad idea as I was still doing intensive rehab, but I was struggling with all of the losses in my life and living with my parents put all of those losses in my face every day.

After living on my own for only a month, I discovered how terribly lonely it really is when all you have to think about is your injuries, your pain, and what you can't do. And your day is focused on going to therapy. Then inspiration hit—I decided to get involved with a rescue group and foster a puppy and my life was again turned around— but this time it was a positive turn. I started volunteering with The Animal Rescue Foundation of Ontario that rescues stray dogs and cats from local First Nations communities. And this was how I met Suzy, a Cattle Dog mix puppy.

Suzy was four months old, with a pretty severe case of demodex that needed a lot of care. It was a whole lot for me to take on, but caring for her gave me a new purpose. Although I was initially concerned that I might have taken on more than I could handle, having a little mangy mutt to look after shifted my focus away from me, from myself, my parents, and my therapy team.

As Suzy grew into a beautiful, strong, and healthy dog, a bond has grown between us that is simply indescribable. She helps me when I am in pain. Most times when my neck, back, and hips are causing me pain (which is most of the time), I can go out and take Suzy for a walk. Getting myself moving and my joints loosened up makes me feel better. I spend numerous hours daily walking with her, and there is something special that happens with us in that time. I can see she loves her time with me, and I, of course, love my time with her. Rather than staying cooped up inside the house and inside my own misery, Suzy takes me out—out of the house, out of myself, and out of my pain.

Having a brain injury has impacted my ability to control my emotions at times. Suzy seems to be very intuitive about when I am moving into an emotionally elevated state. Sometimes it's anger; often it's

Figure 10.1. Jodi enjoys time spent with the Cattle Dog mix Suzy, who lifts Jodi out of her pain.

sadness. Either way, she knows and will come and nudge me to let me know she's there. Stroking and cuddling her brings me down to a manageable emotional state almost immediately. Without her comfort, these unchecked emotions seem to rev up both my misery and my pain. Suzy helps keep that from happening.

Suzy has changed my life. She's been the best rehab therapist and pain killer I could have. We folks in animal rescue truly understand that we do not rescue the dogs or cats—they rescue us. And Suzy definitely rescued me.

Facing a life of constant pain is tough. And when you've been diagnosed with a severe, degenerative condition as a youngster, it's hard to see a light at the end of the tunnel. For Judy Fridono, it took a pull from a couple of persistent Golden Retrievers to see that life could be more than the limitations she knew from decades of debilitating pain.

When Judy was sixteen, she was diagnosed with rheumatoid arthritis, a severe, degenerative autoimmune disease. Most people think about rheumatoid arthritis as a bone disease, because the joints swell from inflammation. This swelling is very painful and results in damage to delicate joints. So, with rheumatoid arthritis, people often develop deformed joints with severe limitations in joint movements. Because of her joint damage, Judy has joints that are misshapen and others that are chronically dislocating. She has also had to go through surgeries. If that's not bad enough, rheumatoid arthritis also causes fatigue, severe muscle aches, and weakness. Also, there is no cure. Today, there are new medicines that help limit joint destruction, but these weren't around when Judy was younger. The older medicines didn't work very well, and they had a lot of their own unpleasant side effects.

So, at sixteen, Judy learned that she would have a life of constant pain. She also learned that she wouldn't be able to do the same things that her friends were doing; for example, her doctors told her that she couldn't participate in most sports or other physical activities. She also knew that as she got older, she'd probably find herself able to do less and less. That's a tough message to hear at any time in your life— and even tougher when the world should just be starting to open up for you.

As Judy entered her forties, she developed additional autoimmune problems that ramped up her muscle and soft tissue pain and sapped her energy:

> *Every cell in my body hurts. The pain is constant—it's with me all day, every day. I don't think I've had a day without pain since I was eighteen. And I don't know what's worse—the pain or the fatigue. The fatigue can become unbearable. I wake up every day saying, "I'm tired." And it goes downhill from there. The pain and fatigue have kept me from being able to work full time, and I can only be productive for a few hours a day before needing to rest. This makes me frustrated, irritable, and depressed.*

As things seemed to be going downhill for Judy, she was joined by two dogs that have turned Judy's life around—Golden–Lab mix Rina and Golden Retriever Ricochet:

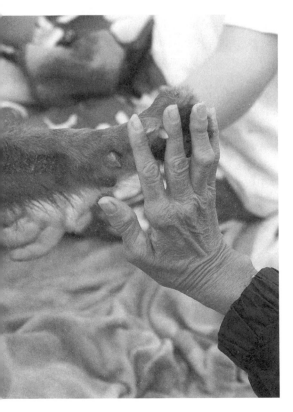

Figure 10.2. Although showing joint damage from years of rheumatoid arthritis, Judy knows Ricochet will always offer her a comforting paw. Photo courtesy of Rob Ochoa from Pawmzing Pets.

You can't stay in bed all day when you have the responsibility of caring for dogs. Regardless of how miserable you might feel, the dogs still need to go out, eat, and play. Having the dogs has forced me to get up, get out, and get involved. Rina and Ricochet push me to get out of bed—literally! They'll stand next to me and lick my face until I get up.

And by getting Judy up and out, the dogs brought her unexpected comfort:

Before Rina, I was caught in downward spiral of pain, doom, and isolation. I had no energy to go out and do things. I wouldn't go when friends invited me to dinner or the movies—it was just too hard, too painful, and too exhausting. But I knew I couldn't beg off of taking Rina out. When I'd go out with Rina, I'd meet other people and we'd start talking about our dogs. Rina gave me an outlet outside of my pain. These outings kept me from feeling isolated from others and drew me out of myself and my own misery—Rina brought me back into the world—away from my miserable and lonely seclusion.

Ricochet has opened up even more worlds to Judy. Whereas Rina is now a sedate seven-year-old, Ricochet is an energetic two-and-a-half-year-old. More than that, Ricochet has incredible balance and a passion for surfing:

Growing up with a chronic illness kept me from participating in sports and other physical activities with my friends. While they were having fun, I was getting medical treatments and surgery. Not being able to be a "regular teen" made me feel depressed and very negative. Life just felt miserable. Ricochet has changed all that. I still can't do sports, but I can experience the joy of the athlete through her and her eyes. I can now live vicariously through Ricochet's athleticism even though I was never able to participate. That's why I work so hard to continue her surfing—even though I can't physically surf and need someone to help her on days she's surfing. When she wins something—it shows me I'm winning at life, too. The memory of all those times when I was a kid and I couldn't even participate get washed away and replaced with pride in Ricochet's accomplishments. Being a part of Ricochet's life has given me joys I never thought I'd know.

Ricochet has also brought a new focus and meaning to the now–fifty-two-year-old Judy's life. Ricochet's love of surfing and people led Judy to train Ricochet to help others. Ricochet now provides goal-directed therapy, helping people with disabilities and working as a tireless fundraiser for charity. And in case you wonder whether a Golden Retriever can *really* raise money, Ricochet raised over $30,000 in an eight-month period—so yeah, this is *serious* charity work. In 2010, Ricochet was one of five dogs to receive the prestigious American Kennel Club Humane Fund Awards for Canine Excellence for her tireless charity work and the inspiration she provides to others.

Managing Ricochet's schedule and charity work has given Judy new purpose and meaning:

> *Ricochet has helped me give back to others—to be a participant in my community, rather than feeling like just a spectator. Ricochet has made such a difference in so many people's lives, that I feel a responsibility to keep that good work going. So instead of lingering in bed, I'll get up to answer her emails and manage her Web site and Facebook page. Ricochet has helped me lose my negative attitude. She has shown me that I can turn my life of disappointments into positive opportunities that help others—and help me.*
>
> *When you have a chronic pain condition, it's easy to think, "I can't do anything!" Through Ricochet, I've changed the way I think about my pain and my life. I now say, "I can't do everything—but I can sure do something!" And that something can be very positive.*

Have Rina and Ricochet cured Judy's pain? Nope. Have they cut down the suffering and despair from her pain? Absolutely! They have helped push that pain a little more into the background, where it's less disruptive:

> *Rina and Ricochet help me turn my focus away from my pain, away from my fatigue, away from my misery. By shifting my focus onto them and other people, I've lost the negative attitude that just made everything worse. I still have pain and fatigue—but they are no longer overwhelming and all consuming. I may have pain, but I also now have a life. And with the help of Rina and Ricochet, it's a productive, fulfilling life that I'd never have believed was possible.*

Susan Ambridge also didn't expect an easy life—she was a single mother raising two small boys alone. Life got even tougher when she forgot her seatbelt and then was in a car accident, colliding into the dashboard and windshield. Susan was alive but bruised all over her body. She has never had a day without pain since the accident. Her doctors assured her everything was all right, but there was nothing they could do for the pain she complained about. Despite the pain, she continued to work up to two jobs and care for her growing boys.

Four years later, Susan's life took a further turn for the worse when her pain became more unbearable and an imaging study showed a tumor on her spine. The surgeons were able to remove the tumor, although the surgery damaged the nerves going into her right leg and foot. Now, in addition to pain, she also had problems walking and needed to go onto disability. The doctors also told her that the new tests they had run showed that the earlier car accident had caused problems with her discs that were likely to get progressively worse over time:

> I'd lost all hope. What was I going to do? I couldn't work. I had young boys that I needed to raise. I still had bad pain everyday and couldn't sit or stand for very long. And now my walking was terrible. I had an awful limp that would draw stares and comments for people I'd walk by. So I didn't get out of the house much—and that just made things worse.

Unsure of how he could help Susan, her boyfriend introduced her to Binx, an eight-week-old Sheltie puppy.

> I'd never had a dog before—so this was a learning experience for both me and Binx. I knew I had to take Binx's training seriously and that got me out of the house and walking. And when I walked with Binx, people no longer stared at my awkward lurching. They were too busy noticing how cute Binx was. This really helped me feel less self-conscious when I walked and was a big step toward getting me walking better and starting to feel better about myself.

Susan started talking to people she met about dogs and dog training and also met people who trained service dogs. Susan began to see that Binx could do more than just motivate her to get out of the house.

To start Binx's training, Susan enrolled them both in a Canine Good Citizen class. After a lot of hard work, he earned his certificate:

> *Binx and I learned a lot together in our classes—we really became a team. He was doing so well, I thought, 'I wonder if I can teach him to do useful things to help me?' So I tossed the phone on the floor and asked him to retrieve it. He brought it right back and I knew he was going to help me regain a lot of the independence I'd lost.*

Retrieving a phone on command may not seem like much, but for Susan it was a lifeline to safety. She has previously fallen in the bathtub when no one was home to help her and, because she couldn't reach a phone, she couldn't call for help. "Now Binx gets the phone for me as

Figure 10.3. When Susan graduated from technical school, she made a companion cap and gown for Binx: "Binx was there for me each step of the way. And without him—I never would have made it. My diploma was really a graduation for both of us."

soon as I say 'phone.' I'm no longer scared to be alone, knowing he's watching out for me."

Binx now does a lot to help Susan. Binx picks up things she drops, closes doors and drawers, and provides a stabilizing brace for her when Susan walks:

> *Binx has changed my life! I no longer worry about going out or being alone at home. Binx has taught me that I don't have to just sit home and suffer. I look at Binx and say, "Binx and I are going to do it together!"*

And Susan has taken that pledge seriously—enrolling at Winter Park Technical School, where she was inducted into their honor society and earned a degree in medical transcription. Inspired by her success and looking toward the future, she's now a student in her local community college, completing a degree in business. Does she still have pain every day? Unfortunately, yes. Does the pain control her life any more? No way: "If you knew me before Binx and then saw me now, you'd think I was a whole different person."

In many ways, Susan is a different person. Binx has helped her break free from the suffering of chronic pain, leading her to the full life that still lies ahead.

TAKE A LESSON FROM FIDO FOR MANAGING CHRONIC PAIN

I have been working with chronic pain patients and doing pain research for a couple of decades. This has taught me two things. First, chronic pain doesn't get better quickly or easily. Second, like many unpleasant things in life, chronic pain often does get better over time for people who don't have an ongoing, degenerative illness.

For many people with chronic pain, like Jodi, Judy, and Susan, pain management therapy includes a lifestyle overhaul. Luckily, you can learn many pain-relieving healthy lifestyle habits by watching and listening to Fido.

Did you ever notice how your dog gets up in the morning, doing a play bow—with his front legs and head down on the ground and tail and butt up in the air—and then stretching out each of his hind legs? He'll probably go through this same routine several times a day and again in the evening. Fido knows the importance of keeping muscles stretched out. Simply petting Fido, working your fingers through his fur, and brushing him after breakfast can be great ways to help move stiff joints in the morning.

If you are someone with a chronic pain problem, your doctor has probably recommended that you do fifteen or twenty minutes of stretching a couple of times each day, too. Do you wonder if stretches really can make a difference? In one study, 200 patients with chronic low back pain were treated with either an analgesic medication or stretching and strengthening exercises at home twice a day (Shirado et al., 2010). The effects of daily therapy were measured after a year, with better relief of both pain and disability with exercises:

- Pain scores dropped by forty-four percent with exercise and thirty-five percent with the pain medication.
- Disability dropped by seventy-two percent with exercise and forty-seven percent with the pain medication.

So, the next time you notice your dog taking a stretch, be sure to do some stretching yourself.

Tail Waggin' Tip

Start and end your day like Fido, with a good body stretch. Research shows that regularly doing exercises that include stretching relieves the pain and disability of chronic pain better than pain medication.

Excess weight is often the result of a simple formula: Too many calories in without enough calories burned means added fat. Any good veterinarian will tell you to avoid feeding Fido too many treats. "Your dog gets enough nutrition at mealtime. Just give small training treats infrequently." The same is true for us humans.

Excess weight puts you at higher risk for developing a chronic pain problem, including pain in the shoulder, back, and knee (Jakosson, 2010; Jinks, Jordan, & Croft, 2002; Miranda et al., 2001; Webb et al., 2003).

- A study in the journal *Spine* found that obese people have a seventy percent increased risk for having back pain and disabling pain (Webb et al., 2003).
- Excess weight also affects your likelihood of developing a chronic pain condition after a work injury (Fransen et al., 2002): The risk of pain after a work injury increases by fifty-six percent if you're a little overweight and eighty-five percent if you're obese.

Excess weight also makes it less likely that you'll get relief from pain treatments. A recent study showed that obese patients did not get as much pain relief from the same treatment as patients who weren't obese (Sellinger, Clark, & Shulman, 2010):

- Pain severity scores decreased by four percent in obese patients and fourteen percent in non-obese patients getting pain treatment.
- Non-obese patients experienced significantly more improvements in disability, quality of life, and emotional functioning with treatment compared with the obese patients.

Tail Waggin' Tip

Exercise Fido to help you keep your weight in check if you have a pain problem. Excess weight increases pain risk and pain severity. Excess weight also blocks the pain-relieving effect of pain treatment.

Fido also understands the refreshing powers of a good sleep. Most people don't get enough sleep. The National Sleep Foundation (2010) recommends getting seven to nine hours of sleep each night. Unfortunately, only about two in every five adults get a good night's sleep most nights.

Having a sleep problem puts you at risk of developing chronic pain. A survey in the journal *Sleep* found that almost half of everyone with sleep problems had a chronic pain complaint, compared with only seventeen percent of people without insomnia (Taylor et al., 2007). In an interesting study of rats, sleep deprivation made the rats become more sensitive to pain and less responsive to the pain-relieving effects of morphine (Nascimento et al., 2007). Interestingly, allowing the rats twenty-four hours to "catch up" on lost sleep didn't improve their pain responses. Another study showed that, like the rats, when healthy women were deprived of good sleep they were more sensitive to pain and actually developed pain complaints (Smith et al., 2007).

Tail Waggin' Tip

Take a sleep lesson from Fido. Adults need about seven to nine hours of sleep each night. Not getting enough sleep makes you feel more pain.

All of the women with pain who shared their stories in this book talked about how getting moving and out of the house with their dogs helped distract them from the misery of their pain condition. Moving your muscles, talking with others, and getting involved in the world outside of yourself can help distract you and your brain from your pain. Doctors actually prescribe what are termed *distraction techniques* like these to help shift people's focus away from their pain as a routine part of pain management.

Distraction techniques are commonly used to reduce a wide range of chronic pain symptoms (van der Hulst et al., 2010). The idea behind distraction is that the brain can only focus on so many things at a time. For example, when you're trying to balance the checkbook, you probably have a harder time when your toddler's running around the house, your teen's playing loud music, and the dog's barking at the neighbor's cat. If enough other signals bombard the brain, it's also harder for the brain to focus on pain messages. In their stories described in this chapter, Jodi, Judy, and Susan help illustrate the power of distraction. None of them said their dogs cured their pain or helped them become pain free. Each one experienced getting involved in other things to keep mind and body busy, and they found that when they did this, the suffering from their pain was less. They still had pain, but it wasn't controlling their lives so much anymore. Going for a walk, attending a dog class with Fido, socializing with friends, and getting engrossed in a new book about dogs are all great ways to distract yourself from chronic pain.

 11

Managing Your Metabolism With Molly: Diabetes and Weight Control

---

WHAT IS MY METABOLISM?

Metabolism describes how your body makes, uses, and stores energy. So, what happens to the food that you eat—does your body use it efficiently, or do you store too much energy as unwanted fat? You've probably been hearing a lot about *metabolic syndrome*. Patients with metabolic syndrome have abnormalities in their blood levels of fats, cholesterol, and glucose. They typically have high blood pressure and are overweight. Patients with metabolic syndrome are more likely to develop a wide range of serious health problems:

- Diabetes
- Heart disease
- Thyroid disease
- Stroke
- Breast cancer
- Kidney disease
- Liver disease

Metabolic syndrome affects about one in every three adults in the United States (Ervin, 2009), and over half of all seniors over age sixty-five have metabolic syndrome (Kuk & Ardern, 2010). Being inactive and overweight are major risk factors for developing metabolic syndrome.

 Metabolic syndrome occurs when your body doesn't use energy efficiently. People with metabolic syndrome have a combination of problems, including excess weight, high blood pressure, high cholesterol, and diabetes.

The most important steps for preventing and treating metabolic syndrome are exercising and losing weight. This is where your dog can really help. Nutrition experts at Colorado State University found that seniors who lived in a home with a dog experienced better metabolism (Dembicki & Anderson, 1996):

- Dog owners walked eighty-three percent more than seniors without dogs.
- Extra walking improved blood lipids. Triglycerides are an important blood lipid linked to increased risk for heart disease. Triglyceride levels were forty-three percent lower in seniors who owned dogs.
- The more time the seniors walked, the lower their triglyceride levels were.

The great news is that even ten-minute walks can make a big difference. Researchers at Harvard and MIT showed that walking on a treadmill changed concentrations of a variety of naturally produced compounds that are important for burning calories and controlling your blood sugar (Lewis et al., 2010):

- Exercising for ten minutes resulted in significant changes in metabolism chemicals.
- Improved metabolism lasted for at least an hour after exercising.

So, if you walk your dog for ten minutes three or four times a day, you'll be able to keep your metabolism revved up throughout the day.

Stick with your fitness program even if you are not losing weight. Don't despair if you have features of metabolic syndrome and get frustrated when you start a new fitness program because you seem to be working hard and not losing the weight you'd like. A study in the journal *Mayo Clinic Proceedings* found that cardiorespiratory fitness, but not weight alone, was linked to long-term risk of death (Lyerly et al., 2009). Women who had never had heart disease or diabetes were included in this study if they had an abnormal fasting blood sugar level that showed they were at risk for developing problems with their metabolism. Over 3,000 women were included. The women's level of cardiovascular fitness was tested using an exercise treadmill test, with women assigned into categories of low, moderate, or high fitness. At the start of the study, women were an average age of forty-seven. These women were then followed for sixteen years:

- Risk of death during follow-up was thirty-six percent lower in the women in the moderate- or high-fitness groups compared with the low-fitness group.
- Baseline weight alone did *not* predict who would die during the study.
- Being overweight or obese *and* having low fitness resulted in over twice the risk of death compared with women who were of normal weight and at least moderately fit.

 Aerobic Exercise Helps Your Metabolism and Reduces Your Risk of Dying (Lyerly et al., 2009)

- Aerobic fitness reduces your risk of death by over thirty-five percent.
- Aerobic fitness is a stronger predictor of longer life than weight alone.
- Being a couch potato—overweight *and* aerobically unfit—more than *doubles* your risk of death.

So, help your metabolism by adding daily exercise into your routine.

DIABETES

Diabetes is a metabolic disease whereby problems with insulin affect how well you can get energy from the foods you eat and your blood sugar becomes abnormal. People with diabetes either don't make enough insulin, or their body ignores the insulin they do make. According to statistics at the American Diabetes Association (2010), nearly eight percent of the U.S. population has diabetes:

- Eighteen million people have been diagnosed with diabetes.
- Nearly six million have diabetes but have not been diagnosed.
- Over one and a half million new cases of diabetes are diagnosed in adults every year.

When blood sugars get too high or too low, people can feel irritable, confused, and sick. Very abnormal blood sugars can even cause people to lose consciousness and sometimes even die. In addition, abnormal blood sugars can damage the heart, nerves, kidneys, and eyes. To control their blood sugar, people with diabetes need to monitor the food they eat, stay physically active, take their diabetes medications, and keep track of their blood sugars. When you exercise, your body burns sugars. If your activity level and amount of food you eat stay the same each day, it's easier to keep your sugars under good control.

Diabetes is tough, because it can affect the whole family. My mom was diagnosed with diabetes when I was in junior high school, and the whole family made a lot of changes. We had to make sure mealtimes were on a strict schedule, food choices were changed, and regular exercise became more important. The whole family tried to stick to Mom's routine for a few weeks—until most of us slid back into old habits. My mom, however, was incredible: After spending weeks flat in bed before learning why she felt so sick, she very carefully measured everything she ate, taped lists of exercise routines onto her bedroom door, and measured her blood sugar frequently. Though we might tempt her with our dishes of ice cream, she stuck to her snack of one-half of a graham cracker and small glass of skim milk, and while we plopped on the sofa for a family TV show, she'd join us with her exercise sheets.

I saw first hand that staying motivated to make, and then keep up with, the many lifestyle changes prescribed for treating diabetes can be tough. For some people, taking care of a tail-wagging, energetic dog is just what the doctor ordered. Rose Mary Mulkerrin and her husband, Jim, had no idea that Jim was going to develop diabetes when they visited a shelter after recently losing their little dog and deciding it was time to add another small dog to their home. They didn't know they not only would they be getting a dog but also that Jim was going to find the best personal trainer at a time when it was essential to his health. Sometimes we chose a dog—carefully selecting his breed, temperament, and expected level of care. Other times, a dog seems to choose us. On rare and special occasions, we're chosen by a dog because he seems to know that his therapeutic powers will be needed in our lives. This was the case in the Mulkerrin family, who were chosen by a one-year-old Border Collie mix named Lucky D.

At the shelter, Rose Mary searched each room for another cute lap dog. She stood outside one room that held four Border Collie mix dogs from the same litter. One had his back to the window, and as Rose Mary casually glanced into the room, he turned and stared deeply into her eyes:

> *That dog gave me "The Look," which startled me a bit. But I knew I wanted another lap dog, so I moved down to the next few windows to find "my dog." Besides, we live in the city, so I didn't even think about getting a breed that would need as much exercise as a Border Collie. A few minutes later, Jim was calling me, "Rose Mary! You've gotta see this dog. He just looked right at me!" And sure enough—it was the same Border Collie that had looked so directly at me.*
>
> *We tried to look at other dogs, but we just kept getting drawn in by this Border Collie's intent look at us. When we went into the room, the dog came right over to Jim without hesitation—he really picked us! The people at the shelter warned us that this dog was normally very shy and had had a lot of medical problems and was lucky to be alive. They told us, "He's a lucky dog!", so we took him home and named him Lucky D.*

Lucky D couldn't have picked a better time to join the Mulkerrins. Jim had just been diagnosed with diabetes and had received strict instructions from his doctor to exercise and lose weight:

> *Because of Lucky D, Jim went out every day for a two-mile walk. If it was going to be too hot to walk later in the day, Jim would make sure he and Lucky D went out early so they could walk in cooler temperatures and wouldn't miss their walk. I don't think anything else could have gotten Jim up and out exercising at the crack of dawn except for Lucky D. And all this walking paid off—Jim lost forty pounds and was able to stop his blood sugar medications.*

Without a doubt, Lucky D picked the Mulkerrins at a time when they would need him. They didn't know it that day when they were looking for a quiet little lap dog. But Lucky D knew. And the Mulkerrins were very lucky he did!

Controlling blood sugars can be tricky. Changes in routine or additional health problems can affect blood sugar levels and drive them out of whack. When blood sugar levels start to get too low, people can feel

Figure 11.1. Jim is picked by Border Collie mix Lucky D, who becomes Jim's personal trainer to get his blood sugars under control.

hungry, shaky, and nervous. They may sweat or feel lightheaded. These can all act as alarms telling the person that it's time to eat to bring the blood sugars back into a more normal range. Sometimes when blood sugars get too low, people become confused, weak, and have problems communicating. When this happens, the person may not realize the problem is his or her blood sugar. When my mom's blood sugar would go a little low, she'd understand what was happening and eat something to feel better. If it got too low, she'd become confused and belligerent, and getting her to eat then could be a struggle. People with diabetes can also have their blood sugars fall too low when they're sleeping.

A partner or family members are often helpful in letting people know that they're "acting funny" or starting to sweat and that it's time to get their sugars up. Interestingly, dog owners with diabetes often note that their dogs can alert them when their blood sugar starts to go low. Researchers at Queen's University in Belfast, Northern Ireland, surveyed 120 dog owners with diabetes (Wells, Lawson, & Siriwardena, 2008):

- Two of every three owners reported that their dog reacted with a noticeable change in behavior when they had a low blood sugar or hypoglycemic reaction.
- One in three owners said their dog had reacted to their low blood sugar nearly a dozen times or more.
- One in three people felt that their dog usually reacted when their blood sugars were low *and* the dog reacted *before* the person was aware that anything might be wrong.

 How Do Dogs Let Their Owners Know Their Blood Sugar Is Getting Too Low? (Wells et al., 2008)

- Sixty-two percent of dogs bark or vocalize their distress.
- Forty-nine percent lick their owners.
- Forty-one percent nuzzle their owners.
- Forty-one percent stare intently into their owners' faces.
- Thirty percent jump on their owners.

The dogs became a warning beacon to check their sugar levels and take some glucose. Most animals reacted by trying to get the owner's attention.

Dr. Mortimer O'Connor from Victoria University Hospital in Cork, Ireland, described how his patient's dog saved him from a dangerous low blood sugar reaction (O'Connor, O'Connor, & Walsh, 2008). The patient was a seventy-two-year-old man, living at home with his wife. One night, the wife was startled awake by their Cavalier King Charles Spaniel, Beauty, barking, running in and out of the room, and acting strangely. Alerted by Beauty, the wife found her husband unconscious in bed. The man was hospitalized, treated, and sent back home. Six months later, the man started having stomach problems and, again, Beauty became agitated and started acting strangely—like she had when the man's blood sugar had dropped dangerously low. Back at the hospital, Beauty's diagnosis of low blood sugar was again confirmed. *Hypoglycemia* is the medical term for low blood sugar, and Dr. O'Connor started calling Beauty his "hypoglycemia detector."

Dr. Mortimer's report was no surprise to Cindy and David Etling. The Etlings are real dog lovers who share their home with three big dogs: a German Shorthaired Pointer, a German Shepherd, and a Newfoundland. Cindy has a passion for rescuing dogs—bringing them to her home for medical care, food, and love and then helping them find permanent homes. Cindy takes this rescue work very seriously, even offering new families dog sitting services from her children to help make the placement a success. When Cindy brought a starved, matted, flea-infested little Pomeranian named Charlie home for her usual rehabilitation, she had no idea that Charlie would save her husband, David's, life.

David had been diagnosed with diabetes in 2003 and needed insulin shots to control his blood sugar:

> *Although I'd originally planned to place Charlie in another home, he bonded so well with our family that we couldn't bear to have him leave. My biggest surprise was how he bonded with David. David's a big man and he's always had big dogs. Somehow, this big man and tiny Pomeranian just clicked and became inseparable!*

Cindy would later discover that Charlie's bond to David would be a lifesaver:

> *One evening, David appeared to be sleeping peacefully. All of a sudden, Charlie was licking David all over his face and nipping at his nose and ears. I got cross with Charlie, who ignored me, and called to David, "You better get that silly dog away from you before he bites your nose off." Suddenly, I noticed David wasn't responding and wasn't waking up. Then I got in the act of getting David awake. The doctor told us that David's blood sugar had gotten dangerously low and he had developed sleep apnea, where he'd temporarily stop breathing. Without Charlie's alert, I'm afraid of what might have happened to David. Since then, David always tells people that he owes Charlie his life.*

Figure 11.2. Pomeranian Charlie became a guardian and sentinel for David.

Now, both Cindy and David have learned to respect Charlie's signals:

> When we see Charlie acting funny by excessively kissing David's nose, we know something's wrong with David. Charlie has become an indicator for us. If Charlie's seeming to be overly affectionate and won't leave David's nose alone, we know it's time to check his blood for a problem.

With Charlie helping to monitor things, Cindy knows David's health is in good hands—in this case, in four furry Pomeranian paws.

Carol Estades's seven-and-a-half-year-old Boston Terrier, Phoebe, likewise made detecting low blood sugar her job:

> I've been a diabetic for the last ten years. Five years ago, I underwent gastric bypass surgery to help lose weight. I did lose weight, but like some patients developed problems with low blood sugar or hypoglycemia after surgery.
>
> As my health changed, so did Phoebe. She suddenly started getting in my face, staring at me, barking, and trying to kiss my face. This is something that I generally don't like and would not let her do. But she wouldn't back off. She had always been sensitive and very attached to me, so at first I thought she was developing a behavior problem. After a little while, though, it clicked that Phoebe's new behavior was soon followed by my having a low blood sugar reaction. So I started to pay attention to her. She became my cue that my sugar was crashing—letting me know I better check a blood glucose test. And sure enough, if Phoebe said so, my blood sugar would be low.
>
> One night, my husband Ruben had a big scare. He couldn't wake me up and had to call the paramedics. They found my blood sugar was dangerously low, at 29—my normal blood sugar should be between about 95 and 105. At the time, Phoebe didn't sleep in our bed, but after this scare I decided to put Phoebe to the test to see if she would alert me the next time my sugar crashed while I was asleep. So Phoebe joined us in bed and soon showed me that my sugar was crashing every night! While I was asleep, she would get up, stare at my face, breath her hot breath on me, and tap my head with her paw until I'd wake up. Job well done. Needless to say Phoebe now sleeps with me every night.

Figure 11.3. Boston Terrier Phoebe has a gift for detecting low blood sugars in Carol.

Thanks to Phoebe my glucose levels are now under much better control. I feel truly blessed to have such a special dog in my life, right when I needed her.

Phoebe is a champion dog, with lots of titles after her name. Her official name is Champion Sunwood Cosmic Tyrant, TDI, CGC, RAE, CD. She's a certified therapy dog with Therapy Dogs International

(TDI) and Canine Good Citizen (CGC) certificates and has an American Kennel Club Rally Advanced Excellent title (RAE) and an American Kennel Club Companion Dog Obedience degree (CD). She also carries a new badge: She's certified as a Registered Medic Alert Dog. Phoebe has been "on the job" monitoring Carol's blood sugars for five years now and has really become a lifeline for keeping her blood sugars controlled.

Tail Waggin' Tip

Dogs can get diabetes, too. About one in every ten dogs will develop diabetes. Diabetes typically affects dogs seven to nine years old. Breeds more prone to getting diabetes include Dachshunds, Poodles, Cairn Terriers, Beagles, Miniature Schnauzers, and Miniature Pinschers. Symptoms of doggie diabetes can include:

- sluggishness
- excessive water drinking and urination
- unexplained change in weight

Talk to your vet if your dog develops any of these problems.

OBESITY

Obesity has become a worldwide health problem. In a recent journal article, titled "Are We Facing an Obesity Pandemic?", Drs. Jacobi, Buzelé, and Couet (2010) stated that research suggests the answer is unfortunately a resounding "Yes." According to the World Health Organization (2006), over 1½ billion adults were overweight across the world in 2005, and at least 400 million were obese. Obesity is a global epidemic, affecting about one in every three to four adults in the United States and Europe (Abubakari et al., 2008; Do Corno et al., 2008; Donfrancesco et al., 2008; Haijan-Tilaki & Heidari, 2007; Hopman, Berger, et al., 2007; Wang et al., 2008). Obesity also affects Asia, with about one in every four or five adults overweight or obese in China (Zhang et al., 2009).

> One in every three to four adults in the United States and Europe is obese.

The journal *Obesity* published staggering projections for weight in United States. Using current trends in obesity, researchers at the Johns Hopkins School of Public Health predict that by 2020 three in every four adults will be overweight or obese and by 2030, four in every five adults will be overweight or obese, and half will be obese (Wang et al., 2008). It is estimated that by 2048 every single adult around age forty years will be overweight or obese—*every* adult (Wang et al., 2008).

What exactly *is* obesity? Having a few extra pounds here and there is not obesity. Extra weight puts added stress on your heart and joints, but we're not talking about a few love handles. Obesity is generally considered to be having a weight that's more than twenty percent above your ideal weight.

Most doctors define overweight and obesity using the body mass index (BMI), which takes into consideration your weight and your height. For example, if you are five feet, nine inches (1.5 m, 2 cm) tall, a healthy weight for you could be between about 125 and 168 lbs (57–76 kg). Between 169 lbs (77 kg) and 202 lbs (92 kg), you'd be considered to be overweight, and if you weighted over 202 lbs you would be considered obese. You can find BMI calculators on the Internet (e.g., http://www.nhlbisupport.com/bmi/).

BMI Shows Healthy and Excess Weight

- A normal BMI is less than 25 kg/m².
- Overweight is when the BMI is 25 to 29.9 kg/m².
- Obesity is when the BMI is 30 kg/m² or more.

Gaining unwanted weight is a common problem as we get older, and it's a problem for most people. A Canadian study followed a randomly selected group of more than 8,500 men and women for five years (Hopman, LeRoux, et al., 2007):

- The average man under age forty-five and the average woman under age fifty-five gained an average of 1 lb (0.45 kg) per year.
- This extra weight generally hung on during middle-aged years.

According to Dr. Mark Hyman, author of the New York Times Bestseller *Ultra-Metabolism* (2008), "The average American gains about 20 pounds between the ages of 25 and 55" (p. 85).

Being overweight and obese should not be considered a cosmetic problem. Excess weight increases your risk for a wide range of health problems. A recent report in the journal *The Lancet* detailed the following complications of childhood obesity (Han, Lawlor, & Kimm, 2010):

- Arthritis
- Asthma
- Gallstones
- Heart disease
- High blood pressure
- High cholesterol
- Insulin resistance
- Kidney disease
- Liver disease
- Sleep apnea

These same conditions can be linked to obesity that starts in adulthood.

Obesity has also been linked to an increased risk of cancer. A large study that looked at cancer in thirty countries in Europe estimated that about 124,050 new cases of cancer could be attributed to excess body weight (Renehan et al., 2010):

- Three percent of new cancer cases in men could be linked to excess weight.
- Nearly nine percent of cancers in women were related to obesity.

The Following Cancers Are Most Strongly Linked to Obesity

- Endometrial cancer
- Postmenopausal breast cancer
- Colorectal cancer

The good news is that cancer risk decreases as weight drops. In one study, women undergoing weight-loss surgery decreased their risk of developing cancer during the next ten years by about forty percent (Sjöström et al., 2009). Curiously, however, weight loss with surgery did not decrease cancer risk in men.

Tail Waggin' Tip

People's risk for obesity drops by thirty-nine percent when they walk their dogs (Coleman et al., 2008).

Many of us have a hard time taking care of ourselves. We carefully pack a lunch with a hearty-grain sandwich, fruit, and carrots for Junior, and then grab a hot dog and cola for lunch for ourselves. We'll remind our spouses and kids to get enough rest and exercise, while we stay up too late watching old movies on the sofa.

Need an extra incentive to get in shape? A study published in the journal *Public Health Nutrition* linked obesity in us with obesity in our dogs (Nijland, Stam, & Seidell, 2010). The researchers looked to see what individual factors explained this link. This obesity link couldn't be explained by the gender or age of the owner, or of the dog, or how long the dog and owner had been together. One factor explained this link: The amount of time the dog was walked each day.

Tail Waggin' Tip

Unhealthy extra weight is an increasing problem in our dogs. One in every three adult dogs is overweight or obese (Lund et al., 2006). Research shows that normal weight dogs get exercised every day, whereas overweight dogs get walked only about once each week (Bland et al., 2009).

Remember—you and your dog are a *team*. What helps one, helps the other. And even if you don't think you're worth taking that walk today, I bet you know Bailey's worth a walk. So if you don't want an overweight dog, start walking your dog every day.

Certain Dog Breeds Are More Likely to Develop Weight Problems (Lund et al., 2006)

- Cocker Spaniels
- Dachshunds
- Dalmatians
- Golden Retrievers
- Labrador Retrievers
- Rottweilers
- Shetland Sheepdogs

Most people estimate that walking the dog will burn about 150 to 250 calories per hour. If you decide not to walk and simply sit in front of the television for an hour, you'll be burning only about eighty-five calories. You can almost triple your calorie-burning power by getting off the couch and walking Fido.

Walking Your Dog for an Hour will Burn About 200 Calories

How much food is 200 calories? You eat about 200 calories when you have any of the following foods:

- Two bananas
- Two pears
- Two cups of cooked corn or peas
- One cup of cooked rice
- Two tablespoons of butter or mayonnaise
- One cup of cottage cheese
- Two cups of milk
- One bagel
- Two muffins
- One croissant
- Five or six slices of bacon
- Two breakfast sausage patties
- One hot dog
- A can of cola
- Hershey's chocolate bar

A milkshake has nearly 500 calories, or two and a half extra dog-walking hours. And if you're thinking about a Big Mac with cheese, that's over 700 calories—over three hours of dog walking!

Make smart meal and snack choices to avoid extra calories you don't need. And when you treat yourself to that extra sweet, just add in an extra jaunt with Fido to walk it off!

As you start to lose weight, remember that you'll need to pick up the intensity or duration of your exercise if you want to lose more weight. Simple tips to boost the calorie-burning power of your dog walks include the following:

- Adding an extra walk to your routine
- Adding extra minutes to your walks

Figure 1.4. Cindy with New-foundland–Labrador Retriever mix Lady, Pomeranian Charlie, and German Shorthaired Pointer Winston. Cindy knows dogs make great exercise companions: "There's no excuse for being over-weight when we have pets."

- Walking faster or adding in some skips and jogs during the walk to pick up the pace
- Pumping your arms as you walk
- Choosing a route with hills

Tail Waggin' Tip

- Expect to burn about 150 to 250 calories per hour when walking Fido.
- You'll burn about three times more calories walking Fido compared with watching television.
- You'll burn fewer calories as you start dropping your weight. So increase your pace, add hills, or include extra walks to keep the weight loss going.

Are some people just plain more likely to put on unwanted extra weight? Absolutely. However, being prone to being overweight doesn't mean you're doomed to carry around unhealthy extra pounds. The same steps that reduce weight in others—reducing calories and increasing exercise—will also help you lose weight even when your genes predispose you to being overweight.

New research in the *Archives of Pediatric and Adolescent Medicine* showed that daily exercise curbs obesity, even in children who are genetically predisposed to be overweight (Ruiz et al., 2010). In this study, over 750 teens who have a gene shown to increase your risk for becoming obese were compared with teens without this gene. If the teens who were genetically at high risk for obesity exercised less than an hour a day, they were more likely to be obese, as expected. Teens genetically at high risk for obesity who did exercise at least an hour a day were no heavier than teens who were not at high risk for becoming obese.

So, although genes are important—it's *not* all in your genes. Just because parents struggle with obesity, their children don't have to travel down the same path, even when their genes suggest they will likely follow in their parents' heavy foot steps. This is great news; it means you *can* control your weight. Even individuals whose genes suggest they have a higher risk of becoming obese benefit from exercise and can keep their weight in check with generally recommended exercise guidelines.

WATCH THAT WAISTLINE

You might have heard your doctor talk about the importance of "belly fat"—that bulge that readily grows around the middle. Researchers are taking a second look at belly fat as perhaps a more important weight loss target than overall weight. Researchers have linked bigger waist measurements with increased risks for developing a number of serious health problems (Cameron et al., 2009; Seidell, 2010):

- Cancer
- Diabetes
- Heart disease
- High blood pressure
- High cholesterol
- Diabetes
- Heart disease

Still not convinced it might be important to focus on your waist? A year-long study conducted in Italy found that waist measurements rather than weight alone predicted risk of dying in patients with chronic heart failure (Testa, Cacciatore, & Galizia, 2010).

Researchers with the American Cancer Society similarly found a strong link between belly fat weight and mortality in over 100,000 adults age fifty and older in the United States (Jacobs et al., 2010). Belly fat was identified by measuring the waist. The researchers noted the following observations:

- People with the biggest waists had double the risk for dying over a ten-year period—regardless of their overall weight.
- Having extra belly fat increased risk of death from lung disease, heart disease, cancers, and other illnesses.
- People carrying an extra four inches (ten centimeters) around the waist increased their risk of dying by fifteen to twenty-five percent.
- Women who still weighed in the normal weight category with four extra inches (ten centimeters) around the middle had the highest increase: a twenty-five percent increased risk for dying.

Tail Waggin' Tip

Healthy waist measurements should be forty inches (102 centimeters) or less in men and thirty-five inches (88 centimeters) or less in women.

A study published in the journal *Gastrointestinal Endoscopy* confirmed an important link between belly fat and cancer. In this study, having a large waist increased the risk for having colon cancer (Hong et al., 2010):

- Having a waist measuring more than thirty-five inches (ninety centimeters) in men or thirty-one inches (eighty centimeters) in women was linked to a fifty-seven percent increased risk for colon cancer, with more than double the risk for advanced cancers.

This study is particularly important because the researchers studied younger adults forty to fifty-nine years old who were not at high risk for developing colon cancer, making this study an important lesson for all of us around this age group.

Nobody would ever say forty-seven-year-old Cheryl Noethiger was fat. But this pretty mother of four busy boys began to notice the waistband on her pants was starting to tighten:

> *At first, I wasn't really worried and thought I could just cut down on desserts and I'd be fine. When I was younger, cutting back on desserts a little always kept my weight in check. But this time, it didn't help. When I realized I could no longer close my jeans, I knew I had to do something.*

Cheryl enlisted the aid of her in-home personal trainer: a six-year-old Yellow Labrador Retriever named Honey Bear. Together, they walk two and a half miles each evening after the kids go to bed—every evening, rain or shine. After several months, Cheryl was happy to once again button her jeans with ease. When Honey Bear went for her annual visit to the vet, the vet was pleased to report that Honey Bear had also lost a couple pounds and looked trimmer than the previous year's visit. Motivated by their success, Cheryl and Honey Bear have added a pre-school, pre-work morning walk to their routine:

> *Honey Bear keeps me motivated because I know she needs to go for walks. When she sees me getting ready and it's around walk time, she stands at the door and barks. She won't let me skip a day—which is good for us both!*

 12

Get Off Your Butt!
Let Your Dog Show You How

M ost of us think we're doing a good job exercising. The General Electric Better Health Study surveyed Americans about lifestyle habits (General Electric, 2010). Over 2,000 people and their doctors were asked to grade how well they were doing at getting in enough exercise. Whereas one in every three people gave themselves an "A," over nine in every ten doctors gave these same people a "C."

 According to the U.S. Bureau of Labor Statistics (2010), the average working-age adult spends about five hours of leisure time each day. Only about fifteen minutes, however, are spent doing any form of exercise, sport, or recreation.

Why don't we keep up with a regular exercise program? This question was asked to 100 women enrolled in a research program in which they were asked to walk ninety minutes each week (Nies & Motyka, 2006). The vast majority of these women reported that adding exercise to their routine made them feel more fit, healthier, and less stressed. They also found that sticking with their program was tough. Most women said they were too busy to fit in exercise. Data from the Bureau of Labor Statistics (2010), however, show that few people are actually too busy to exercise.

- The average adult between ages twenty and fifty-five watches television about two hours every weeknight and three hours on the weekend.
- After age fifty-five, television viewing increases to three to four or more hours on weekdays and four or more hours on weekends.

If we just turned off the television for a little bit each day, there should be plenty of time for exercise.

 See If You Can Spot Common Exercise Myths

Choose each statement about exercise that is false:

- Once you reach middle age, daily exercise is no longer important.
- You need to get a least one 30-minute exercise session each day.
- Exercising less than thirty minutes at a time won't improve your health.
- You need to sweat to make sure you're exercising hard enough.
- Walking doesn't count as real exercise.
- Don't include your dog in exercise, because this will slow you down and reduce your cardiovascular workout.

If you chose every statement as incorrect, you're right on target! (Especially that last one—imagine not wanting to include Precious in your daily exercise.)

WHY IS REGULAR EXERCISE IMPORTANT?

Regular exercise can reduce your risk for developing many serious health problems (Kruk, 2007):

- Regular exercise reduces your risk of breast cancer by seventy-five percent.

- Heart disease risk decreases by forty-nine percent.
- Diabetes risk decreases by thirty-five percent.
- Colon cancer risk decreases by twenty-two percent.

A recent study that followed over 2,400 seniors for an average of eight and a half years found a lower risk of death among seniors who spent more leisure time engaged in physical activities (Gillum & Obisesan, 2010b).

Many people are not aware that exercise has important prevention effects for a number of serious health problems (Sanderson et al., 2009):

- Only half of adults know physical inactivity is a risk factor for heart disease.
- Only seven percent of adults know that inactivity increases cancer risk.

HOW MUCH EXERCISE IS ENOUGH?

The World Health Organization (2010) recommends that adults exercise a total of 150 minutes per week. Scheduling your daily exercise with regular dog walks can be a great way to motivate yourself to start and stick with a new exercise program.

World Health Organization (2010) Recommendations for Adequate Exercise to Promote Good Health

- Sixty minutes of moderate to vigorous activity daily for children five to seventeen years old
- Thirty minutes of moderate-intensity exercise five days per week for adults eighteen to sixty-five years old, plus strengthening exercises two days per week
- Thirty minutes of moderate-intensity exercise five days per week, with modifications as needed, in seniors over age sixty-five, plus flexibility and balance exercises

In a study published in the *Journal of Physical Activity and Health*, adults were asked about leisure time physical activity (Merom, Bowles, & Bauman, 2009). Interestingly, people often forgot to include walking (including dog walking) among their listed activities. Walking was often mentioned only if the researchers suggested walking as a possible leisure activity. Apparently, people don't associate walking or dog walking with exercise.

Dog walking can be an ideal routine for achieving regular exercise. Research studies show that breaking exercise into several, shorter segments is more beneficial than one long session. Researchers at the University of Pittsburgh randomly assigned overweight adults to one of two exercise programs (Jakicic et al., 1995). People in both programs were asked to exercise about twenty to forty minutes a day on five days each week. One group was told they should break up their exercise minutes into several short exercise periods of about ten minutes each. The other group was told to do one long fitness session each time they exercised. The researchers noted the following:

- After five months, the people who used several short exercise periods were exercising about twenty-five percent more days than those doing the single long workout.
- People who exercised in short segments were working out for almost twenty percent longer in total duration compared with those needing to get their exercise done in a single, long session.
- People who used the short exercise sessions also lost about forty percent more weight.

So, you can probably get better exercise and weight loss by walking your dog for ten minutes each walk two to four times a day than you will get from trying to stick to an exercise video.

The other great news is that you don't have to huff and puff to lose weight. A researcher in Texas compared weight loss among overweight, sedentary women who performed one of four exercise programs for one year (Chambliss, 2005). The women all started walking 100 minutes per week at moderate intensity. This would be equivalent to a brisk walk during which you are still able to talk while you're walking. If you can sing while you're walking, you need to increase your intensity level. Exercise duration was increased to 150 to 300 minutes per week, and intensity varied from moderate to vigorous. During what is considered vigorous exercise you would feel too winded or out of breath to carry on a conversation. The study results indicated the following:

- At the end of the year, weight loss and heart benefits were similar in all of the exercise intensity groups.
- It was more important to walk at least 150 minutes per week than to use a vigorous intensity of exercise.

Dog Walking Guidelines

- Plan to walk your dog at least twice daily.
- Plan to walk for at least ten minutes per walk.
- Try to walk a total of at least 150 minutes per week.
- Walk briskly—you shouldn't be able to sing while you walk, but you should still be able to chat comfortably.

Walking with a canine companion provides important motivation and social support that encourages and reinforces dog owners to get great health benefits from walking (Cutt et al., 2007). Research proves that people who walk with their dog are more likely to exercise regularly and get fit compared with people who walk with only human companions (Cangelosi & Sorrell, 2010; Christian nee Cutt, Giles-Corti, & Knuiman, 2010). Here are the results from one study that evaluated over 480 people (Christian nee Cutt et al., 2010):

- People who routinely walked their dogs in the neighborhood walked an average of over five times each week for an average of almost 200 minutes per week.
- People who didn't walk their dogs regularly walked the dog only about twice each week and only got in about forty-five minutes of weekly physical exercise.
- Therefore, two in every three regular dog walkers got their needed weekly exercise, compared with one in four dog owners who did not make walking a regular routine.

Researchers in Japan similarly found that dog owners who walked their dogs spent more time doing moderate to vigorous physical activity and walking than people without a dog (Oka & Shibata, 2009):

- Total weekly calorie-burning potential from walking was almost twenty percent higher for dog owners than those without dogs.
- Dog owners who walked their dogs were also more likely to get in other moderate to vigorous physical activity, in addition to dog walking.
- Total weekly calorie-burning potential from moderate to vigorous physical activity (including dog walks and other exercise) was fifty-six percent higher for dog owners than those without dogs.

In sum, dog owners were one and a half times more likely to get in their necessary exercise requirements. That's the good news. The bad news is that, although dog owners exercised more, only thirty percent of dog owners were getting enough exercise to meet standard daily exercise recommendations.

Walking your dog keeps you living healthy longer. A large study conducted by researchers at Howard University looked at mortality in people with and without pet dogs. In this study, over 11,000 Americans ages forty and older were followed for an average of eight and a half years (Gillum & Obisesam, 2010a):

- Risk of dying was twenty-five percent less among dog owners.
- When the researchers took into consideration healthy lifestyle factors in dog owners compared with those without dogs—such as exercise level, weight, blood pressure, and high cholesterol—the risk of dying dropped to nineteen percent lower in dog owners. This smaller amount was not statistically significant, meaning it wasn't any better than could be explained by chance alone.

What does this study tell us? Is having a dog good for a longer life? Absolutely. However, the increased life span benefit is not caused by simply added companionship but also from your dog helping you stay more fit.

Dog Owners Are More Physically Active

- Dog owners walk nineteen more minutes per week than people without pets (Yabroff, Troiano, & Berrigan, 2008).
- People who walk their dogs are fifteen percent more likely to met daily physical exercise requirements than people without a dog (Coleman et al., 2008).
- Seniors with dogs are more likely to walk, for example, walking the dog, walking to the store, walking to church (Thorpe, Kreisle, et al., 2006).
- Older seniors (age 71–82) who walk their dogs are more likely to continue to have good mobility three years later (Thorpe, Simonsick, et al., 2006).

Dogs can become great motivators to maintain an exercise program long term. A survey of dog owners conducted at the University of Western Australia and published in *Health Promotion Journal of Australia* revealed that dogs are great motivators for walking, for several reasons (Cutt et al., 2008):

- Dogs provide a strong motivation to maintain a program.
- Dogs are good walking companions.
- Dogs offer good social support when exercising.

So, if you want a consistent exercise partner, make Toby your workout buddy.

It's easy to forget about healthy walking plans, so set the stage for a successful program.

• Establish a walking schedule: Plan to walk thirty minutes total each day. This might include a ten-minute neighborhood walk in the morning and a twenty-minute romp at the dog park after work, or maybe three 10-minute walks or one 30-minute walk fit in better with your day.

— If dog walking is scheduled into each day, you'll feel more responsible for sticking with your program. Fluffy with also get used to the routine and remind you when "it's time."

- Track your progress
  — Post a calendar on the refrigerator and add a sticker for each ten minutes of walking you do each day. This will reinforce your good behavior and make you pause before opening the door to grab a calorie-laden snack.
  — You can download a walking progress calendar from http://www.fitasfido.com
- Keep a basket of walking supplies handy at the door
  — Leash
  — Water bottle for you and collapsible bowl to use for Duke—so you'll both stay hydrated
  — Training treats—turn your walks into training sessions to reinforce good behaviors and new tricks. Your dog will love it, and walks won't become boring.
  — Poopie bags
  — Rain gear
  — Good walking shoes and boots
  — Grooming supplies to remove dirt, mud, and twigs before Daisy enters the house

So grab a leash, whistle for Fido, and go for a walk—today and every day. Dog walking is a great way to jumpstart a healthy lifestyle program.

If you or your dog have health problems or are seniors, check with your doctor and veterinarian before starting a new exercise program. Then follow these tips to make your program a success:

- Schedule dog walks into each day. You'll feel more responsible for sticking with your program and Fluffy will get used to the routine and remind you when "it's time."

Sunday	Monday	Tuesday	Wednesday	Thursday	Friday	Saturday	Week Total
□ Fit As Fido	□ Fit As Fido	□ Fit As Fido	□ Fit As Fido	□ Fit As Fido	□ Fit As Fido	□ Fit As Fido	
□ Fit As Fido	□ Fit As Fido	□ Fit As Fido	□ Fit As Fido	□ Fit As Fido	□ Fit As Fido	□ Fit As Fido	
□ Fit As Fido	□ Fit As Fido	□ Fit As Fido	□ Fit As Fido	□ Fit As Fido	□ Fit As Fido	□ Fit As Fido	
□ Fit As Fido	□ Fit As Fido	□ Fit As Fido	□ Fit As Fido	□ Fit As Fido	□ Fit As Fido	□ Fit As Fido	
□ Fit As Fido	□ Fit As Fido	□ Fit As Fido	□ Fit As Fido	□ Fit As Fido	□ Fit As Fido	□ Fit As Fido	
□ Fit As Fido	□ Fit As Fido	□ Fit As Fido	□ Fit As Fido	□ Fit As Fido	□ Fit As Fido	□ Fit As Fido	
□ Fit As Fido	□ Fit As Fido	□ Fit As Fido	□ Fit As Fido	□ Fit As Fido	□ Fit As Fido	□ Fit As Fido	
□ Fit As Fido	□ Fit As Fido	□ Fit As Fido	□ Fit As Fido	□ Fit As Fido	□ Fit As Fido	□ Fit As Fido	
□ Fit As Fido	□ Fit As Fido	□ Fit As Fido	□ Fit As Fido	□ Fit As Fido	□ Fit As Fido	□ Fit As Fido	
□ Fit As Fido	□ Fit As Fido	□ Fit As Fido	□ Fit As Fido	□ Fit As Fido	□ Fit As Fido	□ Fit As Fido	
□ Fit As Fido	□ Fit As Fido	□ Fit As Fido	□ Fit As Fido	□ Fit As Fido	□ Fit As Fido	□ Fit As Fido	
□ Fit As Fido	□ Fit As Fido	□ Fit As Fido	□ Fit As Fido	□ Fit As Fido	□ Fit As Fido	□ Fit As Fido	

Figure 12.1. A Fit As Fido monthly walking calendar. Check a Fit As Fido box every time you walk for ten minutes. Your target is to walk at least 150 minutes per week, so fifteen or more boxes should be checked each week. Write your total number of ten-minute walks in the Week Total column. If the number is fifteen or more, circle Fido. Reprinted from Marcus, D. A. (2008). *Fit As Fido: Follow Your Dog to Better Health*. Bloomington, IN: Universe.

- Track your progress by using a walking diary, like the Fit As Fido walking log (http://www.fitasfido.com).
- Trade in your walking shoes for a new pair every 300 miles or at least twice a year. Exercising in old shoes increases your risk for injury.
- Make sure both you and Lucky take a drink of water before and after each walk to stay well hydrated.
- If you don't have your own dog, consider walking a neighbor's dog, or volunteer to be a dog walker at your local animal shelter.

SPICE UP YOUR EXERCISE ROUTINE

Keep your daily activity fun by changing your routine. Try out new routes for your walks, or walk your old route in the reverse direction. Use the suggestions given later in this chapter from exercise experts

Figure 12.2. Take a lesson from therapy dog Lexi: Beef up your aerobic power by adding skips, jumps, and jogs to your daily walk.

Dawn Celapino and Janet Atutes to turn your daily dog walks into a whole-body workout routine. Adding in short bursts of more intense exercise—such as running sprints, chasing Fido, and fast retrieving—can boost your heart and breathing fitness.

Have you ever used the excuse "But I simply don't have time to do any effective exercise"? Thanks to researchers at the University of Glasgow, that excuse won't work anymore. They tested ten sedentary, overweight men with fitness measures (Whyte, Gill, & Cathcart, 2010). Then the men participated in two weeks of sprint interval training. They did six sessions of four to six repetitions of thirty-second sprints, with about a five-minute recovery between sprints. Doesn't sound like much exercise, does it? Well, not only were measures of heart disease risk lower after two weeks, but also waist and hip circumferences dropped significantly.

So, if you thought doing some quick runs in the yard with Lucky, throwing a ball vigorously for your enthusiastic Goldie for a few minutes, or taking some quick sprints down the street with Tip was fun for your dog, but not really good for you, think again. And when you try the excuse of "I can't find a whole thirty seconds for a quick sprint activity," it'll sound so lame that you'll be unable to complete this poor justification for continuing unhealthy habits and will be on your way to a healthier you.

Remember: Short, high-intensity exercise bursts should be included as part of your daily exercise routine. Don't forget the daily dog walks, too! Short bursts of high-intensity exercise are terrific for boosting heart fitness, while steady exercise is generally more helpful for keeping you weight down and blood lipids in check (Nybo et al., 2010). By focusing on daily dog walks with added exercise bursts, you can get the best of both worlds.

DAWN CELAPINO HELPS YOU "LEASH YOUR FITNESS"

Dawn Celapino is a certified personal trainer in San Diego, California. She has over eighteen years of experience helping people reach their fitness goals. She has a bachelor of science degree in kinesiology from San Diego State University with an emphasis in nutrition and health. Dawn has found the perfect way to make fitness a fun treat: she developed "Leash Your Fitness," a company specializing in adding Fido to your workout. Her motto? *Take your dog walks to the next level!*

Dogs play an important part in Dawn's exercise classes:

I didn't want to leave my own dog at home when I worked out, so I started doing my exercises outside where my dogs could stay with me. I enjoyed this so much that I started incorporating my clients' dogs in the human exercise routine and it took people's minds off of exercises and made the workouts more fun. Boosting your exercise sessions with your dog can be as easy as adding simple exercises to your regular dog walks. A variety of terrific exercise moves can be added to dog walks—sprints, squats, lunges, push-ups, balance, core exercises, etc.

In class, we incorporate jumps, sprints, lunges, squats, push-ups, and band work for the person. Dog obedience training is included for the dog throughout the class, so the dogs get mentally stimulated and have to keep thinking. Adding mental stimulation to the exercises tires the dog out faster than just exercising alone.

Another fun exercise we do is Doga Yoga, which is basically yoga with your dog as your buddy. For much of the class, the dog stays by the person's side. In some cases, we're able to actually incorporate the dog into some of the poses. People love having the comfort of their dog nearby during yoga. Your dog reads your energy so if you are calm— the dog will follow suit. In this way, your dog helps act as a good barometer to let you know if you're getting the most from yoga.

Dawn has found that adding dogs to the exercise routine improves the bond between dog and owner and turns the drudgery of daily exercise into fun:

Exercising with your dog can help improve your dog's obedience for basic commands—sit, stay, down, and heel. By working on both exercise and obedience together, you strengthen the bond and working relationship between dog and owner.

People LOVE being with their dogs. Including their best canine buddy in exercise helps make the exercise more fun and provides important distractions to help keep people motivated throughout the whole exercise session. When people start getting tired during an exercise session, they begin to focus on what their dog is doing and it takes their minds off of the pain of the exercise and keeps exercise fun!

Dawn encourages her students to take what they learn in class home to spice up their daily dog walks:

Dog owners everywhere can easily add exercises to their daily dog walks. A walk is great, but you can turn a walk into a full body

Figure 12.3. Dawn and Cairn Terrier exercise buddy Jack.

workout by adding in other exercises. You can work on balance exercises, core strengthening, and the big muscle groups as you are on your walk. For example, you can add lunges to your walk or stop at a park bench to add an upper body workout with push-ups for the biceps or triceps exercises.

THE FIT AS FIDO PROGRAM

On the other side of the country, aerobics instructor Janet Atutes and I teamed up to develop a Fit As Fido exercise class, based on my book,

Fit As Fido: Follow Your Dog to Better Health (Marcus, 2008). Janet started teaching aerobics in 1978:

> *I was never very athletic as a kid, with dance lessons and cheerleading my only physical activities. When I went to college, running was so unpopular for the average person that I used to carry my Adidas to the track, change there, run a mile, and come back to the dorm. After I graduated and got a dog, I expanded my running for the dog's benefit. Later, aerobics seemed like the perfect way to combine my need to exercise and love of dance.*

Janet found that having a dog helped make her own exercise routine more consistent:

> *Since 1974, I could probably say I've missed only a few weeks total of walking or running. The reason—I always felt that I had to get my dog out. Whether it was dark, raining, snowing, blazing hot—I had to figure out how to get my dog outside. Sometimes it was a just a twenty-minute walk before work, but I felt obligated. My first dog Jack lived over sixteen years; my next dog Bailey died in her sixteenth year. And both dogs had major traumatic medical episodes midway through their lives— Jack swallowed a pine cone and had to have surgery, and Bailey was hit by a car, with major injuries. While Bailey was recovering, I would carry her to our favorite trail in the park each day. The vet said she would use it as inspiration to heal. In a matter of days, Bailey could stand, then walk a few steps, then eventually jog. While the vet thought this would inspire Bailey—it also inspired me. It changed my life. Bailey lived another twelve years. My current dog, Truly, gets the retirement benefit—we go to the park every day.*

Although Janet retired from teaching public school, she still teaches aerobics, step, and lifting. We worked together to develop a fun way to exercise with Fido:

> *I tried offering a traditional aerobics class to which people could bring their dogs, but most people found it too confusing to do the typical*

Figure 12.4. Janet and her eager aerobic student, Truly.

aerobics routine and try to keep their dog under control. Meanwhile, people coming to regular aerobics complained that they had trouble finding the time to fit in a routine. By combining exercise that focuses on moving a range of muscles with basic dog obedience practice, people can get in their exercise, have fun with their dog, and reinforce good training skills.

Our Fit As Fido class is an enjoyable break from traditional exercise classes. Fit As Fido exercise is entertaining—and you get a great workout. You can also adjust the exercise to your comfort

Figure 12.5. The Fit As Fido exercise circle. A center lane is formed with a chair for the human and a towel or mat for the dog. When you go back and forth, you'll be moving between chair and towel. The outer circle is formed here with logs on the left, which can be used for making small jumps, and the flags on the right, which can be used for making weaves. You can make the circle bigger or smaller depending on your needs and available space.

level. Class time combines fun exercise with a different opportunity for training. And ideally, people use some of the ideas they learn in class to put together their own "regularly scheduled" Fit As Fido program between classes.

The Fit As Fido exercise program uses an outer circle for longer walks and a lane across the circle for you to practice individual skills with Fido. You can set this up in your yard, using the example in Figure 12.5. If you have a friend or a few friends joining you for your workout, just widen the circle and add extra lanes with more chairs and mats. Space the lanes farther apart if your dog has trouble getting distracted by the other dogs. Interestingly, most dogs who know basic obedience skills do fine with just about three feet between lanes, because all the activity seems to keep them focused on you rather than getting distracted by a potential playmate.

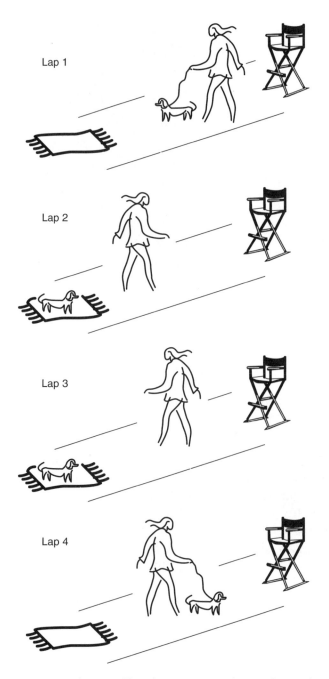

Figure 12.6. Exercises make use of laps between your chair and your dog's mat. This series of drawings shows the lap pattern for the Fit As Fido exercises.

Table 12.1 describes a full one-hour Fit As Fido exercise program. Each exercise uses a repetition of four laps that you can see described in Figure 12.6.

- Lap 1: Walk your dog from your chair to the mat.
- Lap 2: Leave your dog at the mat using a stay command and return to your chair.
- Lap 3: Return to your dog.
- Lap 4: Pick up your dog's leash and walk him back to your chair.

Repeat this sequence of four laps for the duration of each exercise interval.

Table 12.1. Suggested Stretching Exercises

Stretch	Instruction
Lower leg stretch	• Step 1: Holding onto the back of your chair, step one foot back and lean forward (see Figure 12.7). Keep both heels on the floor for a good stretch. Hold for 10 seconds. • Step 2: Lean back and bend your knee (see Figure 12.8). Hold for 10 seconds. • Switch sides and repeat Steps 1 and 2 for a total of 5 times.
Butt stretch	• Hold onto the back of your chair. • Step back and then bend forward from the waist so that you're looking at the floor. • Bend your knees and flatten your back (see Figure 12.9). Hold 10 seconds. Relax. • Repeat 5 times.

(Continued)

Figure 12.7. Lower leg stretch, Step 1. Rosebud approves of Gloria's form for Step 1.

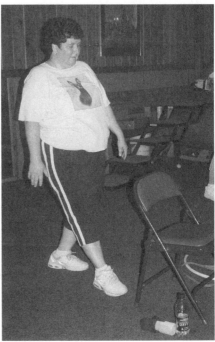

Figure 12.8. Lower leg stretch, Step 2. Janet gets a good stretch.

Figure 12.9. Butt stretch. Lannie watches Marleen get into good form.

Table 12.1. Suggested Stretching Exercises (*Continued*)

Stretch	Instruction
Upper leg stretch	• Turn so your side is next to the back of your chair and hold on with one hand. • Step one foot back as far as you can and bend that knee to the floor (see Figure 12.10). Hold 10 seconds. • Switch legs and repeat. Repeat 5 times.
Back stretch	• Move away from your chair and place your feet 1–2 feet apart. • Step 1: Place your hands on your thighs and slowly round your back up, pulling in your stomach muscles (see Figure 12.11). • Step 2: Flatten your back (see Figure 12.12). Relax. • Repeat 5 times.

(*Continued*)

Figure 12.10. Upper leg stretch. Janet demonstrates correct form for stretching the quadriceps muscles.

Figure 12.11. Back stretch, Step 1. Rosebud sits obediently by while Gloria rounds her back into an arch (Step 1) and then flattens her back (Step 2).

Figure 12.12. Back stretch, Step 2. Gloria flattens her back as Rosebud continues to sit obediently by.

Table 12.1. Suggested Stretching Exercises (*Continued*)

Stretch	Instruction
	• Step 3: Turn your left shoulder to the ground and hold for 10 seconds (see Figure 12.13). Then turn your right shoulder to the ground and hold for 10 seconds.
	• Repeat 4 times
Upper body stretch	• Interlace your fingers together in front of your body.
	• Round your back and "press your cares away!" (See Figure 12.14.) Hold 10 seconds. Relax.
	• Repeat 5 times.

Figure 12.13. Back stretch, Step 3. Miki rotates under Spinner's watchful eye.

Figure 12.14. Upper body stretch. Janet finishes the stretching routine by pushing her cares away.

Janet and Dawn's One-Hour Fit As Fido Exercise Routine

- **Getting started**

You'll need the following items:

- — A sturdy chair, like a folding chair. You will use the chair for some exercises and a place to take breaks, when needed.
- — A mat, blanket, or towel as a place for Fido to wait
- — Obstacles for jumps and weaves. You can use logs and flags (like in Figure 12.5) or whatever you have handy—such as traffic cones, two-liter soda bottles, or stacks of books.
- — A water bottle for you
- — A water dish, leash, and treats for Fido

- **Set up**

- — Set up your exercise course in a large, open room or a fenced yard.
- — Place your chair and Fido's blanket about ten to fifteen paces apart on a flat area. This is your fitness lane for doing your laps.

- **Stay hydrated**

- — Make sure you keep a water bottle for you and water dish for Fido behind your chair.
- — Take a big drink before starting your exercise.
- — Take breaks between intervals to catch your breath and get drinks.
- — Make sure you've finished at least one water bottle by the time your exercise is done.

- **Pace yourself**

- — Adjust your pace so you can do this program comfortably and can still talk to Fido.
- — If you can't comfortably talk, slow your pace.
- — If you can sing to Fido, pick up the pace.

Janet and Dawn's One-Hour Fit As Fido
Exercise Routine   (*Continued*)

- **Basic obedience**
  - — Your dog will need to understand basic obedience skills.
  - — Reward Fido with small treats during the program as needed to help reinforce his skills.
  - — If your dog gets up from his waiting position, don't get upset. Correct him by returning him to his spot, and remember: As long as you're moving, you're getting a workout.
  - — Your fitness program is not a competition. Don't worry about not being perfect.
- **Making the workout work**
  - — Do this program in ten intervals.
  - — It will take you about sixty minutes to complete the whole circuit—including setting up and cleaning up.
  - — As long as you keep the warm-up stretch and cool down, you can pick and chose intervals to do if you don't have a full hour for your workout. For example, complete the stretches in Table 12.1 and the select exercise numbers 1, 2 through 5, and 10 from Table 12.2 for a thirty-minute workout one day and numbers 1, 6 through 9, and 10 for your next workout.
- **Have fun**
  - — Exercise should be fun for you *and* Fido.
  - — Have fun, smile, and enjoy getting Fit As Fido!

Start your workout with body stretches, which are important to get your muscles ready for a workout. Forgetting your stretches before you begin exercise can increase your risk for getting exercise-related injuries. It's also healthy to do stretches before daily walks and in preparation for bed at night.

After finishing your stretches, your workout program will continue with a series of exercises described in Table 12.2. Use Figures 12.15 through 12.26 to help check your form.

Table 12.2. A Fit As Fido Exercise Routine

Intervals	Descriptions
1. Warm-up stretch	• Walk around the big circle with your dog on a heel for 2 minutes.
	• Return to your chair and put Fido in a sit–stay next to your chair.
	• Complete your 5 body stretches.
2. Walking: Sit–stay	• Lap 1: Take your dog's leash and briskly walk from your chair to Fido's blanket.
	• Lap 2: When you reach the blanket, put your dog in a sit–stay position and walk briskly back to your chair.
	• Lap 3: Turn in front of your chair and return to your dog to pick up his leash.
	• Lap 4: Walk your dog back around your chair and back to the blanket for another sit–stay.
	• Keep up this pattern for 4 minutes. If your dog has trouble staying, ask him to sit at the blanket, then pick up his leash and walk him back toward your chair. Continue the pattern, using sit instead of sit–stay.
	• After 4 minutes, take a 1-minute break by walking around the big circle.
3. Triceps dips: Down–stay	• Lap 1: Walk your dog to the blanket and put him in a down–stay.
	• Lap 2: Briskly return to the front of your chair and do 8–12 triceps dips (see Figure 12.15 and 12.16).
	• Lap 3: Go back to your dog and pick up his leash.

(Continued)

Figure 12.15. Triceps dip. Janet shows the starting for a triceps dip.

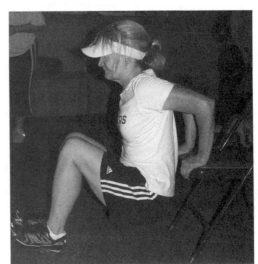

Figure 12.16. Triceps dip. Janet shows the ending position for a triceps dip.

Table 12.2. A Fit As Fido Exercise Routine (*Continued*)

Intervals	Descriptions
	• Lap 4: Walk him back around your chair and back to the blanket for another down–stay while you go back to do more triceps dips.
	• As before, if your dog won't stay, replace the down–stay with a brief "down" command and keep your dog with you.
	• Continue for 4 minutes and then take a break with a 1-minute break by walking around the big circle.
4. Lunges: Sit–stay	• Lap 1: Take your dog's leash and walk to the blanket.
	• Lap 2: When you reach the blanket, put your dog in a sit–stay and walk back to your chair.
	• Lap 3: Turn in front of your chair and return to your dog to pick up his leash.
	• Lap 4: Walk your dog back around your chair and back to the blanket for another sit–stay.
	• When you walk with and without the dog, walk slowly, doing lunges (see Figure 12.17). If you're not able to do lunges, just take slow, wide steps. If you want to beef up your workout, make each lunge slow and deep.
	• Continue for 4 minutes and then take a 1-minute break by walking around the big circle.

Make sure you and Fido take a water break.

(*Continued*)

Figure 12.17. Lunges. Walking with wide steps and lunges gives a great workout and adds interest for a curious Coonhound.

Table 12.2. A Fit As Fido Exercise Routine (*Continued*)

Intervals	Descriptions
5. Upper body–shoulder: Down–stay	• Lap 1: Walk your dog to the blanket and put him in a down stay.
	• Lap 2: As you walk back toward your chair without your dog, work your upper body by reaching your arms overhead and then pulling down an imaginary rope (see Figures 12.18 and 12.19). Then reach your arms forward and pull back (see Figures 12.20 and 12.21). Continue the pattern of reach up, pull, reach out, pull until you are back with your dog.
	• Lap 3: Return to Fido.
	• Lap 4: Walk a lap with Fido and repeat.
	• Continue for 4 minutes and then take a 1-minute break by walking around the big circle.

(Continued)

In Figures 12.18, 12.19, 12.20, and 12.21 Janet shows the four movements in this upper body and shoulder reach up–pull–reach out–pull pattern.

Figure 12.18. The first reach is over the head.

Figure 12.19. Then pull back to the shoulders.

Figure 12.20. The second reach is in front.

Figure 12.21. Try to push your shoulder blades together with the second pull.

Table 12.2. A Fit As Fido Exercise Routine (*Continued*)

Intervals	Descriptions
6. Weaves and jumps	• Continue walking around the big circle.
	• When you get to your obstacles, alternate weaving through obstacles one time (see Figure 12.22) and then jumping over them or next to them the next.
	• Continue for 4 minutes.
Take a water break and give Fido a chance to relieve himself if needed or take a sniff while you're getting an extra drink.	

(*Continued*)

Figure 12.22. Weave through obstacles with your dog at your side. Here, cones are used as weave markers.

Figure 12.23. Push-ups. Gloria gets an upper body workout between walks with Rosebud.

Table 12.2. A Fit As Fido Exercise Routine (*Continued*)

Intervals	Descriptions
7. Upper body push-ups: Sit–stay	• Lap 1: Walk your dog to the blanket and put him in a down stay.
	• Lap 2: Briskly return to the back of your chair and do 8–12 push-ups (see Figure 12.23).
	• Lap 3: Go back to Fido and pick up his leash.

(*Continued*)

Table 12.2. A Fit As Fido Exercise Routine (*Continued*)

Intervals	Descriptions
7. Upper body push-ups: Sit–stay	• Lap 4: Walk him back around your chair and back to the blanket for another down–stay while you go back to do more push-ups. • As before, if your dog won't stay, replace the down–stay with a down command and keep your dog with you. • Continue for 4 minutes and then take a 1-minute break by walking around the big circle.
8. Freestyle: Recall	• Lap 1: Walk your dog to the blanket and put him in a sit–stay. • Lap 2: Return to your chair doing a brisk walk, lunges, jogging, skipping, dancing—whatever strikes your mood (see Figures 12.24 and 12.25). Go crazy and have fun! When you reach your chair, call Fido to you and love him up. • Lap 3: Return Fido to his blanket for another sit–stay and repeat. • Continue for 4 minutes and then take a 1-minute break by walking around the big circle.
9. Squats: Recall	• Lap 1: Walk your dog to the blanket and put him in a sit–stay. • Lap 2: Slowly return to your chair, doing squats with each step or every other step (see Figure 12.26). Adjust the depth of the squat as is comfortable for you. When you reach your chair, call Fido to you and love him up. • Lap 3: Return Fido to his blanket for another sit–stay and repeat. • Continue for 4 minutes and then take a 1-minute break by walking around the big circle.

(*Continued*)

Figure 12.24. Mary Ann (May) entertains Lhasa Apso Latte and gets a great aerobic workout with some fancy dance moves during her freestyle walk.

Figure 12.25. Miki boosts her aerobic exercise and gives Long-Haired German Shepherd Spinner some extra distractions when he has to do his down–stay while she does her freestyle walk stepping over him.

Figure 12.26. Barbara adds some thigh work to her walk with squats, flanked by Maltese Sadie.

Table 12.2. A Fit As Fido Exercise Routine (*Continued*)

Intervals	Descriptions
10. Cool down	• Spend about 4 minutes walking around the circle at a more casual pace. • Weave around obstacles and tell Fido how proud you are of him for being such a great workout buddy. • Promise Fido you'll make this into a regular routine.

Try doing this program with a friend or two and their dogs for added fun for you and distractions for Fido to improve his skill level. Just add another chair next to yours and blanket next to Fido for as many people as you need.

Try these adjustments for the Fit As Fido exercise program to make your routine shorter or longer:

- Change the time for each interval
- Leave out some of the middle intervals
- Repeat intervals more than once

You can also incorporate some of the exercises from the Fit As Fido routine into your daily dog walks to spice up your walks and boost your workout power:

- Add squats or lunges every time you get to a new block
- Jump over sidewalk cracks
- Weave between trees, signs, or other obstacles on a not-so-busy sidewalk
- Do a few push-ups or triceps dips when you find a bench.

 13

Thanks for the Memories: Helping Seniors Connect With Their Past and the Present

Therapy dog visits can be especially important for seniors—particularly for those living alone or in nursing homes. Seniors who also have memory problems may become especially isolated. As memory problems worsen, people often become distressed and agitated. They also typically engage less and less with others around them, losing important stimulation of their memory and a chance to engage in daily activities. Visits from therapy dogs have been medically proven to significantly reduce agitation in seniors with marked memory problems and improve their social interaction with others (Richeson, 2003). Therapy dogs can often reach people whose memory problems seem to have pushed them out of the reach of medical staff and family members.

When memory loss becomes more severe, people can develop *dementia*, which is defined as a loss of memory plus loss of other mental functions, such as understanding language, identifying common objects, setting and achieving goals, or thinking abstractly. Alzheimer's disease is the most common type of dementia, although dementia can also be caused by other diseases and strokes. People with dementia often become confused, agitated, and withdrawn. According to a recent report from the Alzheimer's Association (2010), over five million seniors in the United States have Alzheimer's disease or another type of dementia. That's one in every eight people ages sixty-five and older.

The Alzheimer's Association estimates that someone in the United States develops Alzheimer's disease every seventy seconds.

THERAPY DOG VISITS CAN HELP PATIENTS RECONNECT WITH THEIR PAST AND PRESENT

Therapy dog visits can be an important part of the day for seniors. The dog and handler can become a much-anticipated part of the senior's week—giving him or her something to look forward to, an eager ear to hear tales of younger days, and a connection to what's happening in the outside world today. Research has convincingly shown that the addition of therapy dog visits to a nursing home significantly improves socialization among the residents (Fick, 1993).

Tail Waggin' Tip

Handler Barbara Pohodich frequently hears people say, "I had a dog like that," when she brings her Poodle and Maltese therapy dogs for visits to nursing homes. "Seeing my dogs helps remind people of stories in their past—good stories about them and their dogs."

A small study conducted at the Department of Public Health of Hamamatsu University in Japan evaluated the effects of therapy dog visits every other week for three months for seniors with dementia attending adult day care (Kanamori et al., 2001):

- After three months, memory actually improved slightly, by eight percent, among those seniors who received the therapy dog visits, compared to a seven percent *decline* in memory for seniors who did not visit with the therapy dog.
- Overall behavior problems also dropped significantly, by thirty-five percent, among seniors visited by the therapy dog, while worsening by four percent among those who did not have the dog visits.

The researchers also measured chromogranin A in the saliva. Chromogranin A is a protein produced by the adrenal gland and released when the nervous system is stressed. Researchers used chromogranin A levels as a marker of mental stress. After the final visit, chromogranin levels had dropped by fifty-seven percent in the seniors who visited with the therapy dog, compared with a nineteen percent increase in residents who did not receive visits.

 The following benefits from weekly therapy dog visits to seniors with severe memory problems have been observed (Tribet et al., 2008):

- Calming effect
- Improved communication with others between dog visits
- Increased interactions
- Increased self-esteem

When Mary Ann (May) Seman visits with her six-year-old Lhasa Apso therapy dog Latte, nursing home residents get a taste of their homeland:

One of the nursing homes where Latte and I visit has many residents of Slovak and Polish descent; also some of them are fellow church parishioners. I was visiting with one of my fellow parishioners and probably spending more time in that room than Latte thought I should. She was getting restless and was eager to move on. The lady I was visiting looked at Latte and said, "Sediet seba." In Slovak, this means, "Sit down." Amazingly, Latte sat down. This prompted me to teach Latte a few basic commands in Slovak (come, sit, down, wait, and turn around). It is now one of our favorite performances at the nursing home. Of course, Latte is responding to the hand signals, but the residents just love it. One resident told me Latte understands Slovak better than her grandchildren!

Figure 13.1. May brings Lhasa Apso therapy dog Latte to entertain seniors in a nursing home and bring them a taste of their home culture.

THERAPY DOGS FILL A SPECIAL ROLE FOR PEOPLE WITH SEVERE MEMORY LOSS

A recent review identified a number of benefits of animal-assisted therapy for patients with dementia (Filan & Llewellyn-Jones, 2006):

- Patients with dementia show reduced agitation after visiting with a therapy dog.

- Therapy dog visits reduce aggressive behavior in seniors with dementia.
- After a therapy dog visit, patients with dementia had increased social behaviors, including more smiling, looking, leaning, touching, and verbalization.

Interestingly, the benefits from pet therapy were independent of the severity of dementia.

To see whether having therapy dogs visit patients with dementia really makes a difference, Dr. Richeson from the University of Southern Maine measured agitated behaviors in nursing home residents with dementia during a three-week period before a therapy dog had visited residents, during a three-week period during which therapy dogs regularly visited residents, and during a three-week period after the dogs had stopped making visits (Richeson, 2003). Compared with the period before having visits, agitated behaviors dropped by twenty-three percent during the weeks when dog visits occurred. Agitated behaviors increased nine percent during the weeks when the dogs were no longer visiting. This study tells us three things about therapy dog visits for patients with severe memory problems:

1. Regular visits from a therapy dog have a calming effect and reduce agitated behavior.
2. Benefits for seniors last after the dog leaves the facility.
3. Continuing to make visits is important to help maintain benefits over the long term.

This study highlights that therapy dog visits make a difference. So if you ever wonder whether you should bother to head out to keep your regular visit on a given day, the answer should be a resounding "Yes."

Mary was an older woman living in a nursing home who struggled with dementia. She spent her days confused and disengaged from the world around her. Usually, Mary would sit in her wheelchair with her head down and grab a hand railing in the hallway of the nursing home where she lived. She'd use that railing to pull herself up and down the hall, over and over throughout the day, seemingly oblivious to staff and others around her. Try as they might, the staff couldn't find a way to get through to Mary. One day, when the Rev. Danielle Di Bona was visiting the nursing home, she spotted a photo of a Golden Retriever in Mary's room and decided to bring her therapy dog, Naomi, in for a visit:

When Naomi came, I put her right in front of Mary's chair as Mary made her daily journey up and down the hall. I was a bit concerned because Mary would often not stop once she'd started her day's travels, even when someone was in her path. When Mary got to Naomi, Mary stopped. Still hunched over in the wheelchair, Mary silently reached out a hand and began petting Naomi. After five minutes, Mary sat up straight in her wheelchair and looked directly into my eyes and clearly announced, "You have the most beautiful dog!" Naomi is a gorgeous Wheaten Terrier, so I wasn't quite sure why the nurses looked so startled until they told me that this was the first time Mary had uttered a word in over three years.

Therapy dogs can reach into the world of patients with dementia when others have been unable to reach them. Danielle is very familiar with patients with severe memory problems and dementia as part of her work as a hospice chaplain:

Once I saw a group of dementia patients seated in their wheelchairs in a circle. The activities director was trying to get them engaged by encouraging everyone to toss a beach ball back and forth around the group. Despite her best efforts, many people seemed completely unaware of the ball and few people got engaged in the game. My therapy dog Naomi was with me as I watched, and we took away the ball and let Naomi enter the center of the circle. Naomi slowly circled the group, stopping before each person as everyone interacted with her. Some people touched her, while others just leaned forward. But the biggest change we saw was the brightness that came over faces as people who had previously seemed lost in their own confused worlds gazed at my little terrier and smiled.

Naomi also provided one-on-one therapy to dementia patients. The late afternoons can be especially difficult for patients with Alzheimer's disease and their caregivers. The decrease in dementia patient's general condition around this time of day is called *sun-downing*, and it can really become a major problem, especially in nursing homes where midafternoon shift changes frequently coincide with these times of increased patient agitation, aggression, and confusion. For Rachel, a 2:00 p.m. visit from Naomi helped improve her afternoon behavior:

> *The nurses would tell Rachel that Naomi would be coming, which seemed to help Rachel keep her behavior in check before we got there. Naomi and Rachel always had a wonderful time together, and the nurses told us that Rachel would remain well behaved for the rest of the day after a visit from Naomi.*

THERAPY DOGS CAN OPEN DOORS TO PEOPLE CLOSED OFF FROM DEMENTIA

As dementia becomes more severe, people can become withdrawn from the world around them, retreating into a place closed off to their loved ones and caregivers. These patients may become lost to those around them—not interacting, not talking, not involved with what's going on in the world outside of themselves. Seeing Mom or Dad drift away like this can be especially hard on those who love them the most.

Doctors at the Research Institute on Aging investigated whether dogs could help bring patients with dementia out of their shells and help them reconnect with the world and people around them. They had seniors living in a nursing home with dementia spend three minutes with a dog-related activity: watching a puppy video, being given a dog coloring book, holding a plush dog, playing with a robot dog, or having a visit from a real therapy dog (Marx et al., 2010). As you might have guessed, patients preferred the real dog to anything else. Each dog activity produced an increase in speaking, although people talked the most when they were with the real dog. These seniors said an average of twenty-three things during the three minutes with the real dog, fifteen things when playing with the robot dog or watching the puppy video, five things when coloring, and only three things when holding the stuffed dog.

Investigators in Japan likewise showed benefits from therapy dogs visiting older women with dementia in a nursing home (Kawamura, Niiyama, & Niiyama, 2009). Dog visits occurred monthly. The researchers made the following observations:

- Seniors with dementia enjoyed therapy dog visits.
- Therapy dogs were seen as stress relievers.

- Therapy dog visits provided a break from the loneliness and daily irritations from living in a nursing home.
- Residents commented that having the dogs visit was "like a breath of fresh air."
- Dog visits brought residents a sense of purpose—they connected with the dogs and developed a responsibility for making sure the dog was happy during each visit.
- Having dog visits improved the residents' interaction and communication with the staff and fellow residents.

 How Do Therapy Dogs Help People With Dementia? (Filan & Llewellyn-Jones, 2006; Kawamura et al., 2009)

- Reduce agitation
- Reduce aggression
- Encourage healthy social behavior
- Provide a break from the loneliness and daily stresses
- Bring back fond memories of times with their own dogs
- Increase self-confidence

Benefits occur even in people with severe dementia.

The results of these studies come as no surprise to Marleen Ashton, who makes therapy dog visits with Lannie, a gentle, friendly four-year-old German Shepherd:

Lannie has always been a big hit. He's quite the showman. When he first comes into a room, he shakes paws and, if people lower their heads, will present them with a big, slobbery kiss. When we visited one lady in an assisted living facility, she insisted Lannie join her in her bed. I didn't think the bed could possibly hold both of them. But my eighty-five-pound Lannie gingerly snuggled up to this little lady in her tiny bed. She just held Lannie and hugged him tightly with a priceless grin from ear to ear.

One of Lannie's most memorable visits was to an assisted and skilled nursing facility:

> *As Lannie and I followed a nurse into one room, she announced, "Ray—you've got a visitor!" When a sullen-looking Ray didn't react, I asked, "Would you like to pet my dog?" Again, there was no response. Lannie walked in front of Ray and just stared at him, while the nurse and I turned our attention to the man in the next bed, who started asking questions about Lannie. As we became engaged in a conversation with Ray's roommate, Ray reached out a hand and started petting Lannie. A few minutes later, Ray began to softly talk to Lannie. Ray and my Lannie had had quite a conversation by the time we left the room. Once outside, the nurse pulled me aside, "You're not going to believe this, but Ray hasn't spoken to anyone for months. Nothing we could do would break down those walls around him. I can't believe I finally heard him speak."*
>
> *In the weeks that followed, we visited Ray regularly, and Ray also started talking to me. He was no longer the sullen, disengaged man we had first met but now greeted us each week with a smile. The supervisor was amazed at the tremendous change in Ray after Lannie's first visit—Ray started smiling, opening up, interacting with others, and enjoying life.*

Who knows how many lives have been touched by seemingly simple visits like those between Lannie and Ray. Lannie's gift to Ray changed

Figure 13.2. Marlene commends therapy dog Lannie on a job well done. You can almost hear Lannie responding, "All in a day's work for a therapy dog, Ma'am. All in a day's work."

his life and the lives of everyone Ray touches. When Ray turns to smile at his nurse tomorrow, part of that smile belongs to Lannie.

Keeshonden, also known as *wolf spitzes* or *Dutch barge dogs*, are beautiful dogs with fluffy manes and curled tails, known for their excellence in obedience and agility. These beautiful, bright, intelligent dogs have qualities that make them superb therapy dogs: They're outgoing, affectionate, good natured, and friendly. Just ask Marlene Miller, who has had three wonderful Keeshonden St. John Ambulance therapy dogs.

Marlene's Keeshonden have served people of all ages, from young children needing help reading to lonely elderly residents of a nursing home. Marlene will never forget one very special visit she and one of her dogs, Mitsu, made to an older man with Alzheimer's disease:

> *For almost five years now, my angel-dog, Mitsu, and I have visited a small nursing home. Actually, Mitsu visits—I just drive, hold the*

Figure   13.3. Proud Marlene and Keeshond Mitsu become a certified therapy dog handler team for St. John Ambulance therapy dogs.

leash, and open the doors. We had been visiting the nursing home regularly for about three months and Mitsu had a regular routine. First, Mitsu would visit Bill, who couldn't talk but would wave his arms to get Mitsu's attention, and then on to Sarah, a dear lady whose totally blank eyes always sprang to life the moment I held the dog up to her bed and a nurse guided Sarah's hand to stroke Mitsu's fuzzy Keesie coat.

One day, Mitsu had finished her rounds and, as we were about to leave, a young man reached over to stroke Mitsu. It is unusual to say the least to see youthful skin in this house of age and fragility. This young man with tears in his eyes was talking to Mitsu when he wistfully said, "I wish my dad could see you. We had a Keeshond when I was little, named Sheba, but she died a long time ago." Without hesitation, Mitsu and I followed the man to his dad's room, where Mitsu walked purposefully up to the bed, ignoring all the other people in the room.

Mitsu has always been extremely well behaved on visits and would never dream of putting even a paw on furniture. So I was startled as Mitsu began to climb onto the man's bed, one paw at a time. Slowly, she crept up towards the old man's face until she could burrow her nose in his neck. The man opened his eyes and focused his dying gaze on my lovely Keeshond and her alone. "Sheba, my beautiful Sheba," he crooned as he hugged her close and kissed her face.

After about five minutes, I quietly took Mitsu down. The young man followed us out to thank us. (Thank us!? What for!? Mitsu simply did what she was born to do and I was in total awe of her.) A few hours later, the old man died. And we know he was met by his beloved Sheba on the other side.

But that wasn't the end of this story for Marlene:

Three years later, I went on a cruise to Alaska and, not being a party-goer, retreated to the top deck every evening for a cup of tea and conversation with like-minded travelers. When you have a dog, it's hard not to include stories about them in your conversations.

One evening, I was telling a companion about Mitsu's work as a therapy dog in a nursing home in Newmarket, when suddenly an older woman grabbed my arm and shook me. "What home, what home?" she asked. When I told her, she hugged me crying and sob-bing. "You have the Keeshond!" she cried in my arms. "And you must be Sheba's mom," I concluded, crying myself.

This woman told me that that visit with Mitsu was the first time her husband had spoken in almost four years. She had wanted to send us a thank you note for giving him such happiness in his final moments, but she never got around to it. Her sons had sent her on this cruise to help cheer her up, but she really didn't want to be there. Now she knew the reason she was there.

Some people might say this encounter was just coincidence. I don't believe so—and neither does Mitsu.

Tail Waggin' Tip

"When people are greeted by a therapy dog, memories take over."— Ann Cadman, Health and Wellness Coordinator, Animal Friends

DOES VISITING SENIORS WITH FIDO *REALLY* MAKE A DIFFERENCE?

Researchers at the Veterans Affairs Medical Center in St. Louis, Missouri, answered this question by evaluating the effects of therapy dog visits on the loneliness of residents of nursing homes (Banks & Banks, 2002). There was a significant drop in loneliness among residents who received therapy dog visits, compared with those who did not receive visits. Also, interestingly, loneliness dropped about the same for folks who had a visit once a week and those who had one three times a week. This study highlights that occasional visits with therapy dogs can have enduring effects that last between visits.

Tail Waggin' Tip

Therapy dog visits—even occasional visits—have long-lasting effects in curbing loneliness in seniors.

Encouraging seniors to stay active can be another important goal for therapy dogs. Why is exercise important for seniors, and why are we talking about exercise when we've been focusing on memory? Researchers at Rush University in Chicago recently published research linking muscular and intellectual health in seniors in the *Archives of Neurology* (Boyle et al., 2009). In their study, a group of over 900 seniors without dementia were followed for over three years. During that time, 138 developed Alzheimer's disease. They found that seniors with increased muscle strength at the beginning of the study had a slower rate of declining intellectual function over time.

 Seniors with increased muscle strength have a forty-three percent *decreased risk* of later developing Alzheimer's disease (Boyle et al., 2009).

The protective effect of exercise on preventing memory loss was supported by additional work from researchers at Columbia University. Dr. Scarmeas and colleagues reported in the *Journal of the American Medical Association* that physical activity was linked to a reduced risk for developing Alzheimer's disease in seniors (Scarmeas et al., 2009):

- Compared with seniors doing essentially no physical activity, those doing some physical activity reduced their risk of Alzheimer's by one-fourth (twenty-five percent).
- Seniors doing much physical activity reduced their risk of developing Alzheimer's by one-third (thirty-three percent).

A subsequent study from this same research group showed that once people have Alzheimer's disease, physical activity doesn't affect their rate of additional memory loss (Scarmeas et al., 2010), although people who remain physically active do live longer.

Tail Waggin' Tip

Seniors who stay active and physically fit are less likely to develop Alzheimer's disease and more likely to live longer.

Unfortunately, a study conducted by researchers at the University of London and published in the *British Journal of Sports Medicine* found that most seniors don't get enough regular physical activity (Harris et al., 2009). Less than three percent of seniors were getting the recommended 150 minutes of weekly moderate-intensity exercise broken up into bouts of ten minutes or longer per session. That's fewer than three of every 100 seniors. And two of every three seniors got no—yes, that's not a typo—*no* moderate exercise.

What's the good news from this study? Well, there *were* folks getting their necessary weekly exercise. What two factors were linked to getting appropriate exercise? Taking long walks and *dog walking*. Yes, once again, science proves that having a pooch in your life gives you a big boost toward achieving important health and fitness goals. So if you're a senior with a dog: Congratulations—you've taken the first step to getting in your daily exercise. And if you know a senior, include him or her in your daily dog walks.

 14

The Healing Power Witnessed by Dog Handlers

Therapy dog handlers are special people, and each has a unique story to share. Before becoming therapy dogs, some dogs were in a shelter on the schedule to be euthanized, some had been beloved family pets, and some had successful careers as show dogs. But in each dog, their owners found special gifts that would make them extraordinary therapy dogs.

As a doctor, I'm used to seeing people during emotional times, but I'm still surprised by the healing release of emotions that occurs when I see patients with my dogs as well as how often it seems like these visits occur for the last person you see during an otherwise seemingly uneventful outing. Mr. Harrison was our last visit of the day for me and Wheatie when Wheatie was just starting to make hospital visits. Wheatie and I cheerfully knocked on the doorjamb and walked into Mr. Harrison's room, asking if he'd like a visit from a dog. When I saw the whole family clustered around Mr. Harrison in his bed, I knew the news couldn't be good and expected them to ask us to try again another time. Mr. Harrison's wife, however, turned around and said, "Why, I think that would be very nice." Turning back to her husband, a frail-looking middle-aged man in the bed, she said, "Honey, look who's coming to visit." As a doctor, I recognized the signs of severe liver disease in Mr. Harrison, the yellowed skin and markedly bloated belly. We rounded the bed, and before I could announce that this was Wheatie, Mr. Harrison sat up in bed, buried his hands deep into Wheatie's soft hair, and burst into sobs. Tears streamed down Mr. Harrison's face as

Wheatie showered him with kisses, with Mr. Harrison's fingers capturing every sensation from Wheatie's soft coat. I looked up to see his wife beaming, reporting that their daughter had two beloved Wheatens that Mr. Harrison missed very much. Soon, her eyes were a bit glossy, and I noticed his other visitors were all crying as well. Although their sorrow was foreign to me, and I really didn't understand their tears, it was very hard to fight back my own tears, surrounded by their grief. When we left, the family thanked us for the visit, stating, "You'll never understand what this visit meant to him." And they were right, I never would. I continued to be haunted by this visit and the combined joy and pain unleashed by the gentle kisses from a little terrier.

Wheatie and I couldn't resist returning to find out how Mr. Harrison was doing a few days later. Fearing the worse, we approached his doorway, hoping we wouldn't find that Mr. Harrison had been replaced by another patient. We were delighted to see that Mr. Harrison had returned to a more normal color, his belly had flattened, and his face looked bright. He was scheduled for discharge to a rehabilitation facility the next day and we knew he'd be taking a little bit of Wheaten love with him.

My other therapy dog, Toby, also a Wheaten, has only started making hospital visits and sees patients as well as family members waiting for their loved ones getting operations or being cared for in a trauma intensive care unit. As Toby makes his circuit around the waiting room, people often reach out to him, pull him to them, and bury their teary faces in his fur before telling him softly how they really needed a puppy hug. One attractive woman was waiting for her husband to come out of surgery and was expecting to hear bad news. She sat with her family and maintained a cheerful face when she spoke with me. Her attention soon turned to Toby and she grabbed his face on both sides by his full beard, drawing him to her. They sat nose to nose, with Toby occasionally giving doggie kisses and the woman sharing whispered secrets with him. The cheer she had showed the rest of us melted, and tears streamed down her cheeks as Toby ministered to her. When it was time to leave, she told Toby, "You have no idea what you did for me. It's such a sad day, and your being here makes me so happy."

Patients and their families who are visited by a therapy dog usually thank the handler for sharing the dog and spending time doing this important volunteer work. When this happens, most handlers look a bit surprised and embarrassed. If you try to tell a handler that they should be rewarded for the volunteer work they do, you'll most likely hear how they've already been rewarded—that their therapy–dog handler experience has been a blessing for the handler. Most handlers insist, "I get as much or more out of these visits as the patients we see."

Dana Wilson is no exception. She and her four-year-old Golden Retriever, Noel, have been a therapy dog–handler team for the last year. They make weekly visits to a nursing home and a hospital. While seeing patients at the hospital, Dana and Noel often stop in the trauma unit waiting room, where family members wait for the times when they might visit patients in the intensive care unit for trauma victims. This area is filled with tension, fear, and tears, as family members hope and pray for good news:

> The first time we walked into the trauma waiting area, we immediately saw a woman who looked like she'd been there quite a while, surrounded by pillows and tissues. She frantically waved us over and immediately started hugging and kissing Noel. As she was petting Noel, she and I both noticed the matching "Defending Freedom" bracelets we wore—mine for a cousin and hers for her son, who were both stationed overseas. Through Noel's visit, I was able to connect with this woman and share a bond that will long outlast the few minutes of our encounter.
>
> Working as a therapy dog handler has helped me become a better person. I've developed a deeper compassion for others, and better appreciation for my own health and happiness. The gifts I've received through Noel's work have inspired me to want to share her love of life and appreciation of the small things (mostly treats, but pets and ear scratches are okay, too) with as many people as possible. In fact, I strive to be more like Noel. I am grateful every day that Noel is my dog and my teacher.

Mary Ann Hirt has a pack of therapy dogs: ten-year-old Newfoundland mix Walker, seven-year-old Chocolate Lab mix Siena, and three-year-old Merle Great Dane Cooper. While I was writing this book, Mary Ann lost her beloved eight-year-old Black Labrador Retriever therapy dog, Sam. All four of her therapy dogs have taught

Figure 14.1. Noel and handler Dana share a passion for helping others.

her that it takes a special dog to be a therapy dog—although the dog's healing gifts may not have been initially recognized:

> *All of my dogs were shelter dogs who someone else had abandoned before I was lucky enough to have them come into my life. These dogs that other people "threw away" have made fabulous therapy dogs— giving back so much to so many people.*

The Rev. Danielle Di Bona rescued Naomi from the streets of Cleveland, Ohio. At the time, Danielle was working as a hospital chaplain at the Cleveland Clinic, and Naomi had found a soft heart in the hospital kitchen staff, who supplied her with pancakes. Danielle already had two dogs at home, but she was touched by this scruffy, dirty, eight-month-old puppy, so she took Naomi home with the intention of getting her cleaned up, properly trained, and ready for someone to adopt.

When Naomi was cleaned up, she turned out to be a very active Soft-Coated Wheaten Terrier, although Danielle and her husband usually referred to Naomi as the "Wheaten Terror." Danielle persevered and diligently worked with Naomi in obedience classes until Naomi was ready for adoption. Two days after leaving Naomi with her new family, Danielle got a call to come pick Naomi back up. Naomi had more obedience classes and another adoption—and this time she stayed three days before her high energy was too much for the family. Danielle and her family moved to Boston, Naomi a part of the pack. Danielle continued to take Naomi to obedience classes and, after twenty months of training, proudly got Naomi Canine Good Citizen, Temperament Tested, and Therapy Dogs International certified. And by this time, Naomi was Danielle's dog for good.

Danielle had relocated to Boston to work as a hospice chaplain, and therapy dog Naomi liked accompanying Danielle on her rounds:

> *Naomi took a lot of work, but she has become a wonderful therapy dog. People tell me that Naomi shows her soul in her eyes. I sometimes wonder if her suffering while she was living on the streets helped her recognize and understand suffering in others. She really hones in on those people who need her the most. I'm so lucky to have Naomi.*

It sort of makes you wonder—who rescued whom?

Callie is a seven-year-old Whippet–Wirehaired Fox Terrier mix whose path seemed destined to cross with that of the unsuspecting Sandy Grentz. A long-time dog lover, Sandy had lost her own dog to Cushing's disease six months earlier. Arriving home from a vacation in Kanab, Utah, Sandy decided to check out the pet section of her local newspaper:

> *I had never looked for a dog in the paper before, and I'm not quite sure why I did that day. But as I scanned through, I was drawn to the story on dogs rescued from Hurricane Katrina since my dad was born in New Orleans and had lived there until his early twenties.*

Figure   14.2. Whippet–Wirehaired Fox Terrier mix Callie and her fabulous mohawk.

I went online to read more about these Katrina dogs and saw Callie's picture. I knew I just had to meet this dog with a mohawk.

Sandy met Callie, and it was love at first sight. When she was told Callie's story, she knew destiny had intervened in matching her up with this wonderful dog:

Callie had lived in a home with two other dogs—both of whom were killed during Katrina. Callie had been left out on her own for a month before being rescued. She must have been very wily to have survived the lack of food and clean water and also the roaming packs of bully dogs. Callie was rescued by volunteers from Best Friends Animal Society in Kanab, Utah. They kept Callie in New Orleans for a bit, later sending her to Mississippi and eventually to a shelter closer to me in Washington, PA. The link with Kanab was freaky enough—but it turns out Callie lived in Jefferson Parish, the same parish-like county where my dad's family still lives!

Today, Sandy and Callie are a therapy dog–handler team. Callie's specialty is working with children. Callie has had amazing moments at Children's Hospital in Pittsburgh, Pennsylvania. She touched the life of a seven-year-old transplant recipient from Iceland whose mother acted as translator for him. Although neither boy nor Callie spoke the same verbal language, they shared a connection and a bond that transcended words and brought tears to Mom. Another small boy found Callie a pillar of strength. When Mom said to say hello to the dog, the sick little boy put his arm around Callie and placed his head on her back. This precious moment also needed no exchange of words. And in an intensive care unit, a little girl was in a bed too high to see Callie and too full of tubes for Callie to jump up. Although she was very sick, this bright little girl was an avid dog lover, eagerly sharing everything she knew about dogs with Sandy. Knowing how much the little girl longed to see Callie, her mother asked if the girl's male private duty nurse could lift Callie up for the girl to see. Sandy agreed, although no stranger had ever lifted Callie before. The man gently lifted Callie and held her for the girl to touch. Callie seemed to understand—never flinching or squirming in this stranger's arms.

Sandy's face lights up as she talks about Callie's visits:

> The visits mean so much to these children. The other handlers and I give the children wallet-size photos of our dogs when we visit. I take lots of shots of Callie in different hats and costumes to pass out at different seasons of the year—and I always stamp a pawprint and write "Your friend Callie" on the back of Callie's pictures. The kids collect these like trading cards, and they really mean a lot to them. What I like the most is the look on a child's face when he sees Callie and I give him Callie's picture. Families will tell me, "That's the first time he's smiled!" or they'll softly whisper "Thank you so much" in my ear as we leave the room. For the therapy dog handler—that's the payment.

Sadie is a Bouvier des Flandres—a great black dog with a fall of hair covering her eyes and a fabulous beard—who seemed destined for therapy work. Known as a cow herding dog, Sadie fit right in at Jane and Rick Miller's farm. Soon, however, the Jane discovered that Sadie had an extraordinary intuition:

> Sadie has shown an uncanny ability to sniff out a problem in the neighborhood. One day Sadie insisted on going to the back fence. Rick and I stood on the porch and he said, "Sadie, what is it, Girl?"

I chided him that he was talking to her like Lassie when he said, "I think Sadie wants us to follow her." He opened the gate, and Sadie raced up the alley to our neighbor's house. We opened the gate, and Sadie bounded to the back door. That's when our neighbor's grandson, about twelve at the time, opened the door to let her in. The three grandchildren had arrived to pick up Grandma to go to the funeral home for the private family time before their grandfather's services. The three children, Grandma, and their mom patted Sadie, cried, and hugged her, and then Sadie was ready to come home.

About a month after that, Sadie stood at the back door, and I opened it, and she raced to the gate again. This time we didn't have to ask, "What is it, Girl?" I just followed, opened the gate, and again she bounded up the alley to the house of an older neighbor, Judith. Now widowed, Judith lived alone. I didn't wait for someone to come to the door, I followed, and opened the door calling Judith's name. Sadie raced ahead of me to the next room where Judith was lying on the floor. Judith was in great pain and couldn't get up. She just cried and hugged Sadie, saying, "You're worth more than a gallon of morphine!" The next month, I enrolled Sadie in a therapy dog class to prepare her for Therapy Dogs International testing. She'd shown me over and over that she was destined to be a therapy dog.

Patients, their caregivers, and their visitors often need a comforting touch, but it's hard to find that sometimes during a busy day at the hospital and perhaps harder to ask a person for a hug than it is to ask the same from the therapy dogs. Therapy dogs can develop a bit of celebrity status, and handler Anita DeBiase has learned to expect the unexpected when making rounds with her Bloodhound, Louie:

You never know who's going to need some Louie time. One day when Louie and I were seeing hospital patients, we heard a voice in the distance calling, "Hey Doggie!" I turned around to see a young boy literally chasing us down the hall—looking expectantly across the hallway bridge that joined the hospital wing where he was visiting a family member to the one where Louie and I were about to see our patients. He really needed some pet therapy, and it was a privilege to turn and move across that bridge so we could meet this boy halfway for his needed Louie hug.

Louie makes a statement wherever he goes: He's big and beautiful, and he has an instinctive nose to sniff out where he's most needed. Anita and Louie went to an intensive care unit to fulfill a special request to visit a young quadriplegic boy:

> I'd never taken Louie to an intensive care unit before, so I wasn't quite sure how Louie would react. Bloodhounds weigh about 100 pounds—so that's a lot of dog to move around all the tubes, lines, and equipment in intensive care. The boy's father asked us if Louie could get up on the bed, and I helped Louie onto the foot of the bed. Once on the bed, this big Bloodhound stood up and, avoiding stepping on arms and legs that couldn't move away, slowly crept up toward the head of the bed. The boy's father and I watched in amazement as Louie continued until his nose was at the boy's face. Louie seemed to understand—and while the boy couldn't reach up to pet Louie, Louie could give love to the boy. Louie gently nuzzled the boy's neck and face. The boy's face lit up into a great smile, and so did his dad's as tears streamed down his cheeks.

You don't need to be a big dog to make a big impression. Janet Malinsky's previous Toy Manchester therapy dog, Lindsey, was always a big hit at the nursing home, but one lady got a special visit each week:

> Mae really loved my Lindsey and told everyone Lindsey was "her" dog. She'd get the biggest kick each visit when Lindsey made Mae's room her first stop. Lindsey would dash down the hall and into Mae's room and would jump up on her bed. And every week Mae would tell me, "See—she's MY dog."

Therapy dogs also touch the hearts of those they visit and their handlers. Debbie Brown lives with two wonderful St. John Ambulance therapy dogs: twelve-year-old Soft-Coated Wheaten Terrier Hayley and fourteen-and-a-half-year-old Standard Poodle Natalie:

> Both are incredible, but very different girls. Hayley visits a retirement home on Tuesday nights and the people love the fact that her tongue and tail are attached. She kisses everyone and wags her tail continuously. Poodle Natalie visits with special needs adults on Friday nights for an hour before dinner. One of my fondest memories is of Natalie at the L'Arche House.

Natalie visits Brian, a fifty-four-year-old gentleman who is developmentally delayed and has physical disabilities, needing a walker to get around. He loves Natalie so much that I once gave him a stuffed Black Poodle that looks like Natty for his birthday. Natty's proper name is Natalie Cole, so Brian named his stuffed Poodle Coco. The staff tell me that every night Brian goes to sleep with Coco in his arms.

Brian doesn't understand if Natalie misses her regular visit with him and gets very upset. So when Natalie had some eye surgery to remove a small but bothersome skin tag, we visited Brian anyway, even though she was a bit messy from her eye medicine. Brian knew Natty was having eye surgery and deeply touched my heart when presented her with a beautiful candle he'd made just for her in a craft studio where he works. "Put this candle next to your bed and it'll help Natty see better," Brian assured me. I just cried.

Figure 14.3. Brian and Standard Poodle therapy dog Natalie. Photo courtesy of Tomek Sewilski from L'Arche Daybreak.

Like many therapy dogs, Soft-Coated Wheaten Terrier Naomi wore a bit of bling, with several tags recognizing her accomplishments as a therapy dog. The staff in the hospital she visited came to recognize her jingling tags as she'd exit the elevator to cheers of "Naomi's here!" As soon as the staff heard her coming, they'd flock to greet her, saying "I *really* needed Naomi today." At the other end of the leash was Naomi's handler—silent partner Danielle Di Bona:

> *I've even had the staff tell me, "If you're too busy some day, you don't really need to come. Just send Naomi and we'll pay her cab fare!" I know they're making a joke, but I'm also smart enough to know that in a way, they're really not joking.*

In the Glagola household, Pauline says there's one simple rule: "You have to earn your keep by making others happy." That rule applies to dogs and humans alike. Pauline, her husband, and their three therapy dogs have taken that message to heart and go above and beyond just simply earning their keep. Therapy dogs Australian Shepherd–Bernese Mountain Dog mix Rocky and Cocker Spaniels Chip and Sigmund have done it all, from reading programs with young children to bingo with seniors.

Cocker Spaniel Chip died in November 2009, but not before leaving an impact with his visits to Residence at Hilltop and Monongahela Valley Hospital in Monongahela, Pennsylvania. One of Chip's favorite "customers" was Cilly Herman. Cilly had had a tough life—born in Berlin in 1919, she was a Holocaust survivor who came to the United States in 1950, eventually moving to Monogahela, Pennsylvania, where she and her husband ran a successful fur business:

> *Tiny, ninety-pound Cilly would light up when Chip would strut down the hall and call, "Cheep," in her German accent. She'd pet Chip and share amazing stories of her past—seeing Cilly was like a living history lesson. When Cilly became ill and was moved to the hospital at age eighty-nine, a visit from Chip seemed to strengthen her and she surprised the staff by moving back to the residence facility in a week. Through his visits, Chip left pawprints on Cilly's heart.*

Chip must have known he wouldn't be around forever and that Cilly would still need therapy visits when he would no longer be able

Figure 14.4. Glagola family therapy dog Rocky enjoys spending time with Cilly. Photo courtesy of Ron Paglia.

to make them. Chip knowingly rescued a stray cat from a window well, which the Glagolas adopted and named Clyde:

> *One rainy day, we were late to leave for our usual therapy visit and Chip just refused to come—which was so unlike him. Chip was staring into the window well, pacing back and forth. And there, in the window well, we found a stray cat—stuck and soaked to the skin. We brought the wet cat in, Chip gave him a big lick, and their friendship started. We named the cat Clyde and had a new member for our therapy team.*

Naturally, Clyde joined the family in their visits—making Cilly's wheelchair one of their regular stops, even when Chip was no longer around to make visits with him: "Our weekly visits gave Cilly something to look forward to. Cilly knew what day it was because of the schedule for Chip and Clyde's visits to see her."

Saturday, May 15, 2010, Clyde made his usual visit to then–ninety-one-year-old Cilly:

> *When it was time to go, Clyde refused to leave Cilly's side and insisted on nuzzling Cilly for half an hour. I understood something important was happening and sat quietly while Clyde did his work. Finally, Clyde consented to leave and the next day, Cilly passed.*

Although Chip hadn't been able to stay for Cilly, his sidekick Clyde carried on Chip's work, leaving pawprints of love on Cilly's heart.

I have often wondered what families think when a loved one tells them he or she was visited by a dog in the hospital. Anita DeBiase found out when she and Louie made their rounds one day:

> *Soon after we entered one lady's room, we noticed she was talking on the phone. I could tell she really wanted to spend some time with Louie, so I softly promised we'd come back after she'd finished her call. Later, when we walked back past the nurse's station, the head nurse stopped us. "We just got the funniest phone call from Mrs. Miller's sister. Mrs. Miller was talking with her sister on the phone when Mrs. Miller started going on and on to her sister about a big dog outside her room. Once she'd hung up, the sister called us right away and asked if we could check on Mrs. Miller. She thought Mrs. Miller must have gotten too many drugs because she was hallucinating." With a smile on my face, Louie and I went to Mrs. Miller's room with a funny story to share. Mrs. Miller got the biggest kick out of the mistake, and I bet, as soon as we left, called her sister right back and had a bit of fun at her expense.*

Do therapy dog visits really make a difference? Absolutely—just ask Kad Favorite, who has been making visits with her three-year-old Golden Doodle, Lucy, since Lucy passed her Canine Good Citizen test at the very young age of eight months. Kad and Lucy visit residents of nursing home Grace Manor in Allison Park, Pennsylvania, once a month:

It's less than an hour of my time each week, but for many of the residents, that brief time makes their whole month. I've really seen Lucy change people's lives. When Lucy approaches the bedside, people feeling miserable and cut off from everyone else will pop up to greet Lucy. Their whole demeanor changes and they become more engaged.

Margaret just lives for Lucy's visits. When it's time to leave, she stands at the door and watches until we're completely out of sight, which makes it very hard for us to leave. The staff tell me that for the rest of the month, Margaret talks about Lucy over and over and eagerly awaits her next visit.

Therapy dog handlers frequently underestimate the profound impact their dogs make on those they visit. The Rev. Danielle Di Bona often visits terminally ill patients in their homes, providing comfort and spiritual strength during difficult times. On many visits, she takes Naomi:

When I started visiting Sarah, she'd only let Naomi into her kitchen. Sarah had a beautiful home and was very fastidious. Sarah and I would sit in her parlor, but Naomi stayed in the kitchen for months before Sarah finally agreed that Naomi wouldn't cause too much damage by joining us in the parlor.

When Sarah was dying, I got a phone call from her family, "Sarah's asking for Naomi." That's right—she wasn't asking for her chaplain, but for her therapy dog. So I took Naomi to see Sarah, who asked if Naomi could join her on her bed. I sat quietly in the room that afternoon while Naomi ministered to Sarah. Sarah was the last thing Naomi saw before she passed. And I know Naomi—the same dog who was initially banished to the kitchen—gave Sarah great comfort in her last moments in a way that I don't think I could have.

Even a single visit with a therapy dog can sometimes make a lifelong impression. Mary Ann Hirt has been working with therapy dogs for several years. Mary Ann helped show her friend and new therapy dog handler, Claire Rumpler, the ropes by going on some hospital visits together:

Claire and I really were a study in contrasts—she with her seven-pound Maltese–Poodle mix Makena and me with my 120-pound Great Dane Cooper. We brought this canine odd couple to visit Alyssa, a teenager

Figure 14.5. Claire holds up little Maltese–Poodle mix Makena while Thom and Mary Ann surround Merle Great Dane Cooper.

on the neurology floor who had been a patient too long and had become quite depressed. Her family told us they hadn't seen Alyssa smile for over two weeks and were lost for how to help her. It only took Alyssa a short gaze at our silly couple—the great and the small—before she broke out into a huge smile, grinning from ear to ear. Her delight spread to her family, and soon everyone was smiling.

As a therapy dog handler, there are days when you make visits and you really wonder if you made an impact or not. It's often on those visits that seem most ordinary that your dog touches someone in an extraordinary way. Usually, we never learn about this impact, and Mary Ann's story is a great example of how what seemed like only "a little smile" was really much, much more.

It was many months before Mary Ann thought about the visit she and Claire had made and learned about the tremendous impact that short visit had on a young girl's life:

I didn't think much about this visit until about a year later, when the hospital's volunteer director asked me to meet our newest therapy dog volunteer. Imagine my surprise when I was greeted by a beautiful

Bernese Mountain Dog attached to a leash held by Alyssa. "What made you decide to do therapy dog work?" I asked the now–18-year-old Alyssa. She told me, "When I was in the hospital last year, a couple of dogs came to visit me and it really made such a difference. If those dogs could help me so much, I knew dogs could help others, too. So when I got home, I trained my dog to become a therapy dog."

So the gift shared with Alyssa by Mary Ann and Claire has now been passed forward. And who knows—that shy little boy you stop to greet today before visiting his grandma may be tomorrow's therapy dog handler.

After talking with Mary Ann about her visit with Alyssa Applequist, I was lucky to get in touch with Alyssa, who shared her side of what it's like to get a therapy dog visit:

I became motivated to become part of the pet therapy program after I was in the hospital myself and was visited by a Great Dane and Malti-Poo. During the spring of my junior year in high school, I was admitted to Allegheny General Hospital for an autoimmune disease. I couldn't believe how happy seeing these dogs for just ten minutes made me. I immediately thought how happy Troy could make patients in the hospital.

That summer, I started training with Troy at Misty Pines Dog Park in Wexford to get his therapy dog certification. Troy and I passed the test the first time we took it that fall, and I was soon able to start taking Troy to be a therapy dog. That year, I took Troy to a rehabilitation center a couple of times to visit my grandfather as well as the other patients. Then the summer before my senior year of high school, I took full advantage of the program and began taking Troy to, of course, Allegheny General once a week.

During the interview at the hospital, I met with the woman who owned the Great Dane that inspired me to become part of the wonderful program. She was so touched by the story, and this is proof that the program does good.

During my pet therapy visits I have seen many patients, but one story stands out more than others. There was a mentally challenged teenage boy in one of rooms at the hospital who was having a particularly bad week. I went in to find him sitting in a chair holding his toys close, almost as if the action figures were protecting him. The boy's mother was also sitting in the room, and both were happy to see Troy. The boy got somewhat of a smile on his face watching Troy as I was talking to him and his mother. Then the boy said, "Can I pet him?" Of course he could, and I told him that my dog's name is Troy. "Troy," he whispered. Then his mother told me that this was the first time the boy had spoken in almost a week.

Not only does the pet therapy program help the patients in hospitals, but the staff members benefit as well. No one is happier to see Troy than the nursing staff, who know Troy so well and have even bought treats for him. I am so glad that I decided to become a part of the pet therapy program, and I have not only become a better person because of it, but I have become closer with Troy than ever before. I hope more than ever that what Troy and I do brightens the days of others.

The healing power of therapy dogs is not limited to the patients they visit: Patients, their families, hospital workers, and other people

Figure 14.6. Receiving therapy dog visits while she was a patient inspired Alyssa to pursue therapy dog work with Bernese Mountain Dog Troy. Today, Alyssa and Troy pass on the healing from Alyssa's therapy dog visits from Merle Great Dane Cooper and Maltese–Poodle mix Makena to the next generation of future therapy dog handlers.

who spend a few moments with a therapy dog can all be touched in profound ways. Handlers sometimes expect the joy that therapy dogs bring to patients. It's often a surprise when discovering that therapy dogs leave a mark on many lives along the dog's path to a patient's bedside.

Dr. Richard Statman is a mathematician at Carnegie Mellon University. His research focuses on *symbolic computation*, the use of algebra and calculus to solve complex math equations. Yeah—I have no idea what that means, either. But not a lot baffles Rick. If you've got a problem, he'll likely design a complex series of equations to crack it. When Rick started making therapy visits with his buff-colored Cocker Spaniel Pandora, even he was a bit surprised that results added up to far more than he'd thought had gone into the therapy dog equation:

> *Pandora has been making therapy visits for about five years. Together, we've made about seventy-five visits, mostly at the University of Pittsburgh's Shadyside Hospital. We started going to Shadyside because I spent a lot of time there as a patient a few years ago, and I wanted to give something back.*
>
> *There are two things that I didn't anticipate about pet therapy. Number one is that we are there as much for the nurses and staff as we are for the patients. The nurses are under a lot of stress, and playing with Pandora is a great stress reliever for them. Number two is that the most joy Pandora brings is probably to the surgical waiting rooms. Pandora has taken to visiting several of these rooms on her way to see patients. It had never occurred to me before we started making visits how sad and depressing these rooms can be—so full of people waiting and worrying— uncertain about what comes next. Pandora's presence puts smiles on their faces, at least for the few minutes she is there.*

So for Rick and Pandora, one plus one equals countless smiles, joy, and happiness for those many people they greet on their way to patient rooms. Now that's math we all can understand.

Best-selling author, cancer survivor, and founder of the American Wellness Project Greg Anderson encourages people to "focus on the journey, not the destination." Therapy dogs understand that a lot of their work occurs on the journey between visits during seemingly casual contacts with concerned visitors and overworked caregivers. Sandy Grentz also understands that her visits with Callie help patients, as well as their families and the staff:

> *Seeing a therapy dog provides a much-needed and welcome relief for so many people. We see patients in a university teaching hospital, so when we come around a corner, we sometimes run into a group of junior doctors discussing their patients with a senior doctor. I'm always a bit hesitant to interrupt their conversations, but one doctor will turn around, and then another, and before I know it, the senior doctor is waving us over so Callie can meet the whole group. That little break from Callie's visit takes some of their stress away and I leave the group seeing their faces brighter and shoulders held a bit higher. Callie carries some of their burdens away with her.*

Some days when you're making visits, it's easy to get discouraged—especially when you get turned down from people who don't want visits from your dog. One day, Toby and I were seeing hospital patients and we were accompanied by a photographer from our local newspaper who planned to snap photos of Toby with a couple patients for a story on therapy dogs. Normally when we get to our usual nurse's station, we're given a list of eight or ten patients who might like a visit. On this afternoon, the nurses were really too busy to think of patients and we ended up visiting four hospital wings before we were given a list of three patients to see. Although one of these patients didn't want a visit, the man in the next bed was thrilled to see Toby. Toby had a great visit and really lifted that man's spirit. The other patients we visited were equally excited to have a dog visit, and we left both patients with big smiles on their faces and joy in their hearts. We may have been turned down by most of the folks that day, but those who were visited clearly appreciated their time with Toby. Don't let slow days get you down. This work is important.

May Seman used humor when meeting patients not interested in seeing a therapy dog when making visits with Lhasa Apso Latte:

> *Latte and I were at one of the local hospitals visiting the rehabilitation unit. The rooms are marked to show which patients want the dogs and which ones do not. In one particular room, the patient by*

the door wanted therapy dog visits and the other patient did not. The room was divided with the usual hospital curtain for privacy. Latte and I were visiting the patient by the door, and she was receiving much attention from him and his family. However, partially due to her curious nature and her ego not allowing her to think that anyone wouldn't be thrilled to see her, Latte peeked her little head around the curtain. I apologized saying, "Sorry; Latte can't read." Upon seeing Latte, the patient's wife said, "Oh look, how cute she is. Please let her come over." She then informed me that her husband likes dogs but was just having a bad day. Latte promptly walked toward him, looking determined to cheer him up. The man smiled and began to pet Latte—she'd clearly succeeded in her task. And I'm sure, at least for awhile, this man's day was made better. As we were leaving the room I thought to myself, "Latte can't read—but she knows where she's needed."

After Latte's visit, a new sign was posted by this man's door—welcoming therapy dogs.

You'll often find Clyde Schauer and her Soft-Coated Wheaten Terrier Lacey in the winner's circle, earning titles in obedience and rally. Clyde's other Wheaten, Crystal, had a successful start to her obedience career, earning American Kennel Club titles: a Companion Dog title for standard obedience testing in novice competitions and the Rally Excellent title for completing obedience skills through rally courses that combine obedience, agility, and excellent communication between handler and dog. At eight years old, Crystal may not collect winning ribbons these days, but she is still a champion in her role for the last four years as a certified therapy dog. Crystal has won Clyde's heart and the hearts of those lucky enough to be visited by Crystal and Clyde:

Crystal is a lovely little Soft-Coated Wheaten Terrier. Little she is-she weighs only twenty-four pounds, quite a bit under the standard for her breed. While the judges in competitions may not like Crystal's size, she's just the right size to cuddle up next to a patient in a hospital bed. Crystal is certified through the Delta Society and is an active member of the PAWS [Pet Assisted Wellness] team at Stanford Hospital, in Palo Alto, California.

At Stanford Hospital, we are met before each visit in the vestibule by our team coordinator, who gets signed releases from the patients we are to visit. While we wait, a staff member who has experienced a difficult day will often ask if he or she may join us on our bench for a rejuvenating hug from Crystal. They just sit next to Crystal and hold her close to them without saying anything, and after a few minutes, they thank me and tell me they feel much relieved and head on their way. Hospital doctors often sign up for a visit from Crystal in their prep room. Crystal leans against their legs for a petting or pops up onto a lap when invited. These doctors tell me having a visit from Crystal helps reduce their stress—that's good for them and their patients.

One patient we visited was a man who had been in the hospital for six months. He was undergoing detox from prescription pain medications before he could have necessary back surgery. When he spotted Crystal, he took her and held her tight to his chest while tears rolled down his face. He told me that this was the first happy moment he had experienced in his lengthy stay. "I just love this little dog," he said; "She makes me feel as if I have a life to live." Of course, I was teary, too, as was our team leader, who came in as he was speaking.

Another memorable visit we had was with a young man surrounded by his family. He had been thrown from a car and barely survived. Since he was heavily bandaged and somewhat sedated, I held Crystal in my arms as close to him as I could manage. The man had difficulty communicating, but petted Crystal and held onto her leg. We did not stay very long. Two weeks later, the man was moved to a rehabilitation area of the hospital and one of his staff members sent a message to me that the man wanted to let me know how much Crystal's visit had helped him and how the time with Crystal really had made him feel better. It is so nice to know that our visits make meaningful impressions, and that we really do make a change in people's lives.

It isn't always a doctor or patient who values the support of a pet visit. One afternoon, Crystal and I were in the parking lot, preparing to go home after finishing our visits. Crystal still had on her red PAWS scarf and I my red volunteer apron. As we were preparing to get into the car, I was surprised by a man rapidly approaching us. The man never raised his head but crouched down, asking if he could

Figure 14.7. Eight-year-old Wheaten Crystal takes handler Clyde to visit patients in acute care units at Stanford Hospital in Palo Alto, California, and a senior living complex called The Sequoias. Identification tags and the Pet Assisted Wellness (PAWS) apron show everyone Clyde and Crystal are ready to spread the healing power of the therapy dog. Like many therapy dogs, Crystal has her favorite spots to visit, preferring hospital sites, where visits are more predictable and controlled.

pet my dog for a moment. I tentatively said, "Yes." He held Crystal in his arms moaning softly while tears poured from his eyes. I asked him if he was having a sad day, and he replied that it had been a sad day indeed. He thanked me, saying that he really needed that hug from Crystal and felt much better. Then he disappeared from sight.

Visits are draining for both Crystal and me, and when we get home she always goes into her crate and sleeps for an hour or so. It's as though she has given her energy to those who need a boost when she visits them. Being a therapy dog has given Crystal an opportunity to feel very special in an area so different from the drudgery *of obedience classes and the anxiety of dog shows. She eagerly trots into facilities at my side and looks for the first person with a petting hand. She gives love, but she gets love back. A perfect job for a dog.*

As a show dog, Colored Bull Terrier Rufus is a bit of an over-achiever. Best known for winning Best In Show at the Westminster Kennel Club in 2006—the first Colored Bull Terrier to ever achieve this title—Rufus has won a total of thirty-five Best In Show awards and holds 750 titles, including champion titles in America, Canada, world, and the Americas competitions. Rufus's official name in the show ring was "Multiple BIS/BISS, American, Canadian, Mexican, World, Americas, Champion Rocky Tops Sundance Kid, ROM." BIS stands for Best In Show, BISS stands for Best in Specialty Show, and ROM stands for Register of Merit. That's a mouthful of medals.

Since his Westminster win, Rufus went on to earn new titles: Canine Good Citizen and Therapy Dogs International certifications. This Best In Show dog is now usually just called Rufus in his new job as show dog turned therapy dog, visiting patients in nursing homes and hospitals, children in schools, and people in need of a lift on the street. When owner Barbara Bishop modestly talks about ten-year-old Rufus and his work as a therapy dog, you'd never guess this mild-mannered dog was a renowned champion:

> *Rufus is a doll. He's a Bull Terrier, and I think people are drawn to him because he's such an odd-looking dog with his egg-shaped head and triangular eye. I've even had people stop me on the street to say, "Lady, that's the ugliest dog I've ever seen." I just smile and reply that beauty's in the eye of the beholder.*

Barb credits Rufus's unique appearance for some of his success in therapy dog work:

> *I think that since Rufus doesn't have a lot of the features and grace most people attribute to beautiful dogs he appeals to people who also see themselves as not being perfect. Maybe they see themselves as having certain problems, being a bit of an underdog, or as having a different mind set. For whatever reason, Rufus speaks to them. When people see Rufus, they don't see the champion show dog. Instead,*

they see a soft face that's doesn't look like a star and would probably understand their problems.

Since retiring from the show ring, Rufus has done a lot of therapy dog work. He attends programs with special needs children in school. When working with autistic children, kids who have been nonverbal have said their first words when they see Rufus, and children who have been afraid of dogs don't fear Rufus when they see him. Again, Barb credits some of this to Rufus not looking like "a typical dog."

Rufus also enjoys his weekly visits to a nursing home:

People at the nursing home know that Rufus is a retired show dog, and his weekly visits are like having a celebrity come in. I hear more stories about General Patton's famous Bull Terrier, Willie, who followed the general everywhere. Veterans at the nursing home spot Rufus and he brings back memories of their service and younger days. One lady with Alzheimer's disease becomes a different person whenever she sees Rufus. He seems to give her a sense of calm and peace in a way just having me visit never would.

One of Rufus's most memorable visits was to the Walter Reed Army Medical Center to visit wounded soldiers:

We met one woman whose son had been serving as a bomb technician in Afghanistan. He'd suffered severe injuries after a bomb had exploded and was initially sent to Germany to be stabilized before coming home to Walter Reed. When we first went into the room, I didn't see how Rufus could possibly get near this young man. Rufus is a big and clumsy dog, and there were tubes and wires coming from everywhere on the man. When I said I didn't think Rufus could get close enough to the young man, his mother was adamant that she wanted her son to pet Rufus.

Although I didn't think it was possible, somehow Rufus found a teeny open spot where he might get close to this man. It was incredible to see this big dog moving like a ballerina through wires and tubes. It was like magic that he could somehow squeeze into the tiny available spot. But Rufus was able to guide himself next to the man and rose up on his hind legs into the small open area so this wounded warrior could pet him. The soldier seemed mesmerized by

Figure 14.8. Rufus takes owners Barb and Tom to Walter Reed Army Medical Center to visit veterans who have sacrificed so much through their service.

Rufus as he watched Rufus come to him. And once Rufus was in reach, there was just wonderful joy. The man's mother was in tears, and I had trouble holding back tears myself. I didn't think Rufus could possibly get close enough to the wounded warrior, but somehow he was determined and found a way to get close to him and close to his heart.

As Barb, her husband Tom, and Rufus were leaving Walter Reed, they stopped in the Red Cross office to say their goodbyes:

Rufus was just hanging out as we were chatting with the Red Cross workers. A young man came in, spotted Rufus, and yelled, "Chico, Chico!" Chico was the Bull Terrier in the 2000 movie "Next Friday." The young man then got down on the floor and started playing and rolling around with Rufus. Rufus was having the time of his life, playing and giving doggie kisses. I'm a big hip hop fan and have a hip hop song for my ringtone. As the young man was playing with my "Chico," my phone rang and the young man joked, "Hey lady, is that your phone or mine?" He then started telling us about the hip hop groups he enjoyed listening to and finished playing with Rufus. After about twenty-five minutes with this man, it was time to go and we left the Red Cross office.

When we reached the lobby, we were stopped by one of the Red Cross workers, who told us, "I have to tell you something. That young man in the office playing with Rufus has been one of our untouchables. He came back from Iraq last year and no one has been able to break through to him. Today was the first day that he has spoken with anyone. What Rufus did in there was miraculous."

Somehow, my funny-looking dog reached this man, and I hope that day truly was a turning point in this young man's life who sacrificed so much for the rest of us with his service. It was amazing how Rufus could connect with him and reach him in a way others couldn't.

In 2010, Rufus was one of only five dogs nationwide to receive the American Kennel Club Humane Fund Awards for Canine Excellence for his therapy work. He also served as the 2010 Therapy Dog Ambassador at the National Dog Show presented by Purina. But Rufus's work will continue in what Barbara calls his "street ministry—greeting people he passes on the street and leaving smiles behind."

Therapy dog handlers often joke that they're just the one who drives the car, holds the leash, and pushes the elevator buttons—that the real worker on their team is the dog. In many ways, those little quips really aren't jokes at all. Therapy dog handlers soon discover that the therapy dog is the star of the show and the handler often blends into the background.

I always tell people that being a pet therapy handler is easy; it truly is all about the dog. When I first started making visits, someone asked me what I talked about with the patients we visited. After thinking a few minutes, I said, "You know, I really don't say much. I just tell them Wheatie's name and breed and answer any questions they have about him. After that, the patients just talk directly to Wheatie and I'm kind of invisible. Wheatie's really the volunteer; I'm just his transportation." Sometimes I do have lengthy conversations with patients, but when I poke my head in the next week I'm usually greeted with a look of no recognition until the patient's eyes drop down to see Wheatie or Toby. Then the smiles come and the patient says lovingly to my terrier, "Oh, I remember YOU!"

Therapy dog–handler team Janet Malinsky and Barbara Pohodich and their pups follow their patients from nursing home to hospice. When a person does pass, Janet and Barbara often share their respects at the funeral home. Barbara recalled the following experience:

One time, I was getting tentative nods as I offered condolences to family members of a dear man we'd just lost, and I could tell they weren't sure who I was. "You don't recognize me without my dog," I said, explaining that I was Sadie's mom. At the mention of my therapy dog Sadie's name, eyes filled with tears and I received warm, heartfelt hugs, and stories of how Sadie had been a blessing for them and their loved one.

Janet remembers the most memorable viewing she attended:

Linda was an unfortunate woman with severe diabetes. She became blind at age eighteen and had lost her leg from infections when she got older. She had lived for many years in a nursing home and died at age fifty-five. One of the worst things for her about coming to the nursing home was having to give up her own dog—so our therapy dogs really filled an important void. One week, I saw that Linda was sleeping, so I decided to skip my visit with her rather than waking her. Boy, did I catch it the next week! "You better always wake me up when you visit—or you'll be in big trouble." After that, I never missed a visit.

Even though Linda was blind, she always wanted us to take pictures of her with my dogs. Her walls were lined with picture after picture of her with all the dogs who visited her. I was stunned, though, when I saw Linda at her viewing and the inside of her casket was covered with pictures of her and the therapy dogs. I don't think there was an inch of space that didn't have a photo on it. These dogs had been her joy and comfort throughout her time at the nursing home. And now they were her comfort as they carried her through her passing. They talk about dog's crossing over the

*Rainbow Bridge when they die, and I like to think that a bit of our
dogs helped Linda in her crossing, too.*

Barb and Janet touch so many lives so profoundly—all by walking next
to a cute and cuddly therapy dog who really does all the magic.

Gabe O'Neill knows how scary it can be in a hospital. When
his daughter, MaryMargaret, was six years old, the doctor told
him it looked like she had leukemia. After ten frightening days in
the hospital, they received the good news that it was just an infection and that MaryMargaret would be fine. This experience, however, deeply affected both Gabe and his daughter. Working with
his daughter, Gabe later developed the Kids Are Heroes Web site
(http://www.kidsareheroes.org), which recognizes kids who are
doing outstanding things for their communities and encourages
other kids to get involved in making a difference. MaryMargaret,
now eleven years old, raised money to buy 250 MP3 players for
hospitalized children to help them when they get scared or bored.
Her efforts are included with those of other children performing
amazing charity work across the country through the Kids Are
Heroes Web site.

Before getting involved with Kids Are Heroes, Gabe also started
a therapy dog group in Fredrick, Maryland, in 2006 with his dog,
Charlie, called Wags for Hope:

*Charlie and I had been visiting a local nursing home for about two
years when our curiosity got the best of us. We wondered what it
would be like to try another location. Charlie is a 120-lb Bernese
Mountain Dog who is a tad intimidating to some at first, so I wondered what kind of reception we would get. As we walked through
the doors of the assisted living facility, the nurse announced us over
the loudspeaker, "There's a huge dog out here in the lobby." All
of a sudden I looked down both hallways and saw doors opening.
Walkers and wheelchairs appeared from all over and slowly con-
verged on Charlie. Charlie sensed my nervousness and immediately
sat down, looking right at me as if to say, "Don't sweat it—I'll take
care of this one."*

*Charlie sat calmly and patiently letting everyone dote over
him. It was an amazing sight. "When are you coming back? When*

Figure 14.9. Cathy enjoys a visit with Bernese Mountain Dog Charlie and handler Gabe.

will we see Charlie again?" Wow—I have to get people to help me do this, I thought. That was the instant that Wags for Hope was born.

Today, *Wags for Hope* has over 100 therapy dog–handler teams who visit nursing homes, hospitals, assisted living facilities, day care centers for elderly individuals, and elementary school reading programs. Charlie, Gabe, and MaryMargaret understand the importance of volunteering and have found personal ways to make a difference for people in need, setting examples showing how each of us we can make a difference in the lives of people in our neighborhoods.

Resources

A fter reading this book, I hope you're inspired to learn more about the important healing work of therapy dogs. In this Resources section you'll find a variety of places to go to find out more about therapy dog work, including books and Web sites. You'll also find an assortment of other resources about dogs, including Web sites that were described throughout this book.

Since I started this project, each day has been like my birthday, as I often open my e-mails to find a new story or photo from one of the therapy dog handlers you've met in this book. If you'd like to contact me, visit me at my Web site, www.fitasfido.com, and leave me a message about your fabulous therapy dog experience.

BOOKS

There are many wonderful books that describe the healing power of dogs and therapy dogs. The following resources are listed alphabetically by title.

Here's a sample of books describing the important work of therapy dogs:

McPherson, R. (2010). *Every dog has a gift: True stories of dogs who bring hope & healing into our lives*. New York: Jeremy P. Tarcher/Penguin.

McPherson, founder of animal-assisted therapy organization The Good Dog Foundation, shares stories of everyday dogs providing calming, comfort, and healing to those they serve, as well as a chapter on becoming a handler–therapy dog team.

Joseph, M. (2009). *Moments with Baxter: Comfort and love from the world's best therapy dog*. San Diego, CA: Sage Press.
    This is a touching biography of a therapy dog.

Crawford, J. J., Pomerinke, K. A., and Smith, D. W. (2003). *Therapy pets: The animal–human healing partnership*. Amherst, NY: Prometheus.
    This book offers twenty-three profiles of the healing power of animal–human interactions.

Pichot, T. (2009). *Transformation of the heart: Tales of the profound impact therapy dogs have on their humans*. Bloomington, IN: iUniverse.
    This book showcases stories of the impact that therapy dogs have on their humans.

You will also be interested in reading Allen and Sandra Parton's book about service dog Endal, titled *Endal: How One Extraordinary Dog Brought a Family Back from the Brink* (Harper True, 2009).

These books talk about the general healing power of dogs:

Anderson, A., and Anderson, L. (2008). *Angel dogs with a mission: Divine messengers in service to all life*. Novato, CA: New World Library.
    The moving stories in this book describe the healing power of the dogs in our lives.

Masson, J. M. (1998). *Dogs never lie about love: Reflections on the emotional world of dogs*. New York: Three Rivers Press.
    Masson describes the "emotions" of dogs, though at times seeming to excessively attribute human emotions to canine companions.

Sheldrake, R. (1999). *Dogs that know when their owners are coming home: And other unexplained powers of animals*. New York: Three Rivers Press.
    This book includes brief descriptions of the extraordinary power of pets sensing impending crises and pursing long journeys to home.

Doty, M. (2007). *Dog years: A memoir*. New York: HarperCollins.
    Award-winning poet and author Mark Doty recalls how lessons learned from his Retrievers have strengthened him during times of crisis, despair, and profound grief.

Miller, J. (2010). *Healing companions: Ordinary dogs and their extraordinary power to transform lives.* Franklin Lakes, NJ: Career Press.

This book discusses the ability of companion dogs to help people with a variety of emotional problems and describes the best ways to choose and train your dog.

Becker, M. (2002). *The healing power of pets: Harnessing the amazing ability of pets to make and keep people happy and healthy.* New York: Hyperion.

Dr. Becker details the numerous health benefits from contact with pets, such as easing pain and helping to motivate exercise, and helps readers determine which breed is right for them.

Kerasote, T. (2007). *Merle's door: Lessons from a freethinking dog.* New York: Houghton Mifflin Harcourt.

This is a tale of personal growth as one man's life is changed by lessons learned from a stray dog who rescues Kerasote.

Katz, J. (2003). *The new work of dogs: Tending to life, love, and family.* New York: Villard Books.

This book shows how dogs can act as surrogate human replacements to address social isolation and attachment issue in humans.

Sakson, S. (2009). *Paws & effect: The healing power of dogs.* New York: Spiegel & Grau.

Individual accounts of how dogs have helped people through periods of illness and distress.

Anderson, P. E. (2008). *The powerful bond between people and pets: Our boundless connection to companion animals.* Westport, CT: Praeger.

Anderson reviews the history of human–pet relationships and the benefits for humans from pet companionship that leads to an important responsibility to care for pets.

If you're interested in training your dog to become a therapy dog or adding some spice to your visit routine, check out these books:

Pichot, T. (2011). *Animal-assisted brief therapy: A solution-focused approach. 2nd ed.* London: Routledge Press.

This book guides you in how to use animal-assisted therapy effectively for a variety of medical conditions.

Pavlides, M. (2008). *Animal assisted interventions for individuals with autism*. London: Jessica Kingsley.

This special education specialist and dog trainer describes how interacting with animals can help people with autism.

Altschiller, D. (2011). *Animal-assisted therapy*. Santa Barbara, CA: Greenwood Press.

This book details the history of pet therapy and the wide range of areas where animal-assisted therapy can be successfully used.

Lind, N. (2009). *Animal assisted therapy activities to motivate and inspire*. Lombard, IL: PYOW Sports Marketing.

This practical resource provides suggestions for successfully implementing pet therapy.

King, L. (2007). *Animal-assisted therapy: A guide for professional counselors, school counselors, social workers, and educators*. Bloomington, IN: AuthorHouse.

A short, sixty-four-page book on the basics of animal-assisted therapy.

Chandler, C. K. (2005). *Animal assisted therapy in counseling*. New York: Routledge.

This book covers the ethics, selection, and training of dogs for therapy work as well as research describing the benefits of animal-assisted therapy in patients with emotional problems.

Brown, D. P. (2010). *Animal assisted therapy: The layman's guide to understanding AAT and its benefits*. Battle Ground, WA: Learning Life eBooks.

This electronic book is provides an overview of animal-assisted therapy and a wide range of medical conditions that might benefit from animal-assisted therapy.

American Kennel Club. (2010). *Citizen Canine*. Irvine, CA: Kennel Club Books.

This book walks you through the needed skills for teaching your dog to become a Canine Good Citizen on his road to therapy dog work.

Long, L. (2008). *A dog who's always welcome: Assistance and therapy dog trainers teach you how to socialize and train your companion dog.* New York: Howell Book House.

This book explains the whys and hows of basic dog training.

Fine, A. (2010). *Handbook on animal-assisted therapy.* 3rd ed. San Diego, CA: Academic Press.

You know this book is a trusted and valuable resource for therapy dog handlers because it has just been updated into a third edition.

Grover, S. (2010). *101 creative ideas for animal assisted therapy.* Henderson, NV: Motivational Press.

This book provides over 100 practical suggestions for using animal-assisted therapy in a variety of medical situations.

Ensminger, J. J. (2010). *Service and therapy dogs in American society: Science, law and the evolution of canine caregivers.* Springfield, IL: Charles C Thomas.

Attorney John J. Ensminger reviews the development of therapy and service dogs and laws that apply to each.

McConnell, P. B. (2008). *Tales of two species: Essays on loving and living with dogs.* Wenatchee, WA: Dogwise Publishing.

Behaviorist Patricia McConnell, PhD, explains the science behind why dogs do the things they do and provides practical tips for using this knowledge to better understand, train, and love your dog.

Butler, K. (2004). *Therapy dogs today: Their gifts, our obligation.* Norman, OK: Funpuddle.

This book explores the ethics of therapy dog work and is a terrific resource for people developing therapy dog programs.

Davis, K. D. (2002). *Therapy dogs: Training your dog to reach others.* Wenatchee, WA: Dogwise Publishing.

This is an excellent book to help readers determine whether therapy dog work is right for them and their dogs, what skills and responsibilities are needed for therapy dog work, and how to successfully make therapy dog visits.

And be sure to check out Jim Gorant's book, *The Lost Dogs: Michael Vick's Dogs and Their Tale of Rescue and Redemption* (Gotham, 2010) to read more about what happened with pit bull Hector and other fighting dog victims who got a second chance at a better life.

If you have a youngster in your life interested in therapy dogs, try these books:

- *The Adventures of Sheila the Therapy Dog*, by Debbie Fedorovich (Outskirts Press, 2007)
- *Rocky's Trip to the Hospital*, by Sue London (Kristar, 2003)
- *Rosie: A Visiting Dog's Story*, by Stephanie Calmenson (Sandpiper, 1998)

INTERNET RESOURCES

If you type the words *therapy dog* into your Internet search engine, you'll probably get six or seven million possible Web sites identified for you to peruse. Below you'll find recommendations for a number of especially useful sites.

In the book *Service and Therapy Dogs in American Society: Science, Law and the Evolution of Canine Caregivers* (listed earlier in this section), John J. Ensminger provides an extensive listing of additional therapy and service dog organizations, listed by state.

Ian and Olivia check out great Internet sites under the supervision of Miniature Schnauzer Liesel.

National/international therapy dog program	Web site
American Kennel Club's Canine Good Citizen program	http://www.akc.org/events/cgc/
Delta Society	http://www.deltasociety.org
Gabriel's Angels	http://www.gabrielsangels.org
Therapy Dogs, Inc.	http://www.therapydogs.com
Therapy Dogs International	http://www.tdi-dog.org

In you are interested in contacting the therapy dog organizations you read about in this book, check their contact information:

- Angel Paws can be reached through http://www.angelpawstherapy. org
- Animal Friends can be contacted at http://www.thinkingoutsideth-ecage.org
- Gabriel's Angels has a Web site at http://www.gabrielsangels.org/

If you live in Maryland or are otherwise interested, check out Wags For Hope (http://www.wagsforhope.org).

Individuals living in Allegheny County in western Pennsylvania and elsewhere can find out information about the Multiple Sclerosis PAWS program at http://www.mscare.org/cmsc/images/pdf/MS-PAWS. pdf

Additional information on the infection prevention for pet therapy visits can be obtained from the Centers for Disease Control and Prevention Web site, http://www.cdc.gov. Use the search term *animal-assisted therapy* to find resources.

HEALTH LINKS

Online resources, such as the following, can help you estimate how many calories you'll burn with exercise:

- http://caloriecount.about.com lists calories burned with a wide range of activities. Click the "Exercise" link and the search for your desired exercise, including dog walking.

- http://www.fitday.com/webfit/burned/calories_burned.html allows you to estimate how many calories you will burn with a specific exercise, based on your age, gender, height, and weight. And yes, dog walking is one of the available options! When I did the calculation for myself, it was estimated that I would lose about 146 calories per hour of dog walking. And if you walk at a brisker pace and add hills, you'll boost the amount of calories you'll lose.

To determine whether you need to lose weight, check your body mass index with online body mass index calculators such as the following:

- http://www.nhlbisupport.com/bmi/
- http://www.bmi-calculator.net/
- http://www.cdc.gov/healthyweight/assessing/bmi/

If you or someone in your life needs to quit smoking, get tips and a free personal coach at 800-QUIT-NOW (800-784-8669). You can also get information at http://www.smokefree.gov

The President's Council on Fitness, Sports & Nutrition Web site (http://www.fitness.gov/) gives you tips to help determine what your personal fitness targets should be based on your age and other medical conditions. Click on the "Resources & Grants" button, then "Fit Facts & Tips," and then "General Fit Facts."

If you'd like to learn more about the amazing work Dawn Celapino does with her aerobics and yoga classes, visit her Leash Your Fitness Web site (http://www.leashyourfitness.com). And if you're lucky enough to live nearby, schedule yourself for a fun class with Dawn.

Learn first aid and cardiopulmonary resuscitation for you and Fido.

- You can find classes near you at the Red Cross Web site (http://www.redcross.org/).
- You can also purchase *Be Red Cross Ready Safety Series Vol. 2: Dog First Aid* at the Red Cross online store (http://www.redcrossstore.org).

GET CONNECTED WITH THERAPY DOGS

Read more about the incredible therapy and charity work of Surf Dog Ricochet at her Web site (http://www.surfdogricochet.com/). You can click on links to videos detailing her amazing work, although you'll want to have a tissue box ready before you start watching! You can also find out more about the charities Ricochet's work is currently supporting and find a charity that's right for you.

Unless you're lucky enough to live in Canada, you probably won't get a therapy visit from Sue London, but you can hear her inspirational messages and more about how her little dog Rocky helped her develop the positive attitude that has become her trademark by tuning into her radio show (http://www.blogtalkradio.com/life-coach-sue) at Blog Talk Radio—"Get Inspired with Spiritual Life Coach Sue London." This life coach and therapy dog handler will definitely get you inspired!

Pomeranian therapy dog Minnie has her own column in the *Fresno Scene Magazine*, called "Minnie May I." Address your questions for her to Minnie Saroyan, P.O. Box 16404, Fresno, CA 93755. And don't worry if you don't live in California—you can find a digital version online (http://www.fresnoscenemagazine.com). You can also find out more about Minnie's latest work as a reading therapist by visiting her Web site (http://www.minnieandmereadingtherapy.com/).

Therapy dogs are terrific, and you can probably meet therapy dogs in your area by contacting your local animal shelter or dog clubs that offer therapy dog classes. This can be a great way to learn more about therapy dogs and arrange for a therapy dog to visit someone you know who might benefit from a visit.

SERVICE DOG ORGANIZATIONS

There are a large number of terrific service dog organizations, and a complete listing of them is beyond the scope of this book. If you're interested in learning more about service dogs, check out Canine Support Teams, Inc. (http://www.caninesupportteams.org), through which Jennifer Blanchard and Ike work.

You might also be interested in reading about the incredible work Allen Parton does in the United Kingdom helping injured service and emergency personnel get hooked up with service dogs through Hounds For Heroes (http://www.houndsforheroes.com/).

You can also read about the fantastic work being done through The Seeing Eye (http://www.seeingeye.org).

OTHER LINKS TO SPARK YOUR CREATIVITY

Jane Miller has developed an amazing Web site to help promote reading, writing, and expression in children. Her Ruff Writer's Project is a resource of ideas and writing, with tips on bringing reading and writing programs to communities everywhere. You can read more about Jane's incredible work (http://theruffwriters.com).

Check out Soft-Coated Wheaten Terrier owner Maggie Foxmoore's artwork (http://www.foxmooredesignstudio.com/). Her incredible blending of dog cuteness with profound emotional themes and color makes her work priceless.

You can read more about how Gabe O'Neill helps motivate children to get involved in their communities and make real differences through volunteering at the Kids Are Heroes Web site (http://www.kidsareheroes.org).

References

CHAPTER 1

Allen, K., Blascovich, J., and Mendes, W. B. (2002). Cardiovascular reactivity and the presence of pets, friends, and spouses: The truth about cats and dogs. *Psychosomatic Medicine* 64:727–39.

Benjamin, C. L. (1985). *Mother knows best: The natural way to train your dog*. New York: Hungry Minds.

Cangelosi, P. R., and Sorrell, J. M. (2010). Walking for therapy with man's best friend. *Journal of Psychosocial Nursing and Mental Health Services* 48:19–22.

Coakley, A. B., and Mahoney, E. K. (2009). Creating a therapeutic and healing environment with a pet therapy program. *Complementary Therapies in Clinical Practice* 15:141–6.

Garfield, J. B. (1994). *Follow my leader*. London: Puffin.

Kawamura, N., Niiyama, M., and Niiyama, H. (2009). Animal-assisted activity: Experiences of institutionalized Japanese older adults. *Journal of Psychosocial Nursing and Mental Health Services* 47:41–7.

Odendaal, J. S. J. (2000). Animal-assisted therapy—Magic or medicine? *Journal of Psychosomatic Research, 49*, 275–80.

Sobo, E. J., Eng, B., and Kassity-Krich, N. (2006). Canine visitation (pet) therapy: Pilot data on decreases in child pain perception. *Journal of Holistic Nursing* 24:51–7.

CHAPTER 2

American Animal Hospital Association. (2004). *2004 pet owner survey.* http://www.aahanet.org/media/s_pos2004.aspx (accessed January 2011).

Barker, S. B., and Wolen, A. R. (2008). The benefits of human–companion animal interaction: A review. *Journal of Veterinary Medical Education* 35:487–95.

Bufford, J. D., Reardon, C. L., Li, Z., Roberg, K. A., et al. (2008). Effects of dog ownership in early childhood on immune development and atopic diseases. *Clinical and Experimental Allergy* 38:1635–43.

Doty, M. (2007). *Dog years: A memoir.* New York: HarperCollins.

Lappalainen, M. H., Huttunen, K., Ropponen, M., Remes, S., et al. (2010). Exposure to dogs is associated with a decreased tumour necrosis factor-alpha-producing capacity in early life. *Clinical and Experimental Allergy* 40:1498–1506.

Stevens, J. A., Teh, S. L., and Haileyesus, T. (2010). Dogs and cats as environmental fall hazards. *Journal of Safety Research* 41:69–73.

Walsh, F. (2009). Human–animal bonds II: The role of pets in family systems and family therapy. *Family Process* 48:481–99.

CHAPTER 3

Barron, J. S., Tan, E. J., Yu, Q., Song, M., et al. (2009). Potential for intensive volunteering to promote the health of older adults in fair health. *Journal of Urban Health* 86:641–53.

Braun, C., Stangler, T., Narveson, J., and Pettingell, S. (2009). Animal-assisted therapy as a pain relief intervention for children. *Complementary Therapies in Clinical Practice* 15:105–9.

DeCourcey, M., Russell, A. C., and Keister, K. J. (2010). Animal-assisted therapy: Evaluation and implementation of a complementary therapy to improve the psychological and physiological health of critically ill patients. *Dimensions of Critical Care Nursing* 29:211–14.

Harris, A. H., and Thoresen, C. E. (2005). Volunteering is associated with delayed mortality in older people: Analysis of the longitudinal study of aging. *Journal of Health Psychology* 10:739–52.

Haubenhofer, D. K., and Kirchengast, S. (2006). Physiological arousal for companion dogs working with their owners in animal-assisted activities and animal-assisted therapy. *Journal of Applied Animal Welfare Science* 9:165–72.

LeFebvre, S. L., Golab, G. C., Christensen, E., Castrodale, L., et al. (2008). Guidelines for animal-assisted interventions in health care facilities. *American Journal of Infection Control* 36:78–85.

Lefebvre, S. L., Reid-Smith, R., Boerlin, P., Weese, J. S. (2008). Evaluation of the risks of shedding salmonellae and other potential pathogens by therapy dogs fed raw diets in Ontario and Alberta. *Zoonoses Public Health* 55:470–80.

Lefebvre, S. L., Reid-Smith, R. J., Waltner-Toews, D., Weese, J. S. (2009). Incidence of acquisition of methicillin-resistant *Staphylococcus aureus, Clostridium difficile,* and other health-care–associated pathogens by dogs that participate in animal-assisted interventions. *Journal of the American Veterinary Medical Association* 234:1404–17.

Marx, M. S., Cohen-Mansfield, J., Regier, N. G., Dakheel-Ali, M., et al. (2010). The impact of different dog-related stimuli on engagement of persons with dementia. *American Journal of Alzheimer's Disease and Other Dementias* 25:37–45.

Pittet, D., Allegranzi, B., Boyce, J., and World Health Organization World Alliance for Patient Safety First Global Patient Safety Challenge Core Group of Experts. (2009). The World Health Organization guidelines on hand hygiene in health care and their consensus recommendations. *Infection Control and Hospital Epidemiology* 30:611–22.

Rutland, B. E., Weese, J. S., Au, J., and Malani, A. N. (2009). Human-to-dog transmission of methicillin-resistant *Staphylococcus aureus.* *Emerging Infectious Diseases* 15:1328–30.

Sehulster, L., and Chinn, R. W. (2003). Guidelines for environmental infection control in health-care facilities: Recommendations of CDC and the Health Infection Control Practices Advisory Committee (HICPAC). *Morbidity and Mortality Weekly Reports* 52:1–42.

Selli, L., Garrafa, V., and Junges, J. R. (2008). Beneficiaries of volunteering: A bioethical perspective. *Revista de Saúde Pública* 42:1085–89.

Sickbert-Bennett, E. E., Weber, D. J., Gergen-Teague, M. F., Sobsey, M. D., et al. (2005). Comparative efficacy of hand hygiene agents in the reduction of bacteria and viruses. *American Journal of Infection Control* 33:67–77.

Van Willigen, M. (2000). Differential benefits of volunteering across the life course. *Journals of Gerontology: Series B: Psychological Sciences and Social Sciences* 55B:S308–18.

Zamir, T. (2006). The moral basis of animal-assisted therapy. *Society and Animals* 14:179–99.

CHAPTER 4

American Nurses Association. (2010). *Nursing's social policy statement: The essence of the profession, 2010.* Washington, DC: American Nurses Association.

Chinner, T. L., and Daizel, F. R. (1991). An exploratory study on the viability and efficacy of a pet-facilitated therapy project within a hospice. *Journal of Palliative Care* 7:13–20.

Goode, M., Harrod, M. E., Wales, S., and Crisp, J. (2004). The role of specialist nurses in improving treatment adherence in children with a chronic illness. *Australian Journal of Advanced Nursing* 21:41–5.

Havener, L., Gentes, L., Thaler, B., Megel, M. E. et al. (2001). The effects of a companion animal on distress in children undergoing dental procedures. *Issues in Comprehensive Pediatric Nursing* 24:137–52.

Heo, S., Moser, D. K., Lennie, T. A., Riegel, B., and Chung, M. L. (2008). Gender differences in and factors related to self-care behaviors: A cross-sectional, correlational study of patients with heart failure. *International Journal of Nursing Studies* 45:1807–15.

Nagengast, S. L., Baun, M. M., Megel, M., and Leibowitz, J. M. (1997). The effects of the presence of a companion animal on physiological arousal and behavioral distress in children during a physical examination. *Journal of Pediatric Nursing* 12:323–30.

Piette, J. D. (2010). Moving beyond the notion of "self" care. *Chronic Illness* 6:3–6.

Shigaki, C., Kruse, R. L., Mehr, D., Sheldon, K. M., et al. (2010). Motivation and diabetes self-management. Chronic Illness 6:202–14.

CHAPTER 5

Bajtarevic, A., Ager, C., Pienz, M., Klieber, M., et al. (2009). Noninvasive detection of lung cancer by analysis of exhaled breath. *BMC Cancer* 9:348.

Church, H., and Williams, H. (2001). Another sniffer dog in the clinic? *The Lancet* 358:930.

Dosa, D. M. (2007). A day in the life of Oscar the cat. *New England Journal of Medicine* 357:328–9.

Dosa, D. M. (2010). *Making rounds with Oscar: The extraordinary gift of an ordinary cat.* New York: Hyperion.

Fletcher, K. E., Rankey, D. S., and Stern, D. T. (2005). Bedside interactions from the other side of the bedrail. *Journal of General Internal Medicine* 20:58–61.

Gordon, R. T., Schatz, C. B., Myers, L. J., Kosty, M., et al. (2008).The use of canines in the detection of human cancers. *Journal of Alternative and Complementary Medicine* 14:61–7.

McCulloch, M., Jezierski, T., Broffman, M., Hubbard, A., et al. (2006). Diagnostic accuracy of canine scent detection in early- and late-stage lung and breast cancers. *Integrative Cancer Therapies* 5:30–9.

Onukwugha, E., Saunders, E., Mullins, C. D., Pradel, F. G., et al. (2010). Reasons for discharges against medical advice: A qualitative study. *Quality & Safety in Health Care* 19:420–4.

Welsh, J. S., Barton, D., and Ahuja, H. (2005). A case of breast cancer detected by a pet dog. *Community Oncology* 2:324–6.

Williams, H., and Pembroke, A. (1989). Sniffer dogs in the melanoma clinic? *The Lancet* 1:734.

Willis, C. M., Church, S. M., Guest, C. M., Cook, W. A., et al. (2004). Olfactory detection of human bladder cancer by dogs: Proof of principle study. *British Medical Journal* 329:712.

CHAPTER 6

Barak, Y., Beni, A., Savorai, O., and Mavashev, S. (2001). Animal-assisted therapy for elderly schizophrenic patients: A one-year controlled trial. *American Journal of Geriatric Psychiatry* 9:439–42.

Burrows, K. E., Adams, C. L., and Spiers, J. (2008). Sentinels of safety: Service dogs ensure safety and enhance freedom and well-being for families with autistic children. *Qualitative Health Research* 18:1642–9.

Canfield, J., Hansen, M.V., Newmark, A., Diamond, W. (2009) *Chicken soup for the soul: What I learned from the dog: 101 stories about life, love and lessons.* Deerfield Beach, FL: Chicken Soup for the Soul Publishing.

Charnetski, C. J., Riggers, S., and Brennan, F. X. (2004). Effect of petting a dog on immune system function. *Psychological Reports* 95:1087–91.

Chu, C. I., Liu, C. Y., Sun, C. T., and Lin, J. (2009). The effect of animal-assisted activity on inpatients with schizophrenia. *Journal of Psychosocial Nursing and Mental Health Services* 47:42–8.

LaFrance, C., Garcia, L. J., and Labreche, J. (2007). The effect of a therapy dog on the communication skills of an adult with aphasia. *Journal of Communication Disorders* 40:215–24.

Lukina, L. N. (1999). The effect of dolphin-assisted therapy sessions on the functional status of children with psychoneurological disease symptoms. *Fiziologiia Cheloveka* 25:56–60.

Macauley, B. L. (2006). Animal-assisted therapy for persons with aphasia: A pilot study. *Journal of Rehabilitation Research and Development* 43:357–66.

Pavlides, M. (2008). *Animal assisted interventions for individuals with autism.* London: Jessica Kingsley.

Wuang, Y. P., Wang, C. C., Huang, M. N., and Su, C. Y. (2010). The effectiveness of simulated developmental horse-riding program in children with autism. *Adapted Physical Activity Quarterly* 27:113–26.

Zimolag, U., and Krupa, T. (2009). Pet ownership as a meaningful community occupation for people with serious mental illness. *American Journal of Occupational Therapy* 63:126–37.

CHAPTER 7

Allen, K. (1995). Coping with life changes and transitions: The role of the pet. *Interactions* 13:5–6, 8–10.

Banks, M. R., and Banks, W. A. (2002). The effects of animal-assisted therapy on loneliness in an elderly population in long-term care facilities. *Journals of Gerontology: Series A: Biological Sciences and Medical Sciences* 57:M428–32.

Barak, Y., Savorai, O., Mavashev, S., and Beni, A. (2001). Animal-assisted therapy for elderly schizophrenic patients: A one-year controlled trial. *American Journal of Geriatric Psychiatry* 9:439–42.

Barefoot, J. C., Gronbaek, M., Jensen, G., Schnohr, P., and Prescott, E. (2005). Social network diversity and risks of ischemic heart disease and total mortality: Findings from the Copenhagen City Heart Study. *American Journal of Epidemiology* 161:960–7.

Barnes, L. L., Mendes de Leon, C. F., Wilson, R. S., Bienias, J. L., and Evans, D. A. (2004). Social resources and cognitive decline in a population of older African Americans and whites. *Neurology* 63:2322–6.

Cline, K. C. (2010). Psychological effects of dog ownership: Role strain, role enhancement, and depression. *Journal of Social Psychology* 150:117–31.

Conroy, R. M., Golden, J., Jeffares, I., O'Neill, D., and McGee, H. (2010). Boredom-proneness, loneliness, social engagement and depression and their association with cognitive function in older people: A population study. *Psychology, Health, & Medicine* 15:463–73.

Dimitrijević, I. (2009). Animal-assisted therapy—A new trend in the treatment of children and adults. *Psychiatrica Danubina* 21:236–41.

Drageset, J. (2004). The importance of activities of daily living and social contact for loneliness: A survey among residents in nursing homes. *Scandinavian Journal of Caring Sciences* 18:65–71.

Giles, L. C., Glonek, G. V., Luszcz, M. A., and Andrews, G. R. (2005). Effect of social networks on 10 year survival in very old Australians: The Australian Longitudinal Study of Aging. *Journal of Epidemiology and Community Health* 59:574–9.

Hamer, M., Bates, C. J., and Mishra, G. D. (2011). Depression, physical function, and risk of mortality: National Diet and Nutrition Survey in adults older than 65 years. *American Journal of Geriatric Psychiatry* 19:72–8.

Knight, S., and Edwards, V. (2008). In the company of wolves: The physical, social, and psychological benefits of dog ownership. *Journal of Aging and Health* 20:437–55.

Kovács, Z., Kis, R., Rózsa, S., and Rózsa, L. (2004). Animal-assisted therapy for middle-aged schizophrenic patients living in a social institution: A pilot study. *Clinical Rehabilitation* 18:483–6.

Nathans-Barel, I., Feldman, P., Berger, B., Modai, I., and Silver, H. (2005). Animal-assisted therapy ameliorates anhedonia in schizophrenia patients: A controlled pilot study. *Psychotherapy and Psychosomatics* 74:31–5.

Patterson, A. C., and Veenstra, G. (2010). Loneliness and risk of mortality: A longitudinal investigation in Alameda County, California. *Social Science & Medicine* 71:181–6.

Reynolds, R. M. (2001). *Blessing the bridge: What animals teach us about death, dying, and beyond.* Troutdale, OR: New Sage Press.

Saczynsik, J. S., Beiser, A., Seshadri, S., Auerbach, S., et al. (2010). Depressive symptoms and risk of dementia: The Framingham Heart Study. *Neurology* 75:35–41.

Sahyoun, N. R., and Zhang, X. L. (2005). Dietary quality and social contact among a nationally representative sample of the older adult population in the United States. *Journal of Nutrition, Health, and Aging* 9:177–83.

Seitz, D., Purandare, N., and Conn, D. (2010). Prevalence of psychiatric disorders among older adults in long-term care homes: A systematic review. *International Psychogeriatrics* 4:1–15.

Shiovitz-Ezra, S., and Ayalon, L. (2010). Situational versus chronic loneliness as risk factors for all-cause mortality. *International Psychogeriatrics* 22:455–62.

Sockalingam, S., Li, M., Krishnadev, U., Hanson, K., et al. (2008). Use of animal-assisted therapy in the rehabilitation of an assault victim with a concurrent mood disorder. *Issues in Mental Health Nursing* 29:73–84.

Vasiliadis, H., Lesage, A., Adair, C., Wang, P. S., and Kessler, R. C. (2007). Do Canada and the United States differ in the prevalence of depression and utilization of services? *Psychiatric Services* 58:63–71.

Zunzunegui, M., Alvardo, B. E., Del Ser, T., and Otero, A. (2003). Social networks, social integration, and social engagement determine cognitive decline in community-dwelling Spanish older adults. *Journals of Gerontology: Series B: Psychological Sciences and Social Sciences* 58B:S93–100.

Zunzunegui, M., Koné, A., Johri, M., Béland, F., et al. (2004). Social networks and self-rated health in two French-speaking Canadian community dwelling populations over 65. *Social Science & Medicine* 58:2069–81.

CHAPTER 8

Abate, S. V., Zucconi, M., Boxer, B. A. (in press). Impact of canine-assisted ambulation on hospitalized chronic heart failure patients' ambulation outcomes and satisfaction: a pilot study. *The Journal of Cardiovascular Nursing.*

Allen, K., Shykoff, B. E., and Izzo, J. L. (2001). Pet ownership, but not ACE inhibitor therapy, blunts home blood pressure responses to mental stress. *Hypertension* 38:815–20.

American Heart Association. (2010). *Heart disease and stroke statistics— 2010 update.* http://www.americanheart.org (accessed September 2010).

Beulens, J. W., Algra, A., Soedamah-Muthu, S. S., Visseren, F. L., et al. (2010). Alcohol consumption and risk of recurrent cardiovascular events and mortality in patients with clinically manifest vascular disease and diabetes mellitus: The Second Manifestations of ARTerial (SMART) disease study. *Atherosclerosis* 212:281–6.

Beulens, J. W., Rimm, E. B., Ascherio, A., Spiegelman, D., et al. (2007). Alcohol consumption and risk of coronary heart disease among men with hypertension. *Annals of Internal Medicine* 146:10–9.

Bitton, A., and Gaziano, T. A. (2010). The Framingham Heart Study's impact on global risk assessment. *Progress in Cardiovascular Diseases* 53:68–78.

Blackburn, G. (2007). Exercise for women who hate to exercise: Working more movement into your day, such as walking a dog or playing tennis, can help your heart and reduce your waistline. *Heart Advisor* 10:6.

Bos, S., Grobbee, D. E., Boer, J. M., Verschuren, W. M., and Beulens, J. W. (2010). Alcohol consumption and risk of cardiovascular disease among hypertensive women. *European Journal of Cardiovascular Prevention and Rehabilitation* 17:119–26.

Brunckhorst, C. B., Holzmeister, J., Scharf, C., Binggeli, C., and Duru, F. (2003). Stress, depression and cardiac arrhythmias. *Therapeutische Umschau* 60:673–81.

Centers for Disease Control and Prevention. (2009). Prevalence and most common causes of disability among adults—United States, 2005. *Morbidity and Mortality Weekly Reports* 58:421–6.

Cole, K. M., Gawlinski, A., Steers, N., and Kotlerman, J. (2007). Animal-assisted therapy in patients hospitalized with heart failure. *American Journal of Critical Care* 16:575–85.

Curtis, L. H., Greiner, M. A., Hammill, B. G., Kramer, J. M., et al. (2008). Acute and long-term outcomes of heart failure in elderly persons, 2001–2005. *Archives of Internal Medicine* 168:2481–8.

Cutt, H. E., Giles-Corti, B., Wood, L. J., Knuiman, M. W., and Burek, V. (2008). Barriers and motivators for owners walking their dog: Results from qualitative research. *Health Promotion Journal of Australia* 19:118–24.

Cutt, H. E., Knuiman, M. W., and Giles-Corti, B. (2008). Does getting a dog increase recreational walking? *International Journal of Behavioral Nutrition and Physical Activity* 5:17.

Dembicki, D., and Anderson, J. (1996). Pet ownership may be a factor in improved health of the elderly. *Journal of Nutrition for the Elderly* 15:15–31.

Friedmann, E., Katcher, A. H., Lynch, J. J., and Thomas, S. A. (1980). Animal companions and one-year survival of patients after discharge from a coronary care unit. *Public Health Reports* 95:307–12.

Friedmann, E., and Thomas, S. A. (1995). Pet ownership, social support, and one-year survival after acute myocardial infarction in the Cardiac Arrhythmia Suppression Trial (CAST). *American Journal of Cardiology* 76:1213–7.

Giaquinto, S., and Valentini, F. (2009). Is there a scientific basis for pet therapy? *Disability and Rehabilitation* 31:595–8.

Goldstein, L. B. (2010). Physical activity and the risk of stroke. *Expert Review of Neurotherapeutics* 10:1263–5.

Hamer, M., and Chida, Y. (2008). Walking and primary prevention: A meta-analysis of prospective cohort studies. *British Journal of Sports Medicine* 42:238–43.

Johnson, R. A., and Meadows, R. L. (2010). Dog-walking: Motivation for adherence to a walking program. *Clinical Nursing Research* 19:387–402.

Kenfield, S. A., Wei, E. K., Rosner, B. A., Glynn, R. J., et al. (2010). Burden of smoking on cause-specific mortality: Application to the Nurses' Health Study. *Tobacco Control* 19:248–54.

Kuklina, E. V., Yoon, P. W., and Keenan, N. L. (2010). Prevalence of coronary heart disease risk factors and screening for high cholesterol levels among young adults, United States, 1999–2006. *Annals of Family Medicine* 8:327–33.

Marcus, D. A. (2008). *Fit as Fido: Follow your dog to better health.* Bloomington, IN: iUniverse.

Miura, K., Daviglus, M. L., Dyer, A. R., Liu, K., et al. (2001). Relationship of blood pressure to 25-year mortality due to coronary heart disease, cardiovascular diseases, and all causes in young adult men: The Chicago Heart Association Detection Project in Industry. *Archives of Internal Medicine* 161:1501–8.

Ockene, I. S., and Miller, N. H. (1997). Cigarette smoking, cardiovascular disease, and stroke: A statement for healthcare professionals from the American Heart Association. *Circulation* 96:3243–7.

O'Donnell, M. J., Xavier, D., Liu, L., Zhang, H., et al. (2010). Risk factors for ischaemic and intracerebral haemorrhagic stroke in 22 countries (the INTERSTROKE study): A case-control study. *The Lancet* 376:112–23.

Oguma, Y., and Shinoda-Tagawa, T. (2004). Physical activity decreases cardiovascular disease risk in women: Review and meta-analysis. *American Journal of Preventive Medicine* 26:407–18.

Parker, G. B., Gayed, A., Owen, C. A., Hyett, M. P., et al. (2010). Survival following an acute coronary syndrome: A pet theory put to the test. *Acta Psychiatrica Scandinavica* 121:65–70.

Quinn, R. R., Hemmelgarn, B. R., Padwal, R. S., Myers, M. G., et al. (2010). The 2010 Canadian Hypertension Education Program recommendations for the management of hypertension: Part I—Blood pressure measurement, diagnosis and assessment of risk. Canadian Journal of Cardiology 26:241–8.

Rusinaru, D., Mahjoub, H., Goissen, T., Massy, Z., et al. (2009). Clinical features and prognosis of heart failure in women: A 5-year prospective study. *International Journal of Cardiology* 133:327–35.

Sanderson, S. C., Waller, J., Jarvis, M. J., Humphries, S. E., and Wardle, J. (2009). Awareness of lifestyle risk factors for cancer and heart disease among adults in the UK. *Patient Education and Counseling* 74:221–7.

Sattelmair, J. R., Kurth, T., Buring, J. E., and Lee, I. M. (2010). Physical activity and risk of stroke in women. *Stroke* 41:1243–50.

Shafey, O., Eriksen, M., Ross, H., Mackay, J. (2009). *The tobacco atlas*. 3rd ed. Atlanta, GA: American Cancer Society.

Tudor-Locke, C. (2010). Steps to better cardiovascular health: How many steps does it take to achieve good health and how confident are we in this number? *Current Cardiovascular Risk Reports* 4:271–6.

Unverdorben, M., von Holt, K., and Winkelmann, B. R. (2009). Smoking and atherosclerotic cardiovascular disease: Part II. Role of cigarette smoking in cardiovascular disease development. *Biomarkers in Medicine* 3:617–53.

Virués-Ortega, J., and Buela-Casal, G. (2006). Psychophysiological effects of human–animal interaction: Theoretical issues and long-term interaction effects. *Journal of Nervous and Mental Disease* 194:52–7.

Vlastelica, M. (2008). Emotional stress as a trigger in sudden cardiac death. *Psychiatria Danubina* 20:411–4.

Volpe, M., and Tocci, G. (2010). Rethinking targets of blood pressure and guidelines for hypertension clinical management. *Nephrology, Dialysis, Transplantation* 25:3465–71.

Zhang, Y. (2010). Cardiovascular disease in American women. *Nutrition, Metabolism, and Cardiovascular Diseases* 20:386–93.

Zheng, H., Orsini, N., Amin, J., Wolk, A., et al. (2009). Quantifying the dose–response of walking in reducing coronary heart disease risk: Meta-analysis. *European Journal of Epidemiology* 24:181–92.

CHAPTER 9

Friedenreich, C. M. (2010). The role of physical activity in breast cancer etiology. *Seminars in Oncology* 37:297–302.

Friedenreich, C. M., Gregory, J., Kopciuk, K. A., Mackey, J. R., and Courneya, K. S. (2009). Prospective cohort study of lifetime physical activity and breast cancer survival. *International Journal of Cancer* 124:1954–62.

Halle, M., and Schoenberg, M. H. (2009). Physical activity in the prevention and treatment of colorectal carcinoma. *Deutsches Ärzteblatt International* 106:722–7.

Johnson, R. A., Meadows, R. L, Haubner, J. S., and Sevedge, K. (2003). Human–animal interaction: A complementary/alternative medical (CAM) intervention for cancer patients. *American Behavioral Scientist* 47:55–69.

Kruk, J. (2007). Lifetime physical activity and the risk of breast cancer: A case-controlled study. *Cancer Detection and Prevention* 31:18–28.

Kruk, J. (2009). Intensity of lifetime physical activity and breast cancer risk among Polish women. *Journal of Sports Sciences* 27:437–45.

Meyerhardt, J. A., Giocannucci, E. L., Ogino, S., Kirkner, G. J., et al. (2009). Physical activity and male colorectal cancer survival. *Archives of Internal Medicine* 169:2102–8.

Orlandi, M., Trangeled, K., Mambrini, A., Tagliani, M., et al. (2007). Pet therapy effects on oncological day hospital patients undergoing chemotherapy treatment. *Anticancer Research* 27:4301–3.

Pierce, J. P., Stefanick, M. L., Flatt, S. W., Natarajan, L., et al. (2007). Greater survival after breast cancer in physically active women with high vegetable–fruit intake regardless of obesity. *Journal of Clinical Oncology* 25:2345–51.

Pollán, M. (2010). Epidemiology of breast cancer in young women. *Breast Cancer Research Treatment* 123(Suppl. 1):3–6.

Sanderson, M., Peitz, G., Perez, A., Johnson, M., et al. (2010). Diabetes, physical activity and breast cancer among Hispanic women. *Cancer Epidemiology* 34:556–61.

Thompson, H. J., Jiang, W., and Zhu, Z. (2009). Candidate mechanisms accounting for effects of physical activity on breast carcinogenesis. *Life* 61:895–901.

Weiner, J. G., Jordan, T. R., Thompson, A. J., and Fink, B. N. (2010). Analysis of the relationship between diet and exercise benefits and actual behaviors among breast cancer survivors in northwest Ohio. *Breast Cancer* 4:5–13.

CHAPTER 10

Braun, C., Stangler, T., Narveson, J., and Pettingell, S. (2009). Animal-assisted therapy as a pain relief intervention for children. *Complementary Therapies in Clinical Practice* 15:105–9.

Breivik, H., Collett, B., Ventafridda, V., Cohen, R., and Gallacher, D. (2006). Survey of chronic pain in Europe: Prevalence, impact on daily life, and treatment. *European Journal of Pain* 10:287–333.

Fransen, M., Woodward, M., Norton, R., Coggan, C., et al. (2002). Risk factors associated with the transition from acute to chronic occupational back pain. *Spine* 27:92–8.

Jakosson, U. (2010). The epidemiology of chronic pain in a general population: Results of a survey in southern Sweden. *Scandinavian Journal of Rheumatology* 39:421–9.

Jinks, C., Jordan, K., and Croft, P. (2002). Measuring the population impact of knee pain and disability with the Western Ontario and McMaster Universities Osteoarthritis Index (WOMAC). *Pain* 100:55–64.

Lust, E., Ryan-Haddad, A., Coover, K., and Snell, J. (2007). Measuring clinical outcomes of animal-assisted therapy: impact on resident medication usage. *The Consultant Pharmacist* 22:580–5.

Miranda, H., Viikari-Juntura, E., Martikanien, R., Takala, E. P., and Riihimaki, H. (2001). A prospective study of work related factors and physical exercise as predictors of shoulder pain. *Occupational and Environmental Medicine* 58:528–34.

Nascimento, D. C., Andersen, M. L., Hipólide, D. C., Nobrega, J. N., and Tufik, S. (2007). Pain hypersensitivity induced by paradoxical sleep deprivation is not due to altered binding to brain μ-opioid receptors. *Behavioural Brain Research* 178:216–20.

National Sleep Foundation. (2010). *National Sleep Foundation 2010 Sleep in America Poll.* http://www.sleepfoundation.org (accessed September 2010).

Sellinger, J. J., Clark, E. A., and Shulman M. (2010). The moderating effect of obesity on cognitive-behavioral pain treatment outcomes. *Pain Medicine* 11:1381–90.

Shirado, O., Doi, T., Akai, M., Hoshino, Y., Hayashi, K., et al. (2010). Multicenter randomized controlled trial to evaluate the effect of home-based exercise on patients with chronic low back pain: The Japan low back pain exercise therapy study. *Spine* 35:E811–9.

Smith, M. T., Edwards, R. R., McCann, U. D., and Haythronthwaite, J. A. (2007). The effects of sleep deprivation on pain inhibition and spontaneous pain in women. *Sleep* 30:494–505.

Sobo, E. J., Eng, B., and Kassity-Krich, N. (2006). Canine visitation (pet) therapy: Pilot data on decreases in child pain perception. *Journal of Holistic Nursing* 24:51–7.

Taylor, D. J., Mallory, L. J., Lichstein, K. L., Durrence, H. H., et al. (2007). Comorbidity of chronic insomnia with medical problems. *Sleep* 30:213–8.

van der Hulst, M., Vollenbroek-Hutten, M. M., Schreurs, K. M., Rietman, J. S., and Hermens, H. J. (2010). Relationship between coping strategies and lumbar muscle activity in subjects with chronic low back pain. *European Journal of Pain* 14:640–7.

Webb, R., Brammah, T., Lunt, M., Urwin, M., et al. (2003). Prevalence and predictors of intense, chronic, and disabling neck and back pain in the UK general population. *Spine* 28:1195–1202.

CHAPTER 11

Abubakari, A. R., Lauder, W., Agyemang, C., Jones, M., et al. (2008). Prevalence and time trends in obesity among adult West African populations: A meta-analysis. *Obesity Reviews* 9:297–311.

American Diabetes Association. (2010). *Diabetes basics.* http://www.diabetes.org/diabetes-basics/ (accessed August 2010).

Bland, I. M., Guthrie-Jones, A., Taylor, R. D., and Hill, J. (2009). Dog obesity: Owner attitudes and behaviour. *Preventive Veterinary Medicine* 92:333–40.

Cameron, A. J., Dunstan, D. W., Owen, N., Zimmet, P. Z., et al. (2009). Health and mortality consequences of abdominal obesity: Evidence from the AusDiab study. *Medical Journal of Australia* 191:202–8.

Coleman, K. J., Rosenberg, D. E., Conway, T. L., Sallis, J. F., et al. (2008). Physical activity, weight status, and neighborhood characteristics of dog walkers. *Preventive Medicine* 47:309–12.

Dembicki, D., and Anderson, J. (1996). Pet ownership may be a factor in improved health of the elderly. *Journal of Nutrition for the Elderly* 15:15–31.

Do Carmo, I., dos Santos, O., Camolas, J., Vieira, J., et al. (2008). Overweight and obesity in Portugal: National prevalence in 2003–2005. *Obesity Reviews* 9:11–9.

Donfrancesco, C., LoNoce, C., Brignoli, O., Riccardi, G., et al. (2008). Italian network for obesity and cardiovascular disease surveillance: A pilot project. *BMC Family Practice* 9:53.

Ervin, R. B. (2009). Prevalence of metabolic syndrome among adults 20 years of age and over, by sex, age, race and ethnicity, and body mass index: United States, 2003–2006. *National Health Statistics Reports* 5:1–7.

Haijan-Tilaki, K. O., and Heidari, B. (2007). Prevalence of obesity, central obesity and the associated factors in urban population aged 20–70 years, in the north of Iran: A population-based study and regression approach. *Obesity Reviews* 8:3–10.

Han, J. C., Lawlor, D. A., and Kimm, S. Y. (2010). Childhood obestiy. *The Lancet* 375:1737–48.

Hong, S. N., Kim, J. H., Choe, W. H., Han, H. S., et al. (2010). Prevalence and risk of colorectal neoplasms in asymptomatic, average-risk screenees 40 to 49 years of age. *Gastrointestinal Endoscopy* 72:480–9.

Hopman, W. M., Berger, C., Joseph,, L., et al. (2007). The association between body mass index and health-related quality of life: Data from CaMos, a stratified population study. *Quality of Life Research* 16:1595–1603.

Hopman, W. M., LeRoux, C., Berger, C., Joseph, L., et al. (2007). Changes in body mass index in Canadians over a five-year period: Results of a prospective, population-based study. *BMC Public Health* 7:150.

Hyman, M. (2008). *Ultra-metabolism.* New York: Atria Books.

Jacobi, D., Buzelé, R., and Couet, C. (2010). Are we facing an obesity pandemic? *Presse Médicale* 39:902–6.

Jacobs, E. J., Newton C. C., Wang, Y., Patel, A. V., et al. (2010). Waist circumference and all-cause mortality in a large US cohort. *Archives of Internal Medicine* 170:1293–1301.

Kuk, J. L., and Ardern, C. I. (2010). Age and sex differences the clustering of metabolic syndrome factors: Association with mortality risk. *Diabetes Care* 33:2457–61.

Lewis, G. D., Farrell, L., Wood, M. J., Martinovic, M., et al. (2010). Metabolic signatures of exercise in human plasma. *Science Translational Medicine* 2:33–7.

Lund, E. M., Armstrong, P. J., Kirk, C. A., and Klausner, J. S. (2006). Prevalence and risk factors for obesity in adult dogs from private

US veterinary practices. *International Journal of Applied Research in Veterinary Medicine* 4:177–86.

Lyerly, G. W., Sui, X., Lavie, C. J., Church, T. S., et al. (2009). The association between cardiorespiratory fitness and risk of all-cause mortality among women with impaired fasting glucose or undiagnosed diabetes mellitus. *Mayo Clinic Proceedings* 84:780–6.

Nijland, M. L., Stam, F., and Seidell, J. C. (2010). Overweight in dogs, but not in cats, is related to overweight in their owners. *Public Health Nutrition* 13:102–6.

O'Connor, M. B., O'Connor, C., and Walsh, C. H. (2008). A dog's detection of low blood sugar: A case report. *Irish Journal of Medical Science* 177:155–7.

Renehan, A. G., Soerjomataram, I., Tyson, M., Egger, M., et al. (2010). Incident cancer burden attributable to excess body mass index in 30 European countries. *International Journal of Cancer* 126:692–702.

Ruiz, J. R., Labayen, I., Ortega, F. B., Legry, V., et al. (2010). Attenuation of the effect of the FTO rs9939609 polymorphism on total and central body fat by physical activity in adolescents. *Archives of Pediatrics & Adolescent Medicine* 164:328–33.

Seidell, J. C. (2010). Waist circumference and waist/hip ratio in relation to all-cause mortality, cancer and sleep apnea. *European Journal of Clinical Nutrition* 64:35–41.

Sjöström, L., Gummesson, A., Sjöström, C. D., Narbro, K., et al. (2009). Effects of bariatric surgery on cancer incidence in obese patients in Sweden (Swedish Obese Subjects Study): A prospective, controlled intervention trial. *The Lancet Oncology* 10:653–62.

Testa, G., Cacciatore, F., and Galizia, G. (2010). Waist circumference but not body mass index predicts long-term mortality in elderly subjects with chronic heart failure. *Journal of the American Geriatrics Society* 58:1433–40.

Wang, Y., Beydoun, M. A., Liang, L., Caballero, B., and Kumanyika, S. K. (2008). Will all Americans become overweight or obese? Estimating the progression and cost of the US obesity epidemic. *Obesity* 16:2323–30.

Wells, D. L., Lawson, S. W., and Siriwardena, A. N. (2008). Canine responses to hypoglycemia in patients with Type 1 diabetes. *Journal of Alternative and Complementary Medicine* 14:1235–41.

World Health Organization media centre fact sheets. (2006). http://www.who.int/mediacentre/factsheets/fs311/en/index.html (accessed June 2009).

Zhang, X., Sun, Z., Zheng, L., Liu, S., et al. (2009). Ethnic differences in overweight and obesity between Han and Mongolian rural Chinese. *Acta Cardiologica* 64:239–45.

CHAPTER 12

Cangelosi, P. R., and Sorrell, J. M. (2010). Walking for therapy with man's best friend. *Journal of Psychosocial Nursing and Mental Health Services* 48:19–22.

Chambliss, H. O. (2005). Exercise duration and intensity in a weight-loss program. *Clinical Journal of Sport Medicine* 15:113–5.

Christian nee Cutt, H., Giles-Corti, B., and Knuiman, M. (2010). "I'm just a'walking the dog" correlates of regular dog walking. *Family & Community Health* 33:44–52.

Coleman, K. J., Rosenberg, D. E., Conway, T. L., Sallis, J. F., et al. (2008). Physical activity, weight status, and neighborhood characteristics of dog walkers. *Preventive Medicine* 47:309–12.

Cutt, H., Giles-Corti, B., Knuiman, M., and Burke, V. (2007). Dog ownership, health and physical activity: A critical review of the literature. *Health Place* 13:261–72.

Cutt, H., Giles-Corti, B., Knuiman, M., Timperior, A., and Bull, F. (2008). Understanding dog owners' increased levels of physical activity: Results from RESIDE. *American Journal of Public Health* 98:66–9.

General Electric. (2010, February 16). *Study reveals doctor–patient disconnect on healthy living.* http://www.genewscenter.com/Press-Releases/Study-Reveals-Patient-Doctor-Disconnect-on-Healthy-Living-25f7.aspx (accessed August 2010).

Gillum, R. F., and Obisesan, T. O. (2010a). Living with companion animals, physical activity and mortality in a U.S. national cohort. *International Journal of Environmental Research and Public Health* 7:2452–9.

Gillum, R. F., and Obisesan, T. O. (2010b). Physical activity, cognitive function, and mortality in a US national cohort. *Annals of Epidemiology* 20:251–7.

Jakicic, J. M., Wing, R. R., Butler, B. A., and Robertson, R. J. (1995). Prescribing exercise in multiple short bouts versus one continuous bout: Effects on adherence, cardiorespiratory fitness, and weight loss in overweight women. *International Journal of Obesity and Related Metabolic Disorders* 19:893–901.

Kruk, J. (2007). Physical activity in the prevention of the most frequent chronic diseases: An analysis of the recent evidence. *Asian Pacific Journal of Cancer Prevention* 8:325–38.

Marcus, D. A. (2008). *Fit as Fido: Follow your dog to better health.* Bloomington, IN: iUniverse.

Merom, D., Bowles, H., and Bauman, A. (2009). Measuring walking for physical activity surveillance—The effect of prompts and respondents' interpretation of walking in a leisure-time survey. *Journal of Physical Activity & Health* 6(Suppl. 1): S81–8.

Nies, M. A., and Motyka, C. L. (2006). Factors contributing to women's ability to maintain a walking program. *Journal of Holistic Nursing* 24:7–14.

Nybo, L., Sundstrup, E., Jakobsen, M. D., Mohr, M., et al. (2010). High-intensity training versus traditional exercise intervention for promoting health. *Medicine and Science in Sports and Exercise* 42:1951–8.

Oka, K., and Shibata, A. (2009). Dog ownership and health-related physical activity among Japanese adults. *Journal of Physical Activity & Health* 6:412–8.

Sanderson, S. C., Waller, J., Jarvis, M. J., Humphries, S. E., and Wardle, J. (2009). Awareness of lifestyle risk factors for cancer and heart disease among adults in the UK. *Patient Education and Counseling* 74:221–7.

Thorpe, R. J., Kreisle, R. A., Glickman, L. T., Simonsick, E. M., et al. (2006). Physical activity and pet ownership in year 3 of the Health ABC study. *Journal of Aging and Physical Activity* 14:154–68.

Thorpe, R. J., Simonsick, E. M., Brach, J. S., Ayonayon, H., et al. (2006). Dog ownership, walking behavior, and maintained mobility in late life. *Journal of the American Geriatrics Society* 54:1419–24.

U.S. Bureau of Labor Statistics. (2010, June 22). *Table 11: Time spent in leisure and sports activities for the civilian population by selected characteristics, 2009 annual averages.* http://www.bls.gov/news.release/atus.t11.htm (accessed August 2010).

Whyte, L. J., Gill, J. M., and Cathcart, A. J. (2010). Effect of 2 weeks of sprint interval training on health-related outcomes in sedentary overweight/obese men. *Metabolism* 59:1421–8.

World Health Organization. (2010). *Global recommendations on physical activity for health.* http://www.who.int (accessed January 2011).

Yabroff, K. R., Troiano, R. P., and Berrigan, D. (2008). Walking the dog: Is pet ownership associated with physical activity in California? *Journal of Physical Activity & Health* 5:216–28.

CHAPTER 13

Alzheimer's Association. (2010). *2010 Alzheimer's disease facts and figures.* http://www.alz.org (accessed September 2010).

Banks, M. R., and Banks, W. A. (2002). The effects of animal-assisted therapy on loneliness in an elderly population in long-term care facilities. *Journals of Gerontology: Series A: Biological Sciences and Medical Sciences* 57:M428–32.

Boyle, P. A., Buchman, A. S., Wilson, R. S., Leurgans, S. E., and Bennett, D. A. (2009). Association of muscle strength with the risk of Alzheimer's disease and the rate of cognitive decline in community-dwelling older persons. *Archives of Neurology* 66:1339–44.

Fick, K. M. (1993). The influence of an animal on social interactions of nursing home residents in a group setting. *American Journal of Occupational Therapy* 47:529–34.

Filan, S. L., and Llewellyn-Jones, R. H. (2006). Animal-assisted therapy for dementia: A review of the literature. *International Psychogeriatrics* 18:597–611.

Harris, T. J., Owen, C. G., Victor, C. R., Adams, R., and Cook, D. G. (2009). What factors are associated with physical activity in older people, assessed objectively by accelerometry? *British Journal of Sports Medicine* 43:442–50.

Kanamori, M., Suzuki, M., Yamamoto, K., Kanda, M., et al. (2001). A day care program and evaluation of animal-assisted therapy (AAT) for the elderly with senile dementia. *American Journal of Alzheimer's Disease and Other Dementias* 16:234–9.

Kawamura, N., Niiyama, M., and Niiyama, H. (2009). Animal-assisted activity: Experiences of institutionalized Japanese older adults. *Journal of Psychosocial Nursing and Mental Health Services* 47:41–7.

Richeson, N. E. (2003). Effects of animal-assisted therapy on agitated behaviors and social interactions of older adults with dementia. *American Journal of Alzheimer's Disease and Other Dementias* 18:353–8.

Scarmeas, N., Luchsinger, J. A., Brickman, A. M., Cosentino, S., et al. (2010). Physical activity and Alzheimer disease course. *American Journal of Geriatric Psychiatry* 30:7281–9.

Scarmeas, N., Luchsinger, J. A., Schupf, N, Brickman, A. M., et al. (2009). Physical activity, diet, and risk of Alzheimer disease. *Journal of the American Medical Association* 302:627–37.

Tribet, J., Bouchariat, M., and Myslinski, M. (2008). Animal-assisted therapy for people suffering from severe dementia. *Encephale* 34:183–6.

Index

Note: Page references in *italics* denote figures and tables.